MW00595731

Meet the Natives

A Field Guide to Rocky Mountain Wildflowers, Trees, and Shrubs

Bridging the Gap between Trail and Garden

ELEVENTH EDITION

M. Walter Pesman

REVISED AND EXPANDED BY
Dan Johnson

PRINCIPLE PHOTOGRAPHY BY
Loraine Yeatts and **Dan Johnson**

JOHNSON BOOKS
BOULDER

Copyright © 2012, 1999, 1992, 1988, 1975
by Denver Botanic Gardens

All rights reserved.
No part of this publication may be reproduced or transmitted
in any form or by any means, electronic or mechanical, including photocopy,
recording, or any information storage and retrieval system,
without permission in writing from the publisher.

Published by Johnson Books, a Big Earth Publishing company
3005 Center Green Drive, Suite 225, Boulder, Colorado 80301
1-800-258-5830
E-mail: books@bigearthpublishing.com
www.bigearthpublishing.com

Cover and text design by Rebecca Finkel

9   8   7   6   5   4   3   2

Library of Congress Cataloging-in-Publication Data
Pesman, M. Walter (Michiel Walter), 1887-
Meet the natives : a field guide to Rocky Mountain wildflowers, trees, and
shrubs : bridging the gap between trail and garden / M. Walter Pesman ;
edited by Dan Johnson. — 11th ed.
p. cm.
ISBN 978-1-55566-441-1
1. Wild flowers—Rocky Mountains Region—Identification.
2. Trees—Rocky Mountains Region—Identification.
3. Shrubs—Rocky Mountains Region—Identification.
I. Johnson, Dan, curator. II. Title.
QK150.P47 2011
635.9'5178—dc22
2010008618

Printed in Korea

Some people guide you from the beginning.
For instilling respect for, and connection to, the
natural world, I dedicate this book to my parents,
F. Bernard Johnson and Marion B. (Rossier) Johnson.

Some people appear at fortuitous times in life, and
nudge you along in directions you had not seen.
For this, I thank my mentor, Panayoti Kelaidis.

Contents

Foreword
By Panayoti Kelaidis

When *Meet the Natives* first came out, only a handful of books had ever been published about the wildflowers of the Rocky Mountain region. Nowadays, dozens of wildflower guides and many technical floras of the Rockies are available. The wildflower experience in our state has changed almost as drastically: There weren't that many paved roads crossing the higher elevations of Colorado in the early twentieth century, and more roads mean more places to see wildflowers conveniently.

I remember riding along the Peak to Peak Highway with my family as a child in the 1950s. It was gravel then and the bumpy road to Brainard Lake often had no other cars parked at the primitive campground at its end, even on summer weekends. Today, you pay to drive this paved road to multiple, vast, paved parking lots that are so full by early weekday mornings that many visitors drive home discouraged. Don't even think about going on the weekend. Nowadays, a more or less continuous city stretches along the Interstate 70 corridor, which was largely open range and ranchland when M. Walter Pesman was alive. He was the original author of this book back in 1942.

Nothing has amazed me more than the transformation of the sleepy Rocky Mountain hamlets (disheveled mining towns really), little more than a cluster of shops around a gas station and post office to provision the local ranches. Burma Shave signs were some of the most conspicuous human artifacts cluttering the country back then. Today, mountain valleys throughout the West resemble Swiss chalet ski villages crowded with miles of McMansions of America's glitterati. These towns bustle in winter with skiers and in the summer with throngs of tourists attending the dozens of dance, theater, and music festivals. I wonder who would be more shocked if we could bring them back today to wander down the streets of Crested Butte or Vail—a nineteenth century miner, or M. Walter Pesman himself.

Over the decades, more and more countryside has been gobbled up by strip malls and suburbs, shopping centers, asphalt and cement. Vacant lots have all but vanished in the larger cities. You would be hard pressed to find pristine natural vegetation in much of the Front Range megalopolis. Nature has somehow become more desirable as a consequence.

Pesman was one of the most eloquent voices defending natural landscapes and promoting sound horticulture in urban spaces. In fact, he and his compatriot Saco DeBoer were among the first in the state to call themselves landscape architects, dedicating their lives to the art of enhancing the physical setting where we stage our lives.

Growth notwithstanding, the Great Plains, Rocky Mountains, and Great Basin remain the least populated and most pristine parts of the Continental United States. Even Colorado, with far more farming and a bustling Front Range urban corridor, has large areas of prairie and plateau still largely intact. The vast majority of the mountain slopes are National Park, National Forest, or BLM land, much of it never lumbered and much the same as it might have been without human interference.

People escape into wilderness in ever increasing numbers. And hikers inevitably want to know the names of the flowers they wander by. Flower color and elevation are pretty reliable ways to narrow down the choices of possible plants, even though the total flora of the state may be nearly three thousand. Readers now have a guidebook not just for identifying plants, but also to guide them on the plants' potential as garden subjects. *Meet the Natives* has consistently been rated the most satisfactory way for most people to begin their acquaintance with Latin names and our rich native flora.

THE COLORADO NATIVE PLANT SOCIETY was only founded in 1976, but native plant awareness grew exponentially throughout the twentieth century. Periodic drought and increased demand on water resources have made many gardeners receptive to the idea of growing native plants in urban and suburban settings.

Denver Botanic Gardens staff incorporated many natives into the gardens increasingly throughout the fifty-year history of plantings here. It was not until 1998, however, that a staff position of "Curator of Native Plants" was created, and Dan Johnson was the first person to assume responsibility for the various native gardens that had been planted the decade or so before. The Laura Smith Porter Plains Garden, the Xeriscape Demonstration Garden (now renamed the Dryland Mesa Garden) and the Gates Montane Garden were the beginning for Dan. All three gardens had essentially lain derelict for several years due to staff shortages. The prairie had filled up with bindweed, and half dead shrubs and weed trees had grown up all through the Gates Garden and the Dryland Mesa. One of the most gratifying quiet miracles I have observed during my tenure at Denver Botanic Gardens was how quickly Dan rescued these nearly hopeless plots (designed almost along the lines of a revegetation plan), transforming them into the centerpiece displays of the Gardens.

Dan was so successful that a whole new suite of native gardens were mandated by the director at the time. The three vast beds surrounding the main amphitheater near the entrance to DBG were always set-pieces of annual plantings: petunias, zinnias, and such. Three completely new gardens—western panoramas—were planned to showcase the plains, foothills and high mountain beauty of our state, complementing the established WaterSmart garden on the fourth side.

Each border was named for a signature tree: the cottonwood for the plains, the ponderosa for the foothills, and bristlecone for the mountain-flavored panel. Rather than grow plants in the random, naturalistic style of the existing native gardens, grasses and forbs were massed in huge drifts in the bold, romantic style that has become popular among cutting-edge designers in Western and Central Europe in recent decades. Dan Johnson had tens of thousands of plants grown and ordered for these ambitious gardens, and personally placed and planted most of them during the greatest drought in recent history.

I was skeptical. Could these naturalistic gardens really provide the sort of bang that we got year after year from glaring annuals? I gradually came to realize that they delivered so much more. Annual beds are spaded and often fallow for over half the garden year. These glorious beds, full of shrubs and perennials and sweeps of grasses were four-season wonders. For weeks in spring and summer they would brim with colorful flowers, but even in the dullest winter months the textures of foliage was gorgeous. Each year as these gardens mature, it is apparent to me how wise the decision was to use these gardens to further demonstrate the magnificence of using native plants in urban landscapes.

Xeriscape continues to arouse strong feelings—for some it means stark gravelscapes with moribund or sickly plants. Denver Botanic Gardens has created many stunning examples that show that a native garden, properly designed, can rival any formal or exotic garden on the level playing field of beauty.

In *Meet the Natives*, Dan points out which plants he thinks are appropriate in the home landscape, and gives suggestions on where to place them. By expanding and including these cultural notes, this book is not just a wonderful key to wildflowers, but a handbook to help guide you in bringing the majesty and year-round beauty of our Rocky Mountains into your home and garden.

Evolution of a Wildflower Guide

By Dan Johnson

The bronze plaque at the upper end of Mt. Goliath's M. Walter Pesman Trail fittingly dedicates the trail with these words: "He made native plants our friends." In 1942, Pesman, a landscape architect and lover of native plants, wrote the first edition of this book designed "to help the amateur botanist get acquainted with the trees, shrubs, and herbaceous plants so attractive to the visitors to these mountains and high plains."

The earliest editions of this work were self-published. Line drawings and black and white photos accompanied many of the descriptions to assist in identification. Plants were grouped by life zones—a clever premise, and a logical choice when color printing was much more costly. Some features have come and gone over the years, such as the "Treasure Hunt"—a page devoted to a dozen or so rare plants to search for in the wild. Other improvements have been incremental—the inclusion of more drawings or additional plants. By the seventh edition, a partnership with Denver Botanic Gardens brought the book more visibility and produced three subsequent editions.

As Curator of Native Plants at Denver Botanic Gardens, I have revised this eleventh edition with the hope of creating a more timely and useful incarnation of this popular guide. Consultation with other Gardens' staff and regional experts ensures that the information provided will be relevant to those looking for a useful guide to our most conspicuous native trees, shrubs, grasses, and wildflowers. But this edition goes further, and includes the following:

- Organization of herbaceous flowering plants by color, to speed identification

- Color photographs to assist with accurate identification

- Addition of nearly one hundred new entries

- Inclusion of common and useful native grasses, which make up the fabric of so many of our ecosystems, and have proven useful in sustainable gardens

- Discussion of a number of exotic imported plants that have become common, or in some cases aggressively invasive

- Discussion of some of our most charismatic rare plants that may be encountered, to alert you to their fragile status, and encourage preservation

- Quick-reference charts to help with identification

- Horticultural information to assist with incorporating our durable and beautiful native plants into gardens and landscapes

- Recommended Internet sites and other resources that can enhance your familiarity with our native flora

- New, compact, backpack-friendly design

Before using this book for field identification, be sure to review the section, "How to Use this Book" (page 4). We have attempted to use terms that are non-technical, but sometimes there is no familiar substitute. In this case, find definitions in the "Glossary" (page 251). Also, be sure to become acquainted with "About Plant Families" (page 22), for help in recognizing plant species.

Over the decades, many people have contributed directly and indirectly to the production and success of this book, some very recently, and some in the more distant past. Each edition has given its particular credits to groups and individuals, and the list is long. It includes Dr. Moras Schubert, Dr. Jan Wingate, F.H. Wingate, Helen Zeiner, and Aubrey Hildreth, to name a few. The hard work and contributions of many have been preserved here. Some features remain only in previous editions, and some have evolved over time to serve ever-changing needs.

Particular thanks for the eleventh edition go to the following individuals:

LORAINE YEATTS, for her wonderful photographs, the product of a life-long dedication to our native plants and wild places.

Denver Botanic Gardens' PANAYOTI KELAIDIS, MIKE KINTGEN, AND DOMINIQUE BAYNE, for their astute observations and helpful insights about our native plants.

DEB GOLANTY, for her objectivity and attention to detail in proof-reading this edition.

LISA ELDRED, for flogging as needed to produce this volume in a reasonable amount of time.

During the course of ten editions, the world has changed a great deal. While much of Pesman's original language remains, a changing world necessitates an updated context. The prospect of climate change, the expansion of urban areas, and the strain on natural resources have brought new relevance to our understanding and use of native plants. Still, the primary goal of this book remains the same: To introduce the native plants of Colorado and adjacent areas, and to assist in easy identification of many of the most common plants encountered along the region's trails and byways.

M. WALTER PESMAN was the leading landscape architect in Colorado for much of the twentieth century. He was born in the Netherlands, worked briefly with fellow Dutchman S.R. DeBoer when he first came to Colorado, then designed schools and public spaces for the state before concentrating on residential design later in his career. He loved naturalistic gardens: he, Jane Silverstein Reese, and DeBoer essentially crafted the Colorado garden style.

Unto the Hills

Green slopes or golden,
Mountains many-hued,
Sparkling icy waters,
Clouds of summer mood,
Flower-besprinkled meadows,
Crags that pierce the sky,
Serene, majestic, timeless—
Eternity's ally.

Bring not to Glorious Nature
Man's bickering and strife;
Bring love and joy and wonder
For re-creative life.
Search out her myriad secrets
And let no challenge pass:
The life of ferns and mosses,
The glacier's deep crevasse,
Wild creatures not yet fearful,
The strength a storm displays,
The miracles of sunlight,
Of hidden cosmic rays.

Here Beauty was and Poetry
Ere human life began.
To the hills, the hills eternal,
Lift up your eyes, oh Man!

ELIZABETH H. PESMAN
(1893–1987)

About Native Plants…

This is a guide describing over 500 plants that you will be likely (or very fortunate!) to see as you explore both our urban *and* wilderness trails. Along the way, flip through this book and begin to connect the "faces" and names of our long-time residents.

The landscape of the southern Rocky Mountains and Great Plains has existed for thousands of years essentially unchanged—until recently. Not to say that humans have had no influence. Native Americans used fire to manage prairie conditions, supporting their dependence on herds of bison. Natural cycles of planetary warming and cooling, including Ice Age conditions, have certainly shaped today's flora and fauna as well. We can only speculate on the events that removed camels, horses, and wooly mammoths from North American ecosystems.

Most of those changes occurred slowly over many centuries. Today, countless pressures impact plants and their habitats—from agriculture to urban sprawl—and these occur essentially overnight. Many fragile plants are especially susceptible. They may occur only on very specific soils or geological formations or may require specific wetlands or seasonal fluctuations in hydrology. Changes in climate pose new challenges. The sobering prospect of familiar alpine plants being squeezed off their mountaintops as the climate warms was unimaginable just a few years ago.

So, what does all this have to do with a guide to wildflowers? Context. In this book, we define "native" as any plants that existed here before European settlement. It's fair to say that even some of our natives exist now in areas where they likely did not in the past. Big bluestem is one of these, now found scattered in southwestern Colorado, several hundred miles from its prairie origins, finding a niche along irrigation ditches that did not exist pre-settlement. Plants find a way.

Fortunately, many of our wildflowers are resilient, and still find their niche in expansive habitats that continue to thrive. The Rocky

Mountain region is vast, and, for all it has endured, still holds a wealth of beauty and diversity.

Non-Native Plants

Some natives struggle to survive the competition of introduced plants. The unprecedented influx of "non-native" plants can change the dynamics of entire ecosystems. Impacts are unpredictable and controls costly.

You will notice that this book includes a number of plants that are *not* native. In some cases these are very common plants that have naturalized over many decades. Others may be relatively new on the scene. Whatever the case, these are plants that you are likely to see along roadsides or in the wild. They are presented here to increase awareness of the widespread threat that introduced plants can pose. While many persist only in disturbed soils or urban areas, others are aggressive and threaten sensitive plant communities. Millions of dollars have been spent to help restore ecosystems that have been threatened by introduced plants.

Working with national and local organizations, you can play a role in protecting threatened plants and in controlling the spread of aggressive introduced plants. Getting to know them is an important step along the way.

In the Garden

In the process of using this guide, hopefully you will contemplate your own footprint on our changing planet. Native plants don't just belong "out there." Some of our most durable garden plants come to us from our own wild prairies, forests, and deserts. Many are superbly adapted to garden and climate conditions that prevail in the region. They lived here long before we did, surviving frost, heat, hail, drought, and wind better than many traditional garden plants. Many require fewer resources and less water to thrive. Their textures and scale imbue the garden with a sense of place that celebrates our natural landscapes, yet they blend seamlessly with a host of garden plants from similar climates around the world.

Plants should not be removed from the wild for any reason. Most of our rarest plants will never thrive in cultivation, and to remove them from their habitats not only dooms them to a certain death; it reduces already-stressed populations, risking their very survival. Please tread lightly, admire them where they live, and, as they say, take only photographs. Our best native plants are widely grown by nurseries for garden use. Specialty nurseries often grow even the obscure alpine and desert gems favored by collectors and rock gardeners.

While this book is not intended to be a comprehensive horticultural guide, anecdotal tips on cultivation are included wherever relevant. A chart is provided at the back to help you locate plants with similar requirements. Basic "easy/challenging" ratings in the charts provide a general assessment of garden success. Color, habitat, and seasonal traits may help you consider garden combinations. Let the information presented spark further research of your own. Our hope is to introduce you to our diverse native plants, and help to bridge the gap between trail and garden.

How to Use This Book

This edition contains the following sections:

- Descriptions of the major life zones found in the central and southern Rockies, particularly Colorado
- Characteristics of the most common plant families
- Ferns, Horsetails, and Spikemosses
- Grasses and Grass-like Plants
- Trees and Shrubs
- Herbaceous Flowering Plants; Vines; and Cacti grouped by flower color

Plants covered in the Ferns, Grasses, and Trees and Shrubs sections are arranged alphabetically by family and by common name. Refer to photos and the short plant descriptions to determine the identity of your plant. Season of bloom and life zone keys will provide additional help.

The section on flowering plants is arranged by flower color, then by family and common name. Many species can have varying flower color. These plants are listed according to the color that is most often encountered. The reference chart at the back of the book indicates the possible variations that may be found.

Though the focus of this book is identifying native plants, many introduced, or non-native, plants may also be encountered. Some occupy mainly disturbed sites, but others encroach on stable habitats and displace natives. The introduced plants that are included in the book are labeled "non-native."

For quick reference, the chart at the back of the book includes only native plants. It is arranged alphabetically by the family, genus, and species. The chart includes:

- Whether a plant is likely to be found on the Eastern or Western Slope
- Typical growing conditions preferred
- Other color forms that may be encountered
- Whether a plant is considered easy or difficult in cultivation. Where no rating is given, the plant is not usually recommended for gardens

What are Life Zones?

A life zone is a geographic region characterized by a distinct set of plants and animals.

You can leave Colorado Springs in the morning and arrive in the Polar region at noon. Not by plane, but by car via the Pikes Peak Highway—a unique experience, one that is possible because high altitude corresponds to high latitude as far as plant growth is concerned. Going up the mountain, you see wildflowers and trees similar to those in Wyoming, Montana, and Canada, on up to the Arctic Circle and the Arctic Ocean.

Life zone changes are not abrupt. In attempting to create order in an imprecise world, scientists often try to place living things and their habitats into clearly defined categories. It is true that some plants are very precise in their needs. Certain types of flowers and trees belong at certain altitudes (or latitudes), and do not extend much above or below their limits. You will never find the alpine forget-me-not growing in the prairies east of Pueblo.

However, some plants are masters of adaptability. You may well find our common yarrow thriving from the plains on up to the alpine tundra of Mt. Evans. Likewise, you may find a small stand of aspen in the cool shade of a cliff just west of Lyons, but the large characteristic groves may not appear until you are almost to Allenspark, nearly 3,000 feet higher.

Between the Alpine region (above timberline) and the Plains region, scientists have distinguished three rather distinct types of plant (and animal) life, designated as the Subalpine (10,000 feet to timberline), the Montane (8,000 to 10,000 feet), and the Foothills (6,000 to 8,000 feet), each with distinct conditions (elevations indicated here are approximate).

Additionally, the flora at low elevations *east* of the Continental Divide is primarily that of the northern and southern Great Plains, and to a very minor degree related to the northern Chihuahuan Desert. However, the flora of the lower elevations *west* of the Divide is an extension of the Great Basin flora, finding its place in the canyons and plateaus of our western river valleys and high deserts. There are many plants found on the Western Slope that would never, or rarely, be seen on the Eastern Plains, and vice versa.

Riparian areas—where rivers, streams, and small lakes occur—thread their way between all these zones, often carrying elements from adjacent zones out of their expected range. The hydrology of these sites often dictates which plants will thrive, as these riparian zones slice through complex soils and geologic features.

In summary, we refer in this edition to six prominent life zones that will help in identifying plants and flowers in their natural habitats. We begin with the Plains, as that is the zone with easiest access from the urban population centers. For those wanting to explore close to home, there is a wealth of wildflowers to be discovered in the state parks, Open Space trails, and around reservoirs and creeks of lower elevations. Most who travel to the mountains begin their journey at lower elevations, and will note the transitions described as they climb in elevation. Travelers from the Western Slope may likely begin their journey in the valleys of the High Desert, from communities such as Grand Junction or Montrose.

The **Plains Zone** (4,000 to 6,000 feet east of the Divide)

The **High Desert Zone** (5,000 to 7,000 feet west of the Divide). Both the Plains Zone and the High Desert Zone are a part of the larger Upper Sonoran Zone (30° to 40° latitude), separated from each other by the central barrier of the Southern Rockies.

The **Foothills Zone** (6,000 to 8,000 feet) corresponds to the Transition Zone (40° to 50° latitude)

The **Montane Zone** (8,000 to 10,000 feet), corresponds to the Canadian Zone (50° to 60° latitude).

The **Subalpine Zone,** from 10,000 feet to timberline, corresponds to the Hudsonian Zone (60° to 66° latitude).

The **Alpine Zone** above timberline, about 11,500 feet above sea level in central Colorado. This corresponds to the Arctic Zone, north of the Polar Circle (66° latitude).

Going up 2,000 feet in elevation marks about the same difference in plant growth as going north 10 degrees in latitude.

Another interesting angle of this relationship between plants and altitude is that the same kind of plant, if found within a certain range of elevations, will bloom later the higher it is found. That makes it convenient: if you find columbines just out of bloom in Idaho Springs at an altitude of 7,500 feet, go up to Central City (8,560 feet) to find them in full glory. They will still be in bud at Breckenridge (9,579 feet).

As you explore the Rocky Mountains and all the microclimates therein, keep this in mind: plants respond to the reality of their immediate conditions, not precise elevations or textbook descriptions. The elevations ascribed to life zones are approximate, and vegetation will be influenced by many other factors, including the availability of water, the direction of a particular slope, the type of soil, prevailing winds, cycles of drought and fire, and human disturbance, to name a few. All of this explains why you find so many different types of trees and flowers and shrubs in such a compact place as the Rocky Mountain region.

Plains Zone
(4,000 to 6,000 feet, east of the Continental Divide)

The great sea of grass that rolls eastward from the Rocky Mountains is the stuff of legends—sometimes undulating in broad swells; sometimes flat as a tabletop; sometimes broken by bluffs and ravines; always wide as the sky. While time seems to have slowed down in this expansive prairie land, it has not stood still. The American Indian and the bison are gone from the Great Plains. The cowboy and his herd are still keeping up some of the traditions of the past—in places. But as short grasses such as buffalo grass and blue grama grass were plowed up and erosion set in; as dust storms replaced the "thundering herd," many wildflowers were greatly reduced in quantity. Cottonwood groves and willows and boxelder gave way to farmland, and much of the picturesque bottomland disappeared. It is a landscape forever changed, and our prairie wildflowers have changed in extent and numbers as well.

So, how about the native plants—are they holding their own? In some places, yes, but rampant development in the late twentieth and early twenty-first centuries has ravaged natural areas like never before. Shortgrass prairie yields easily to the blade of the bulldozer. Rising populations have stretched urban boundaries far into grasslands and farm country that seemed remote just a few decades ago. The extraordinarily rich piedmont along the Front Range is just a memory along most of the urban corridor. From Cheyenne to Pueblo, civilization, or, more accurately "cultivation," is endangering some of our choicest flowers, particularly the tulip gentian, found in August in wet meadow ground. Our showy penstemons must be guarded lest they disappear as man moves in and the original ground surface is gradually destroyed. Aggressive alien weeds pose a further threat, thriving in the disturbed soils that accompany misguided development.

All is not lost however. Preserving our quality of life has become an essential ingredient in planning for the future, and the preservation of "open space" is now seen as an asset to our communities. Complex issues including habitat loss, water rights, and political sway all converge to direct our future, and only active conservation efforts will ensure that our natural landscapes will endure for future generations.

So, in that context, what can be expected from the embattled landscape of the prairie? The high plains can still overwhelm with their vast expanses, a grassy mosaic of sweeping dry hills, low swales, rocky outcrops, and horizons that echo the curve of the Earth. Each subtle variation in exposure presents an array of habitats where tough and beautiful plants find their niche and endure the extremes of heat, drought, wind, and Arctic blast. At the foot of the mountains, especially near Boulder, there are even remnants of tallgrass prairie, small vestiges of a wetter climate from millennia past. To give even an approximate account of the progression of flowers in all these different locations is beyond the scope of this introduction.

Fortunately, there is still a great deal to see if one knows where to look. Even our urban trails preserve a slice of our native flora. Abandoned roads and railways, as well as the shoulders of any rural road, may harbor species long displaced from surrounding areas.

However, in relatively undisturbed habitats, including our Comanche National Grasslands, the Pawnee National Grasslands, the

Pawnee Buttes area, and other remote sections of our eastern counties, cactus and yucca are presenting the same picture as they have for thousands of years. Three-leaf sumac still occupies dry hills. Spring still brings the sand lily and large fields of white evening primrose; summer has loco, bush morning glory and sunflowers galore; fall is still a blaze of color with goldenrod and aster. In the lowlands, many cottonwood groves are still intact—indicators of creeks and rivers and underground water. We find snowberry, golden currant, plum, chokecherry, and some hawthorns where water persists. White native clematis festoons trees and shrubs, and wild gourd and mock cucumber scramble down the banks in these groves.

We owe many dozens of our most dependable garden flowers to the wealth of the prairies, including sunflowers, penstemons, and gaillardias. The adventurous traveler who does not follow the throngs west into the high country, but instead turns east to the prairies, will discover a restful landscape and a wealth of surprising and beautiful natives that rival the rarest of our fabled Alpine wildflowers.

High Desert

(5,000 to 7,000 feet, mainly west of the Continental Divide)

The varied topography of the Western Slope has a character much different from the foothills and plains found east of the Rockies. A complex geology includes thick sedimentary sandstone, dormant volcanic peaks, deep twisting canyons, and countless other features. This results in equally complex habitats, and a wealth of endemic species found nowhere else on Earth. The landscape here has more in common with Utah and points west than it does with the eastern plains.

Many plants familiar on the eastern plains and foothills play a role here, but the plant palette likewise draws elements from the Great Basin, and what is known as the Madrean flora. This brings elements associated with so much of the far West, including manzanitas, cacti, oaks, and sagebrush, and a great diversity of eriogonums, astragalus, and other wildflowers and shrubs.

Here the foothills break away into flat-topped mesas and rolling hills. At elevations of 5,000 to 7,000 feet, ponderosa pine and other

foothills vegetation give way to fields of sagebrush—a good indicator to early settlers of deep rich soils. The rivers course downward, often carving spectacular canyons below red rock walls.

Winters can be cold and dry at lower elevations, with spotty snow cover. Summer is characterized by sporadic precipitation, low humidity, intense sun, and drying heat blown in from the deserts to the west. Rocky hills and bluffs support thousands of square miles of piñon/juniper woodland. Banana yucca and Indian rice grass thrive in sandy soils between layers of shelf rock, and the diminutive Harriman's yucca wards off the high desert sun with curly white threads that shade its rosette of short leaves.

Though subject to dramatic extremes of weather, the temperate river basins boast conditions that, on average, are more moderate than their counterparts east of the Divide. This accounts for the extensive agricultural areas so well known for their fruit and wine production, which would not be possible without a complex network of irrigation ditches and reservoirs.

Such ventures, while productive, come at a price, as does the impact of open grazing and the steady expansion of the Western Slope's small cities and towns. Increasing oil and gas exploration and extraction scar the landscape and damage fragile habitats beyond repair. Still, remote and pristine areas remain, and public lands are plentiful, affording easy access to some of our most scenic and diverse habitats.

Foothills Zone
(6,000 to 8,000 feet)

The Great Plains lap gently against the foothills along the Rocky Mountain Front Range. Along this eastern boundary, open grasslands wash over mesas and hogbacks, their wildflowers mixing in a rich blend with those of the ascending foothills. In the southern and western part of the region it is the High Desert that merges with the foothills vegetation.

To the mountain lover, the Foothills Zone is the intimate region, easily accessible and therefore well known. Here, from 6,000 to 8,000 feet above sea level, a mosaic of grasslands and ponderosa pine dominates on dry south-facing slopes. Along with the ponderosa pine we may find three-leaf sumac, smooth sumac, mountain mahogany, squaw currant, and native roses. Kinnikinnick and common juniper are natural groundcovers, together with Oregon grape holly.

Vegetation of the foothills spills down the cooler north slopes; a mix of Rocky Mountain juniper, Douglas fir, and a wealth of shrubs, grasses, and wildflowers that find this zone their natural home. Boulder raspberry and mountain spray are plentiful. In the higher regions we find Colorado blue spruce in the valleys, and aspens are scattered widely.

Deep canyons slice through the hills, gathering run-off into swift streams and affording enough protection for ferns and a host of plants that prefer cool canyon walls and crevices. Along streams, in addition to willows, native alders and birch abound. In well-drained places, hawthorn, chokecherry, plum, and hazelnut are abundant. Gooseberry and red-twig dogwood are almost always found.

In Colorado's western counties, large areas of the foothills are cloaked in scrub oak, generally accompanied by mountain mahogany, serviceberry, and three-leaf sumac (chaparral region). Here also you can look for piñon pine, Utah juniper, one-seeded juniper, and narrow-leaf cottonwood, especially in lower elevations.

Spring is the colorful time in the foothills, and early hikers will find pasque flowers, Oregon grape holly, and spring beauty. Lambert's loco and Indian paintbrush, penstemon, wallflower, sulphur flower, gaillardia, senecio, and many others bloom in abundance. The elegant columbines never fail to bring excitement. Intricately decorated mariposa lilies hover above meadow grasses. As the weather warms, one flower after another may dominate the scene.

Foothills wildflowers particularly need protection against predatory humans. Easy access belies the complex and unique character of our Foothills Zone habitats. Our urban residents routinely cross one of the great transition zones on the planet with scarcely a thought—

where the vast Great Plains collide with the formidable Rocky Mountains. As pressures increase on these natural resources, be mindful of the fragility of these habitats and do your best to stay on trails to preserve this natural diversity for those who follow.

Montane Zone
(8,000 to 10,000 feet)

"This is the forest primeval …" These words from Longfellow's "Evangeline" embody the haunting solitude found in the Montane forests of the high Rockies. Here are close stands of lodgepole pine, often all of the same age; here, on north slopes, are large woods of Douglas fir. Here the hush of winter lingers long and the splendid isolation on a summer day can seem to be of another era. Yet in these valleys lie most of our mountain communities and ski towns, bustling year round with visitors from around the world. Some resorts even maintain chairlift services all year, creating easy access for hiking the high meadows.

Climbing from the Foothills Zone, the plant palette shifts gradually, depending as always on exposure. On drier hills and warm sunny slopes in the lower elevations, fragrant ponderosa pine still prevails. Left to itself, natural cycles of fire reduce competition and return nutrients to the soil, creating open parklands with widely spaced trees of varying ages. Here, gaillardia reaches perfection; tiny succulent sedums find impossible foothold in gravelly soil and rock crevices, and sulphur flower brightens sunny slopes in shades of lemon-yellow.

Cool north slopes are cloaked in deep woods of Douglas fir. Aspen groves form large patches among the evergreens in moist places and valleys, lime green in spring and breathtaking in their golden glory each fall. Columbines thrive among them, along with meadow rue, black-eyed Susan, geranium, wood lily, various asters, and Indian paintbrush. Red-berried elder brightens forest edges. Bush honeysuckle is found in moist places and is conspicuous with its bright red involucre around the two black berries.

At higher sites we find large stands of Engelmann spruce on northern slopes, often mixed with alpine fir. Sunny grades are dense with uniform stands of lodgepole pine, dependent on fire for its reproduction. Where the ground has been disturbed by timber cutting, fire, or road building, great quantities of fireweed appear. Common ground covers in this zone are kinnikinnick and common juniper. Shrubby cinquefoil thrives particularly well in the more moist habitats of this zone, and yarrow, while found in other zones, makes a beautiful splurge here.

In windswept regions higher up, fingers of Montane and Subalpine vegetation intertwine depending on exposure to sun and wind. Here we may find the five-needled limber and bristlecone pines, so typical of the Subalpine Zone.

But the Montane Zone is not all forest. Quite a different plant growth is found in the so-called "mountain parks"—large open meadows such as South Park, Middle Park, and North Park, as well as numerous smaller ones. Here, among the grasses, some of the most interesting and colorful flowers bloom in great quantities. Here there are shooting star, wand lily, blue-eyed grass, lousewort, loco, potentilla, and different varieties of asters. And here in the fall, wet meadows shimmer with large fields of deep-blue: different varieties of gentians, some delightfully fragrant, some so shy they close upon being picked or when a cloud passes over them.

Much of the Montane Zone is protected to some extent as national forest or some other designation, managing its resources and preserving vital watersheds. Its ease of access makes this zone a favorite haunt of summer hikers seeking adventure within easy reach of services and mountain communities.

Subalpine Zone
(10,000 feet to timberline)

Continuing upward from the Montane forests, the transition to the Subalpine Zone is at first subtle—the mix of conifers become more spire-shaped. Engelmann spruce and alpine fir, pioneers in a slowly warming climate, still follow the receding glaciers up their favored north slopes. Limber pine is found in stony and exposed places, and bristlecone pine appears singly or in small groups. Mountain meadows in forest clearings often show a wealth of colorful wildflowers, such as larkspur, chiming bell, senecio, monkshood, daisy, and aster. Just below timberline is a plant zone of lush growth, brightly colored flowers, and dense forests of spruce and fir.

Many striking wildflowers thrive in the water-soaked soil of the Subalpine area. Marsh marigold and globeflower are found in large colonies (alpine anemone resembles the latter, but is hairy); shooting star, rose crown, and king's crown all like wet feet; and finding the little red elephant for the first time and noticing its long trunk and floppy ears is an unforgettable experience. Parry's primrose, brook saxifrage, and bittercress are commonly found along rushing, crystal clear creeks. Monkeyflower thrives in running water, at pond edges, and on rocky ground, collecting in exciting colonies.

The initiated flower lover knows where to look for the precious and beautiful mountain laurel, and where and when to find fairy

slipper orchids. In soils where peat has accumulated, we may come upon a host of orchids, wintergreen, wood nymph, and pyrola. The dainty twinflower is not as rare as is generally believed, once you have learned to recognize its carpet of delicate roundish leaves.

Shrubs typical of the Subalpine Zone include subalpine black currant, mountain ash (especially on the Western Slope), red-berried elder, bush honeysuckle, and thimbleberry. Some of these are also found in the Montane Zone. Shrubby cinquefoil, with its cheerful golden blooms, continues still higher into the rocky meadows of the Alpine Zone.

Climbing higher, the landscape begins to open, as exposed meadows and ridges lift skyward. Timberline in Colorado varies from 11,000 to 11,500 feet above sea level (or even higher). At these extremes, limber pine and subalpine fir have reached their upper limit of survival—weird, stunted trees with gnarled wood and branches pointing east, like ghost fingers (high winds blow from the west). Here at timberline they are a graphic illustration of "survival of the fittest." Some crouch in the lee of large boulders or form a low shed with a sloping roof. Others are alive on the east-facing branches only;

still others band together in mass resistance to the elements. These form the higher limit of the subalpine forest.

Alpine Zone
(11,500 feet and Higher)

To ascend above timberline is to step into the sky. Hovering high above the rest of our world, the Alpine Zone of the Rockies plies the thin air with ranges of cold granite and basalt. Some ranges extend unbroken for miles, even creating their own weather patterns. Other peaks stand in grand isolation, buffeted by wind and storms from every side. The breath of summer is cool. Here, rare endemic plants have lived for millennia, unable to leap from one range to the next. Other plants find their nearest relatives as far away as Alaska. Still, nearly every slope and crevice harbors some delicate grass or flower that has found its niche.

The delicate appearance of these tiny alpine gems is, on the one hand, deceptive. They endure near-arctic conditions for most of the year. Sunlight is intense, wind almost constant, and stony soils nearly impenetrable. Only durable and highly adapted plants can survive here. By contrast, they are not in the least prepared for the impact of hiking boots, and a misguided step can end decades of growth and create long-lasting scars on the fragile crust of living tundra. Please explore with care. Stay on trails. Where necessary, rock-hopping can minimize the impact of your visit on fragile alpine plants, and also leave the tundra intact for future wildflower enthusiasts.

Finding large fields of richly colored, dwarf, and highly fragrant flowers far above timberline is an unforgettable experience—one that never fails to impress. Here are thousands of tiny sky-blue forget-me-nots crowded one against the other; hundreds of delicate alpine phlox, white with a tinge of blue; highly perfumed white rock jasmine; and cushions of pinkish-purple moss campion. Eight-petaled creamy white flowers are found blooming on tiny mountain dryad shrubs with scalloped leaves.

By the latter part of July, a number of these earlier bloomers have become much less conspicuous or have disappeared altogether. In their place, we are apt to find fields yellow with alpine goldflower (also called old-man-of-the-mountain), looking like a disproportionately large sunflower head on short heavy stalks, and fuzzy as if trying to keep warm. Most abundant are alpine avens, looking somewhat like buttercups, but with deeply cut dark green or even purplish leaves.

Bistorts give character to this landscape by their upright spikes of small white flowers that remain in bloom a long time. And we must not overlook the pale yellow paintbrush and its gaudy rose-purple brother, so typical of this and the Subalpine region. Cushions of alpine sandwort, with moss-like leaves and five-pointed stars, echo the white of alpine phlox, but without their fragrance.

We may find alpine spring beauty with artificial-looking rosettes of fleshy leaves and a halo of pinkish-white blooms, or tiny clovers, or delicate yellow saxifrages, or beautiful (but smelly) sky pilots, and chiming bells and harebells. The Alpine meadows are full of surprises.

One of the most impressive of these surprises is found near melting snowbanks. Here it's not uncommon to find beautiful snow buttercups pushing their way through the edges of the snow. A little lower, in wet places, we are sure to find the rhodiolas (king's crown and rose crown), marsh marigold, globe flower, Indian paintbrush, and many others more typical of the Subalpine region.

Timberline, however, is not the upper limit for shrub growth; shrubby cinquefoil marches bravely on, and tundra willows venture still higher, even though their stature becomes remarkably small compared with their catkins. Arctic willow is only one inch high here. And on the highest peaks we still find the tiny shrub, mountain dryad, with its striking creamy blossoms.

While plenty of Colorado roads can provide access to our Alpine wonders, there are none higher or more accessible than the road to the top of Mt. Evans, just a short drive west of Denver. The chilly summit, at 14,240 feet, can experience snow, hail, sun, wind, and rain almost any day of the year, and often all in one visit. Sunlit snowbanks and frigid lakes sparkle even through late summer.

Along the way, be sure to explore the M. Walter Pesman Alpine Trail on Mt. Goliath, spanning both Alpine and Subalpine Zones. It is here that our fabled bristlecone pines are at their wind-sculpted best, yet they are accessible to even the casual visitor. A short loop trail weaves through the shadows of trees that have stood nearly 2,000 years. For those with time—and energy—the M. Walter Pesman trail climbs from the forest into the rarefied realm of the Alpine Zone.

Many visitors like to start above timberline at the upper end of the trail, about one mile past the Nature Center via the highway. From the upper trailhead, the rapid descent takes you from boulder fields and alpine crevices to the ancient bristlecone groves just below treeline. Alpine habitats and flowers abound. It is best to have a second car waiting below at the Mt. Goliath Nature Center, as the uphill walk back to the upper trailhead can be difficult at this high altitude.

The facility at Mt. Goliath is the result of dedicated effort from many individuals over the course of many decades, but Mr. Pesman was one who gave a great amount of time and effort to it at its inception. Most recently, the U.S. Forest Service and Denver Botanic Gardens* have cooperatively created the world's highest Alpine Rock Garden and an informative Nature Center. Here, rock outcrops and crevices echo the Alpine backdrop, and wildflowers not only thrive— they are identified with labels, helping to enlighten the novice, and discourage needless trampling of fragile tundra nearby.

The season for Alpine flowers is brief—from mid-June to late-September is typical. Sudden storms can include dangerous lightning or blizzard conditions, but exploring our highest peaks and meadows is still the quintessential Rocky Mountain experience.

*Founding partners in the Mt. Goliath project also included: Colorado Department of Transportation; Garden Club of Denver; National Scenic Byways Program; and Volunteers for Outdoor Colorado. A complete list of those who contributed funding, materials, and countless hours of hard work, may be viewed at the Mt. Goliath donor wall at the Nature Center.

About Plant Families

As you become acquainted with native wildflowers, you may want to know about the families to which they belong. Plants are classified into families on the basis of specific characteristics, some of which are quite easily observed and understood, while others are more obscure, yet can be detected with patience and the aid of a 10x hand lens. Once you have become acquainted with these "family traits," you will often be able to recognize the plant family to which a wildflower, otherwise unknown to you, belongs. Determining the family is a very important step toward the identification of a plant.

Here are fifteen of the most commonly occurring plant families in the Rocky Mountain region, with brief tips on how to recognize them. In addition to the common name, included is the Latin family name, which always ends in the letters *aceae*. These Latin names are recognized around the world, whatever the native language. For your convenience, there is a section at the back of this book (page 247) to help with these unfamiliar words.

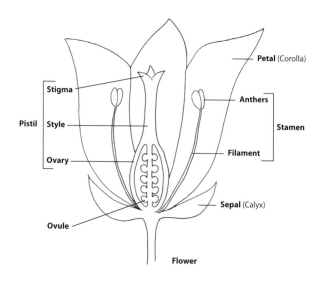

Buttercup Family (Ranunculaceae)

Flowers regular, as in buttercups, or irregular, as in larkspur and monkshood; all flower parts are separate (as opposed to united); 3 or more sepals, often petal-like in the absence of petals, as in pasque flower; petals none to many; stamens many; pistils 3 to many; leaves alternate, simple to compound, often deeply divided or with many leaflets. Members of this family are herbaceous plants or shrubby vines, such as *Clematis*.

Evening Primrose Family (Onagraceae)

Flowers regular with 4 petals united with the sepals to form a slender floral tube; flowers in leaf axils or terminal clusters; stamens commonly 8 or sometimes 4; ovary usually long, slender, 4-sided, and stigma commonly with 4 lobes. Family members include yellow stemless evening primrose, fireweed, willowherb, common evening primrose, cut-leaf evening primrose.

Figwort Family (Scrophulariaceae)

Usually showy flowers with irregular, 2-lipped corollas, the lips usually lobed; stamens are 2, 4, or 5 with 1 not bearing pollen; in the large genus *Penstemon*, the fifth stamen is a conspicuous sterile filament, bearded at the tip, and giving rise to the common name beardtongue because it is attached to the upper lip of the corolla; annual or perennial herbaceous plants with opposite leaves. There are many colorful wildflowers in this family, including Indian paintbrush, kittentail, monkeyflower, bunny-in-the-grass, owl clover, little red elephant, and penstemon.

Gentian Family (Gentianaceae)

Most noticeable members have conspicuous bright blue or purplish-blue flowers, while others have greenish-white or lilac-colored flowers; petals are always united to form a saucer-shaped, funnel-like or tubular corolla with spreading lobes; annual or perennial herbaceous plants with opposite, whorled or basal leaves without petioles and with smooth margins. Gentians usually bloom in the late summer and autumn. Family members include monument plant or green gentian, Arctic gentian, Rocky Mountain fringed gentian, star gentian, rose gentian.

Legume or Pea Family (Fabaceae)

Flowers irregular with 5 petals—uppermost petal generally largest and called the *banner*, 2 at the sides called the *wings*, 2 lower petals joined and folded in a boat-shaped *keel* that encloses the 10 stamens and the simple pistil; flowers often described as butterfly-like or papilionaceous; fruit a 1-chambered, several-seeded pod called a legume, such as bean or pea pods; herbaceous plants, shrubs or trees with alternate compound leaves, often with stipules. Family members include Golden banner, lupine, Lambert's loco, clovers, vetches, locust, wild licorice, peavine, milkvetch.

Lily Family (Liliaceae)

Flower parts in 3s and 6s, the sepals and petals nearly alike in many cases, the flowers often showy; usually 6 stamens; pistil compound, leaves often grass-like, with parallel veins; underground storage organs in the form of bulbs, corms, or fleshy rootstocks usually present. Family members include wood lily, twisted stalk, wand lily, avalanche lily, mariposa lily, alplily, false hellebore.

Mint Family (Lamiaceae)

Irregular 2-lipped flowers with 4 or 2 stamens, commonly 2 long and 2 short; usually aromatic (minty) herbaceous plants with square stems and opposite leaves; fruits are 4, 1-seeded nutlets held within the persistent calyx. Family members include horsemint, skullcap, wild mint, pennyroyal, selfheal.

Mustard Family (Brassicaceae)

Flowers regular with 4 sepals and 4 petals arranged in the form of a cross; 6 stamens, 2 outer ones shorter and 4 inner ones longer; 1 pistil; flowers usually in many-flowered racemes; leaves alternate; herbaceous plants with watery, acrid, peppery-tasting juice. Family members include wallflower, wild alyssum, draba, bittercress, purple mustard, watercress, bladderpod, prince's plume.

Orchid Family (Orchidaceae)

Largest of the flowering plant families worldwide, with most of the species occurring in the tropics or subtropics, yet two dozen or so occur in the Rocky Mountains. More than half of these have small, inconspicuous flowers, but each has the distinctive orchid floral characteristics: calyx and corolla of 6 segments, the 3 outermost are considered sepals (2 are sometimes united) and the 3 innermost are the petals; the lower petal is often much enlarged or otherwise modified to form a lip, a spur or an inflated sac or slipper-like structure; 1 or 2 stamens united with the pistil to form the column, a structure unique to orchids; fruit is a capsule with very numerous minute seeds. Family members include coral-root, ladyslipper, fairy slipper, ladies tresses, green bog orchid, white bog orchid, rattlesnake-plantain.

Parsley Family (Apiaceae)

Very small flowers arranged in umbels, either simple or compound (umbels made up of smaller umbels); sepals tiny or lacking, 5 petals with incurved tips, 5 stamens alternating with the petals and inserted on a disk; aromatic herbaceous plants, the leaves alternate or basal, compound, with petioles enlarged and sheathing the hollow stem at the nodes; fruits are 2-parted, with parts separating at maturity, each containing oil tubules that secrete aromatic oils, often of commercial importance. Family members include salt-and-pepper, sweet cicely, mountain parsley, whiskbroom parsley, giant angelica, cow parsnip, poison hemlock.

Phlox Family (Polemoniaceae)

Showy regular flowers with united 5-parted calyx and corolla, the latter being saucer-shaped, bell-shaped, funnelform, or with a slender tube and abruptly expanded outer portion; corolla lobes appear twisted in the bud; mostly 5 stamens attached inside the corolla tube; most are annual or perennial herbaceous plants with alternate or opposite leaves, simple or compound. Family members include Rocky Mountain phlox, gilia, fairy trumpet, Jacob's ladder, sky pilot.

Pink Family (Caryophyllaceae)

Flowers regular, usually with 5 separate petals; 10 stamens; stems usually enlarged at the nodes, and leaves opposite, simple and entire; annual or perennial herbaceous plants. Family members include moss pink, nailwort, mouse-ear chickweed, Fendler's sandwort, white campion.

Rose Family (Rosaceae)

Flowers regular with a cup-shaped or urn-shaped hypanthium; 5 (or 4) sepals, partly united; 5 petals, separate; 5 to many stamens; 1 to many pistils, separate or united into a 2- to 5-parted compound pistil; alternate leaves, simple or compound, with stipules; shrubs, trees, or herbaceous plants. Family members include cinquefoil, wild strawberry, alpine avens, wild rose, wild plum, chokecherry, mountain ash.

Saxifrage Family (Saxifragaceae)

Flowers regular with 4 or 5 partly united sepals and the same number of separate petals, and with a hypanthium; 5 to 10 stamens; pistils compound, 2-horned at the tip, with 2 styles or stigmas; flowers often borne in a cluster atop a leafless stalk; herbaceous plants with basal leaves, or shrubs with simple opposite leaves and opposite branches. Family members include alumroot, snowball saxifrage, mitrewort, brook saxifrage, dotted saxifrage, whiplash saxifrage.

Sunflower Family (Asteraceae)

One of the largest families of seed plants, with members varying greatly from each other but with a similar inflorescence. Flowers are very small and are crowded into tightly compact heads superficially resembling a single flower. Two kinds of flowers can be found: showy petal-like ray flowers occurring around the outside of the head as in sunflowers and daisies, or tiny tubular flowers forming the disk-like center of the head. In some members only ray flowers or disk flowers may be present in the head. Flower heads are surrounded by modified leaf-like structures called bracts or phyllaries, collectively known as the involucre, which superficially resembles the calyx of other flower types. Petals of both types of flowers are united, and the ovary forms a 1-seeded fruit called an achene. Family members include dandelion, sunflower, aster, goldenrod, blanket flower, black-eyed Susan, coneflower, sneezeweed, sagebrush, rabbitbrush, bull thistle, pussytoes.

Ferns, Horsetails, and Spikemosses

These are non-flowering plants that reproduce by means of spores—no showy flowers to be seen here. Spikemosses look like mosses but have 4-sided cones. Horsetails and scouring rushes, which are common along roadsides, streams, and ditches, have jointed stems that sometimes have whorls of branches and cones on their tips. The true ferns have leaves much like those of flowering plants, but have spore cases (sporangia) arranged in clusters or strips (sori), on the bottom side of the leaf.

Many of these primitive plants prefer moist soil, but in the West, many are adapted to dry conditions, living in rock crevices or stand curling dry and brown as they wait for rain.

eridium aquilinum
Annie Reiser

Bracken Fern

Pteridium aquilinum
ssp. *lanuginosum*
An often abundant fern. Large triangular fronds can reach 6 feet or more; turns brown at the first frost. Bracken ferns are among the most widespread ferns, found in many habitats around the world.

LIFE ZONE: Foothills, Montane

Date _____

Where found _____

_____

Field Horsetail

Equisetum arvense
Rather common along moist roadsides and ditches. The green sterile stems may be up to 2 feet tall and have whorls of branches at their nodes. The short-lived fertile stems are pinkish-brown and bear cones in the spring.

LIFE ZONE: Plains, Foothills, Montane, Subalpine

Date _____

Where found _____

_____

Smooth Scouring Rush

Equisetum laevigatum
A more conspicuous, usually unbranched, plant with noticeably jointed stems tipped by rounded cones. Common in wet spots and along streams. Rough stems have a high silica content and can be used to scrub pots and pans, should the sudden need arise! Aggressive in damp locations.

LIFE ZONE: Plains, Foothills, Montane

Date _____

Where found_____

_____

Fragile Fern
Cystopteris fragilis
A widely distributed small fern found in rock crevices and at the base of boulders. Its finely divided leaves do not have hairs and wither in dry weather.
LIFE ZONE: High Desert, Plains, Foothills, Montane, Subalpine, Alpine

Date _____

Where found _____

_____

Rocky Mountain Spikemoss
Selaginella densa
A low creeping plant that resembles a moss, except for the presence of 4-sided cones. Found on rocks or soil. Looks brown and dead when dry, but returns to green when moisture is available. Also called little club moss.
LIFE ZONE: Foothills, Montane, Subalpine, Alpine

Date _____

Where found _____

_____

Parsley Fern
Cryptogramma acrostichoides
A common small fern of rock outcrops and slopes. The sterile leaves resemble parsley, and the fertile leaves are more erect and have rolled margins.
LIFE ZONE: Montane, Subalpine, Alpine

Date _____

Where found _____

_____

Male Fern

Dryopteris filix-mas
A conspicuous large fern of rocky
slopes. Its fronds are up to 4 feet long
and somewhat evergreen.

LIFE ZONE: Foothills, Montane

Date _____

Where found _____

_____

Oregon Cliff Fern

Woodsia oregano ssp. *cathcartiana*
A small fern that grows in tufts in rock
crevices on open slopes. A related
species, the Rocky Mountain cliff fern
(*W. scopulina*), often has very small
spreading glandular hairs on its stipe
and rachis. It is found throughout the
Rocky Mountains.

LIFE ZONE: Foothills, Montane, Subalpine

Date _____

Where found _____

_____

Grasses and Grass-like Plants

Grasses, rushes, and sedges can be a confusing group of plants to identify. Some of the most basic differences are: Rushes have cylindrical hollow stems, no hairs or leaves; grasses have hollow stems and alternate leaves in ranks of 2 along the stems; sedges have solid triangular stems and leaves in ranks of 3.

Grasses can be generally divided into cool-season and warm-season grasses. Cool-season grasses grow most actively between fall and spring, going dormant during summer's heat. Warm-season grasses are dormant during winter, becoming active as conditions warm in the spring. Grasses can also be distinguished as "running"—those that spread by underground stolons, or bunch forming—those that grow in distinct clumps, spreading only by seed.

The flowers of most grasses are pollinated by wind, so there is no energy wasted on sweet nectar or showy bracts or petals. Flowers are usually held high above the leaves for best exposure to the wind. Most are complete flowers with male and female parts present in one inflorescence. Others, like buffalo grass, produce male and female flowers on separate plants. Some are distinct and easy to identify, while others can challenge even the experts.

In our Steppe climate, true grasses dominate much of the landscape, as they do in our sister climates of South Africa, central Asia, and Patagonia. They form the matrix that ties our landscapes together, from the shortgrass prairies to the alpine tundra. Here we concentrate primarily on our most common grasses and grass-like plants from lower and middle elevations.

Cattail
Typha latifolia
Flowers tiny, crowded into a large, dense, brownish spike; leaves strap-like, tough; plants 3–5 feet tall, usually growing in large, dense patches. Found along borders of standing water and ditches mostly in the plains. Another species, *T. angustifolia*, has more slender spikes and stems and narrower leaves.
BLOOM TIME: July, August
LIFE ZONE: Plains, Foothills

Date _____

Where found _____

_____

Alkali Sacaton
Sporobolus airoides
Warm-season bunch grass. Leaf blades are arching, slender and glossy, up to 18 inches; flowers in cloud-like masses just above the leaves, with a pinkish cast when new, produced over a long season. Found in alkali flats as the name implies, but also in mixed prairies, ditches, and roadsides. Adaptable to garden conditions; fine-textured frothy blooms provide good contrast to coarser plants in the xeric garden. Tends to go flat under winter snows.
BLOOM TIME: June, July, August, September
LIFE ZONE: High Desert, Plains

Date _____

Where found _____

_____

Big Bluestem
Andropogon gerardii
Warm-season bunch grass. Large grass with arching green to blue leaves up to 18 inches long. Flowering stems rise from 4 to 6 feet tall in mid and late summer with distinctive 3-parted spikes scattered along the upper stems, giving it the alternate common name of turkey-foot grass. Most often seen in mesic prairies, ditches, and damp swales, but quite drought tolerant. Infrequent on the Western Slope. Fall color from dark purple or maroon to rust, orange, or coral-pink. Several ornamental cultivars have been selected for garden use.
BLOOM TIME: August, September
LIFE ZONE: Plains, Foothills

Date _____

Where found _____

_____

Blue Grama
Bouteloua gracilis
Warm-season bunch grass. Leaves 6 to 12 inches long, much shorter in harsh conditions. Mid-summer brings a distinctive inflorescence with several horizontal spikes alternating near the top of a 12–18-inch stem. As these mature, they dry and curl, inspiring the common name of "eyelash grass." A delight in meadows and wildflower gardens; can also be mowed as a lawn.
BLOOM TIME: July, August
LIFE ZONE: High Desert, Plains, Foothills

Date_____

Where found _____

_____

Buffalo Grass
Bouteloua dactyloides
Warm-season running grass. A primary component of the shortgrass prairies. Plants always short, under 6 inches; sage green in summer and soft tan in winter, browning after the first hard frost. Male and female flowers on separate plants, female being knobby and close to the ground, male having short spikelets elevated on 4–6-inch stems. Buffalo grass sends its runners above the surface, rooting at the nodes as it spreads. Can make a beautiful low-water lawn.
BLOOM TIME: July, August
LIFE ZONE: Plains

Date_____

Where found _____

_____

Canada Wild Rye
Elymus canadensis
Warm-season running grass. Leaf blades wide, alternating and widely spaced all along the stems; inflorescence wheat-like to 4 inches long, nodding and coarse, atop 4 foot stems. Runs widely, but does not form a dense sod. Found along ditches, roadsides, and riparian areas; appreciates moisture, and tolerates shade better than many grasses. Distinctive, but running habit will challenge even the patient gardener.
BLOOM TIME: June, July
LIFE ZONE: Plains, Foothills, Montane

ate _____

here found _____

_____

Cheat Grass
Bromus tectorum
Widespread annual grass covering many thousands of square miles throughout the West. Germinates early, appearing bright green long before most native plants, and robbing them of early spring moisture. Coarse seed heads are pendulous, maturing to reddish or purplish brown, and sticking in your socks as they dry out. Dramatically increases fuel loads and wildfire potential. **Non-native species.**
BLOOM TIME: March, April, May, June
LIFE ZONE: High Desert, Plains, Foothills, Montane

Date _____
Where found _____
_____

Foxtail Barley
Hordeum jubatum
Cool-season bunch grass. Plants 1–2 feet tall; inflorescence dense, nodding, silky and shimmering in every breeze due to the very long awns on every seed. Often seen along roadsides, drying pond margins, and damp swales, but quite drought tolerant. Similar species are found in higher zones. Ornamental in the sunny garden. Deadhead before seeds shatter. This encourages re-bloom and prevents unwanted seedlings, which can be prolific!
BLOOM TIME: May, June, July, August
LIFE ZONE: High Desert, Plains, Foothills

Date _____
Where found _____

Galeta Grass
Pleuraphis jamesii
Warm-season bunch grass. Leaves grayish-green to 6 inches long and ¼-inch wide, forming dense clumps; flower spikes narrow with short fuzzy hairs among the seeds; leaves curling when dry and dormant. Found in dry open flats and roadsides in Colorado's southeast and western counties, throughout most of the Southwest.
BLOOM TIME: June, July
LIFE ZONE: High Desert, Plains

Date _____
Where found _____
_____

Green Needle Grass
Nassella viridula
Cool-season bunch grass. Leaves green early in the season; tall wand-like flowering stems to about 4 feet; seed spikes slender and brown as they mature. Small flocks of birds give the appearance of organization: one will land and bend the spike to the ground, then the rest will pounce and feast on the large grains. This cool season bunch grass is green well before most other native grasses in the spring.
BLOOM TIME: June
LIFE ZONE: High Desert, Plains, Foothills

Date _____
Where found _____
_____

Indian Grass
Sorghastrum nutans
Warm-season bunch grass. Foliage blue-green; tall feathery plumes to 6 feet; conspicuous lemon yellow anthers. Can reach 8 feet if moisture is plentiful. Ornamental anthers dance by the hundreds on each plume; inflorescence matures into silky brown seeds on dense spikes; leaves shading to pink and yellow in autumn. Tolerant of drought, but found most often in more mesic mid- or tallgrass prairies along the foothills, or along watercourses and ditches onto the plains. Many grasses have a noteworthy inflorescence, but this one is among the most colorful.
BLOOM TIME: August, September
LIFE ZONE: Plains

Date _____
Where found _____
_____

Indian Ricegrass
Achnatherum hymenoides
Warm-season bunch grass. Clumps vase shaped; leaves very slender, wiry; inflorescence arching, straw-colored, openly branched and airy, with a loose zig-zag appearance; large roundish seeds. Found throughout the western U.S., in sandy soils or on dry hillsides, ledges, and along roadsides. Delicate and very attractive among boulders in the xeric garden. Tends to go flat under winter snows.
BLOOM TIME: July, August, September
LIFE ZONE: High Desert, Plains

Date _____
Where found _____
_____

35

Little Bluestem

Schizachyrium scoparium

Warm-season bunch grass. Slender upright leaves, green to quite blue, in dense clumps to 12 inches tall; inflorescence slender, wiry, vertical to 2 feet, with fluffy silver seeds scattered in spikes atop the stems. Found in mixed prairies, roadsides, grassy hillsides, and widespread over much of the U.S. Blue-green effect in the garden is lovely, and autumn shades of rusty pink and red last all winter, standing up even after wet snows. One of the finest native grasses for cultivation, and several named cultivars have been selected.

BLOOM TIME: August, September

LIFE ZONE: High Desert, Plains, Foothills

Date _____

Where found _____

_____

Needle and Thread Grass

Heterostipa comata

Warm-season bunch grass. Narrow stiff leaves to 12 inches; graceful 2-foot blooms of silky bright green that sway in the breeze. The common name is aptly descriptive. At maturity, the sturdy seeds (a nuisance to furry pets) are sharply pointed and barbed, attached to thread-like awns that aid them in burrowing into the soil. Common in sandy soil or disturbed areas on the plains.

BLOOM TIME: May, June

LIFE ZONE: High Desert, Plains

Date _____

Where found _____

_____

New Mexican Feather Grass

Heterostipa neomexicana

Warm-season bunch grass. Plants nearly identical to *Stipa comata*; narrow stiff clumping leaves; wiry stems to 2 feet. Seeds on this species have long awns that are fringed like slender feathers, gracefully twisting as they mature. More commonly found on exposed outcrops and gravelly slopes along the foothills south of Denver, and from Colorado's Western Slope into the Southwest.

BLOOM TIME: May, June

LIFE ZONE: High Desert, Plains, Foothills

Date _____

Where found _____

_____

Pine Dropseed

Blepharoneuron tricholepis
Warm-season bunch grass. Bluish-green leaves generally under 8 inches; inflorescence may have a pink hue as it unfurls, then delicate and airy with tiny white flowers. Very attractive, drought tolerant small grass for sun or part shade among rocks, wildflowers, or in a drift by itself.

BLOOM TIME: July, August, September
LIFE ZONE: Plains, Foothills

Date _____

Where found _____

_____

Purple Three-Awn

Aristida purpurea
Warm-season bunch grass. Leaves very slender, thread-like, to 1 foot; purplish seeds with 3 long prominent awns in a triangular arrangement on stalks up to 14 inches. Best form in dry conditions. Entire plant very fine textured, attractive when grown with more coarse-leaved wildflowers or among boulders.

BLOOM TIME: July, August
LIFE ZONE: Plains

Date _____

Where found _____

_____

Ring Muhly

Muhlenbergia torreyi
Warm-season bunch grass. Short fine leaves under 6 inches. Inflorescence delicate and fine, up to 12 inches, in shades of soft rosy purple. Plants die away in the center as they grow in slowly expanding concentric circles. This accounts for the name, and creates a beautiful effect as rings overlap in sandy fields, dunes, and sandhill prairies.

BLOOM TIME: June, July
LIFE ZONE: High Desert, Plains

te _____

ere found _____

_____

Sideoats Grama

Bouteloua curtipendula

Warm-season bunch grass, sometimes slowly spreading. Leaves narrow, to 12 inches long, but may only reach 2 or 3 inches in very dry conditions; takes on pink-tan shades in fall. Inflorescence is distinctive, with pendulous flowers arranged in two opposite rows up the stem, reaching 2 feet. Nice in a meadow planting.

BLOOM TIME: August, September
LIFE ZONE: High Desert, Plains

Date_____

Where found _____

_____

Silver Beardgrass

Bothriochloa laguroides ssp. *torreyana*

Warm-season bunch grass. Leaves 3–6 inches long, blue-green, alternating along 2-foot stems. Inflorescence a narrow spike 3–4 inches long, fuzzy and silver. Very beautiful when back-lit in the garden. Best form when grown in dry soil; excess moisture creates lanky plants that flop.

BLOOM TIME: August, September
LIFE ZONE: Plains

Date_____

Where found _____

_____

Switch Grass

Panicum virgatum

Warm-season bunch grass. Variable species, generally with blades to ½-inch wide and up to 18 inches long, but appearing longer, as leaves are scattered along the tall flowering stems as well. Inflorescence may rise to 6 feet; nodding branched panicles with many roundish seeds widely scattered on the inflorescence. Found in xeric to mesic sites throughout the plains, and over much of the U.S. This species boasts many named garden cultivars, each beautiful in its own right, and exhibiting great diversity. Fall colors from dusky purple to clear yellow.

BLOOM TIME: August, September
LIFE ZONE: Plains

Date_____

Where found _____

_____

Western Wheatgrass
Pascopyrum smithii
Cool-season running grass. Leaf blades narrow, green to quite blue, rigid and sharp-tipped, rough textured with parallel veins or ridges. Seed spikes up to 2.5 feet, like a slender stalk of wheat. In open grasslands, large patches often create a blue haze compared to surrounding vegetation. Vigorous stolons spread aggressively, making it suitable for revegetation but not for garden use.
BLOOM TIME: July, August
LIFE ZONE: High Desert, Plains, Foothills

Date_____

Where found _____

_____

Grass Family (Poaceae)

Rushes
Juncus spp.
Flowers brownish, in spikes; seed pods contain several small seeds each; leaves stiff, long, and narrow, round in cross-section; stems hollow or spongy and un-jointed. Found in wet places as dark green, grass-like clumps. There are numerous species, difficult to distinguish.
BLOOM TIME: June, July, August
LIFE ZONE: Plains, Foothills

Date _____

Where found _____

_____

Rush Family (Juncaceae)

Bulrush
Scirpus spp.
Flowers are in clusters of brownish spikes at top of main stalk; 2 long grass-like leaves extend above the flower spikes; grows from 3 to 9 feet tall. Found in water around the edges of lakes and ponds, or in marshes. Historically, roots and young shoots were used as food by Native Americans. There are numerous sedge species, difficult to distinguish.
BLOOM TIME: June, July
LIFE ZONE: High Desert, Plains, Foothills, Montane

Date _____

Where found _____

_____

Sedge Family (Cyperaceae)

Sedges
Carex spp.

Sedges belong to a family of grass-like plants. A large proportion of them grow in cold, wet areas; many are found above timberline. Most sedges have 3-cornered stalks without joints, which distinguishes them from grasses. An interesting member of the same family found on the tundra is Kobresia, which forms a grass-like sod. It is conspicuous in late summer, when it turns a beautiful orange-gold.

BLOOM TIME: June, July
LIFE ZONE: High Desert, Plains, Foothills, Montane, Subalpine, Alpine

Date _____

Where found _____

_____

Early Sedge
Carex heliophila

Small clumps of grass-like, yellowish green leaves, flower stalks with small light yellow heads, noticeable because it blooms very early in the spring. Common on mesas and lower foothills, but also found in the Montane. Most sedges have triangular stems.

BLOOM TIME: April, May, June
LIFE ZONE: Plains, Foothills, Montane

Date _____

Where found _____

_____

Trees and Shrubs

Trees and shrubs persist year to year with woody stems, trunks, or branches. Conifers dominate higher elevations where the growing season is short. Deciduous trees are more common in the valleys and middle elevations. Many familiar landscape trees have come to us from far-off lands, which have very different climates. They succeed only with constant care and supplemental water. A few, from similar climates, have succeeded and become weedy.

Native western trees have a distinct advantage: they have adapted over millennia to thrive under natural conditions, each finding its niche in Colorado's varied topography and climate. Very few are native to the lowest elevations where drought, wind, and limited resources favor grasses and desert scrub. Here they only thrive in riparian areas, or struggle, shrub-like, on the fringes of their favored habitats. Native shrubs are even more resilient, occupying every life zone wherever conditions suit them, especially in rocky outcrops and riparian zones. Many do have noteworthy flowers, but we group them separately for ease of identification.

inia neomexicana
Marjorie Leggitt

41

Rocky Mountain Alder

Alnus incana ssp. *tenuifolia*
Tree-like or shrubby, usually 12–20 feet tall, with 2 or more main stems; smooth gray bark; leaves sharply toothed with prominent veins that cause the leaf surface to appear wrinkled; seeds borne in small, dark brown, woody cone-like structures ¾ inch long, persistent for several seasons. Common along streams, frequently associated with western river birch.
BLOOM TIME: March
LIFE ZONE: Foothills, Montane

Date _____

Where found _____

_____

Western River Birch

Betula occidentalis
Large shrub or small tree up to 25 feet; bark reddish brown and shiny; pale horizontal lines on the bark are called lenticels; leaves thin, oval and toothed, dark green above, yellow-green beneath; seeds in light brown papery cones, 1 inch long, shattering when seed is ripe. Common along streams throughout the mountains.
BLOOM TIME: April
LIFE ZONE: Foothills, Montane

Date _____

Where found _____

_____

One-Seeded Juniper

Juniperus monosperma
Small rounded tree, 8–15 feet tall, with several main stems, usually full and bushy to the ground; leaves evergreen, very small, overlapping and scale-like, yellowish green; bluish or copper-colored 1-seeded fruits. Often grows in association with piñon pine. The common juniper of the southern dry foothills and high plains.
BLOOM TIME: May
LIFE ZONE: Plains, Foothills

Date _____

Where found _____

_____

Rocky Mountain Juniper
Juniperus scopulorum
Small tree, 10–20 feet, but taller in some locations, usually symmetrical, but often shrubby with several main stems; leaves evergreen, small, scale-like, gray-green or silvery; smaller branches slender and graceful; light blue fruits, usually with 2–3 seeds. Found in dry soil of lower foothills and mesas. Many named cultivars, including weeping forms, have been selected over the years.
BLOOM TIME: May
LIFE ZONE: Plains, Foothills

Date _____

Where found _____

_____

Utah Juniper
Juniperus osteosperma
Typical small scale-like leaves pressed close to stems, olive-green; cones berry-like, blue to tan with 1 or more seeds; bark shredding in long fibrous strands; trunk usually single or several, but not usually as bushy and multi-stemmed from the base as *J. monosperma*. Usually under 12 feet, but can reach over 20 feet if sheltered and very old. Often forms pure open stands, widely spaced, or mixed with piñon pine. Older specimens have great character, with twisted leaning trunks sculpted by desert winds; often only narrow strips of live bark support the cloud-shaped green canopy.
BLOOM TIME: May
LIFE ZONE: High Desert, Foothills

Date _____

Where found_____

_____

Hackberry
Celtis reticulata
Small tree, often stunted and shrubby; bark light gray and corky; lopsided leaves similar to elm, often badly infested with insect galls. Found on dry, rocky slopes at lower elevations.
BLOOM TIME: April
LIFE ZONE: Plains, Foothills

Date _____

Where found_____

_____

Cypress Family (Cupressaceae)

Elm Family (Ulmaceae)

Elm Family (Ulmaceae)

Siberian Elm

Ulmus pumilus

Tall somewhat vase-shaped tree found in waste places, old homesites, riparian areas. Fast growing; leaves alternate, serrated edges, sometimes shiny on upper surface; seeds are round, papery. An opportunist, springing up along fences, buildings, floodplains. Weak wood and susceptibility to insects and disease often result in poorly shaped specimens and falling branches. **Non-native species.**

BLOOM TIME: March, April

LIFE ZONE: High Desert, Plains, Foothills

Date _____

Where found _____

_____

Legume Family (Fabaceae)

New Mexico Locust

Robinia neomexicana

Large shrub or small tree, 6–10 feet tall, pinnately compound leaves; branches with short thorns; rose-pink to lavender pea-like flowers in clusters; blooms in June. Found along roads and slopes of the lower foothills and mesas, southern Colorado to New Mexico and Texas. A showpiece in the spring garden, though suckering habit and susceptibility to borers may pose a challenge.

BLOOM TIME: June

LIFE ZONE: Plains, Foothills

Date _____

Where found _____

_____

Maple Family (Aceraceae)

Big-Tooth Maple

Acer grandidentatum

Large shrub to small tree, slender in ravines, otherwise full and oval in outline. Leaves firm, maple shaped, broad lobes, with rich fall color; seeds are papery winged pairs (samaras). Found from extreme southwest Colorado and throughout the Great Basin in sheltered ravines or mixed open forests. This medium-sized, colorful, drought-tolerant maple is magnificent in a xeric garden.

BLOOM TIME: April

LIFE ZONE: Foothills

Date _____

Where found _____

_____

Boxelder
Acer negundo

Medium-sized trees up to 40 feet, sometimes shrubby with several trunks; twigs and young branches bluish-gray; leaves opposite, compound with 3–7 leaflets; tiny petal-less flowers in drooping, reddish clusters (staminate and pistillate flowers on separate trees); fruits in winged pairs (samaras) typical of the maple family. Found along streams and moist places in foothills canyons, mesas, and plains.

BLOOM TIME: April
LIFE ZONE: Plains, Foothills

Date _____

Where found _____

_____

Maple Family (Aceraceae)

Rocky Mountain Maple
Acer glabrum

Many-stemmed shrubby tree with smooth gray bark, 8–12 feet tall; leaves palmately lobed, sharp toothed; fruits are twin-winged; young twigs, buds, and leafstalks red, leaves turn vivid red in autumn. Found in canyons and moist hillsides. Colorado's only native maple east of the Divide.

BLOOM TIME: April
LIFE ZONE: Foothills, Montane

Date _____

Where found _____

_____

Scrub Oak
Quercus gambelii

A much-branched small tree or shrub, often forming dense thickets; dark, furrowed bark; leaves leathery, usually with rounded lobes, adding red, brown, and rust to the autumn landscape. Staminate flowers are in long greenish-yellow tassels; pistillate flowers inconspicuous, developing later into small acorns. Common in the lower Montane and Foothill Zones west of Continental Divide, and from Denver southward on the east side. Durable and attractive in a dry garden. Oaks hybridize easily, and variations occur where species overlap, confounding those who need absolute identification!

BLOOM TIME: April
LIFE ZONE: Foothills, Montane

Date _____

Where found _____

_____

Oak Family (Fagaceae)

Oak Family (Fagaceae)

Wavyleaf Oak
Quercus x pauciloba
Shrub or small tree, up to 15 feet tall; leaves deciduous, margins entire, often wavy, sometimes with small teeth. Oaks hybridize easily, and so much variation occurs that precise descriptions are impossible. This species is often single-stemmed; mature specimens with contorted trunks and cloud-shaped form have all the character of a sculpted bonsai. Found in canyons of southeast Colorado and scattered throughout the Southwest. Slow-growing, and excellent as a specimen or informal hedge in the xeric garden.
BLOOM TIME: April
LIFE ZONE: Plains

Date _____

Where found _____

_____

Oleaster family (Eleagnaceae)

Russian Olive
Eleagnus angustifolia
Shrub, becoming a medium-size tree up to 30 feet tall; leaves linear, drooping, willow-like, alternate, very silvery-green; flowers small, yellow, in sweetly fragrant clusters, with 4 recurved petals; fruit mealy, olive-shaped, with large seed having parallel lines. Sometimes found in abandoned fields, farms, windbreaks, but most common in riparian areas and river valleys. Its aggressive nature has resulted in its placement on the noxious weed list in Colorado and New Mexico. **Non-native species.**
BLOOM TIME: May
LIFE ZONE: High Desert, Plains, Foothills

Date _____

Where found _____

_____

Pine Family (Pinaceae)

Bristlecone Pine
Pinus aristata
Medium-sized tree with bushy crown, 15–45 feet tall; 1–1½ inch needles usually strongly curved, in bundles of 5, dotted with white flecks of pitch, making this tree easy to recognize; cones woody with sharp bristle at end of each scale. Found on windy, rocky, exposed slopes and ridges, often growing in gnarled and twisted shapes. Sometimes called foxtail pine because of the round brush-like appearance of the needles at the ends of the branches.
BLOOM TIME: May
LIFE ZONE: Montane, Subalpine

Date _____

Where found_____

_____

Colorado Blue Spruce

Picea pungens

Colorado's state tree, a handsome spruce up to 100 feet tall; needles single, sharp, stiff, and extending from all sides of the twig, may vary from green to silver-blue; cones light brown, up to 5 inches long, hang from upper branches. Found on moist lower slopes of canyons and along streams. A landscaping tree planted worldwide. Surprisingly tolerant of drought considering its riparian origins. Many horticultural forms have been selected.

BLOOM TIME: May

LIFE ZONE: Foothills, Montane

te _____

here found _____

_____

Douglas Fir

Pseudotsuga menziesii var. *glauca*

Evergreen with pyramidal crown, can reach 100 feet; needles often with a blue cast, flat, soft and flexible; cones hang down with protruding 3-pronged bracts between the scales. Commonly found on north-facing rocky slopes and shaded ravines. Economically important for lumber. Variety *menziesii* in the Pacific states grows faster and even larger, but is more tender to cold.

BLOOM TIME: May

LIFE ZONE: Foothills, Montane

te _____

ere found _____

_____

Engelmann Spruce

Picea engelmannii

Tall, slender evergreen to 100 feet; needles 4-sided, stiff, sharp-pointed; cones light brown, small, 2½ inches, hanging downward; old twigs rough with persistent bases of fallen needles; bark of mature trees reddish brown; subalpine slopes but occasionally found in the upper Montane Zone. Forms broad belts of dark green forest with subalpine fir.

BLOOM TIME: June

LIFE ZONE: Montane, Subalpine

e _____

ere found _____

_____

Pine Family (Pinaceae)

Limber Pine
Pinus flexilis
Gnarled, rough-looking with rounded crown, 30–45 feet tall; needles in bundles of 5, 2½ inches long; cones large, 3–8 inches, with broad woody scales; young branches have smooth, gray bark. Found on rocky outcrops and ridges from Montane Zone to timberline, but nowhere abundant. As its common name implies, the branches are extremely flexible.
BLOOM TIME: May, June
LIFE ZONE: Montane, Subalpine

Date _____
Where found _____
_____

Lodgepole Pine
Pinus contorta ssp. *latifolia*
Slender when growing in close, dense stands, as occurs after forest fires, and suffers cyclical periods of demise from fire and pine beetles. Can reach 80 to 100 feet, though usually smaller. Otherwise trees more spreading; needles in bundles of 2, 1–3 inches long, yellow-green, often twisted; cones ¾–2 inches long, egg-shaped to nearly cylindrical, and usually lopsided, cone scales with recurved prickle at tips. Cones are hard, requiring fire to open and release seed, or they may remain on tree unopened for many years. On dry slopes, often growing in pure stands with little or no understory aside from mats of kinnikinnick. The trunks were used by Plains Indians for teepees.

BLOOM TIME: May, June
LIFE ZONE: Foothills, Montane, Subalpine

Date _____
Where found _____
_____

Piñon Pine
Pinus edulis
Common small bushy pine of the southern and western dry woodlands; 15–30 feet tall; needles short, ¾–1½ inches, in bundles of 2; cones small, broad-oval with large edible seeds. Piñon nuts have long been a staple food for Native Americans of the Southwest, and are a popular commodity today, especially in the southwestern part of the U.S.
BLOOM TIME: May
LIFE ZONE: High Desert, Plains

Date _____
Where found _____
_____

Ponderosa Pine or Western Yellow Pine

Pinus ponderosa

Sweetly scented and magnificent, this is likely the most widespread conifer on Earth, occupying vast areas throughout western North America. Several subspecies occur over its broad range. A massive tree when mature, soaring to over 100 feet, with orange-brown bark, open rounded crown; needles in bundles of 2–3, 5 to 7 inches long; cones large, woody, roundish, 3–4 inches long, scales opening wide. These trees are usually widely spaced, and form beautiful open parklands on dry slopes. Important lumber tree.

BLOOM TIME: May

LIFE ZONE: Foothills, Montane

Date _____

Where found _____

_____

Southwestern White Pine

Pinus strobiformis

Tall evergreen, needles 5 per bundle, soft, blue-green, 3 inches long; cones similar to limber pine, but larger. Found scattered from south central Colorado, throughout the Southwest. Sturdy and drought-tolerant, but soft in texture. Similar in habit to eastern white pine (*P. strobus*), but far more durable in the garden, and better suited to the dry climates of the West.

BLOOM TIME: May

LIFE ZONE: Foothills, Montane

Date _____

Where found _____

_____

Subalpine Fir

Abies lasiocarpa

Tall, slender evergreen with spire-like crown; needles flat and flexible, 1–1½ inches; erect dark purple cones on uppermost branches, 3–4 inches long; bark light gray; associated with Engelmann Spruce in the subalpine forest belt. Cones not often seen, as they shatter upon ripening, leaving an upright candle-like stem on the tree.

BLOOM TIME: June

LIFE ZONE: Montane, Subalpine

Date _____

Where found _____

_____

Pine Family (Pinaceae)

White Fir

Abies concolor

Elegant conical tree with silver-gray bark; needles single, flat, flexible, blunt-tipped, about 2 inches long; erect cones on uppermost branches; when the seeds are ripe, cone scales fall, leaving only the slender central stalk. Occurs in canyons and on moist hillsides, Colorado Springs and southwest-ward. This beautiful species may appear very silvery, almost like Colorado blue spruce, but with soft lemon-scented needles. One of the most drought-tolerant firs for the landscape.

BLOOM TIME: May
LIFE ZONE: Foothills, Montane

Date _____

Where found _____

Quassia Family (Simaroubaceae)

Tree of Heaven

Ailanthus altissima

Tall robust trees; single trunk or growing from root sprouts to form large colonies, fast growing, up to 50 feet; leaves large, pinnately compound, foul smelling; small male and female flowers in large panicles on separate trees; fruits papery samaras in large clusters, twisted, with a central seed, bright green or shaded red. Aggressive, unwelcome because of suckering habit, copious seedlings, and alleopathic effects on surrounding vegetation. Listed as a noxious weed in many areas. According to Oregon fossil records, *Ailanthus* had been native in prehistoric times. It was eliminated by natural causes, but alas, a few million years later, humans brought it back! **Non-native species.**

BLOOM TIME: May, June
LIFE ZONE: High Desert, Plains

Date _____

Where found _____

Rose Family (Rosaceae)

Mountain Ash

Sorbus scopulina

Large shrub or small tree, up to 12 feet tall; bark dark brown to gray; pinnately compound leaves of 11–15 leaflets with toothed edges; flowers creamy white in flat-topped clusters; orange to red fruits shaped like tiny apples that serve as food for birds. Found in cool ravines and foothill canyons, chiefly west of the Continental Divide. Highly ornamental substitute for imported species in the landscape.

BLOOM TIME: May, June
LIFE ZONE: Montane

Date _____

Where found _____

Pin Cherry
Prunus pensylvanica
Tall shrub or small tree, usually under 20 feet, smooth brown bark with horizontal markings; flowers white, 5-petaled, in small clusters near ends of twigs; fruits are small bright red cherries; leaves oval, 1–3 inches long; grows in scattered clumps rather than dense thickets. Foothill canyons and shaded slopes, not as common as chokecherry or wild plum. Small stature and gracefully spreading and nodding branches make this a nice addition to a shrub border or informal garden.
BLOOM TIME: April, May
LIFE ZONE: Foothills

Date _____

Where found _____

_____

Western Chokecherry
Prunus virginiana var. *melanocarpa*
Tree-like large shrub can reach 30 feet or more, often shorter depending upon habitat; bark reddish brown; flowers in cylindrical creamy white, fragrant clusters; dark red or black fruits in elongated clusters, puckery, excellent for jelly. Important food for wildlife. Because the seeds pass through birds and are dropped where they commonly sit along fences, look for this species, frequently in rows, along fence lines. Forms thickets in valleys and on hillsides, common throughout the United States. Stoloniferous habit and abundant seedlings can be challenging in the garden.
BLOOM TIME: May
LIFE ZONE: Plains, Foothills, Montane

Date _____

Where found _____

_____

Western Soapberry
Sapindus saponaria var. *drummondii*
Small suckering tree to 40 feet, with pinnately compound leaves; flowers tiny, greenish, in conical panicles; fruits a translucent golden-orange drupe, turning dark brown, with a single stony round seed. More widespread in the south-central plains, and found rarely in canyons, riparian areas, and ditches near Colorado's far southeastern border.
BLOOM TIME: May
LIFE ZONE: Plains

Date _____

Where found _____

_____

Narrow-Leaf Cottonwood
Populus angustifolia
Medium-sized, up to 50–70 feet tall, bark of lower trunk gray and furrowed, branches smooth and creamy white; leaves narrow, 2–4 inches long. Found along streams. Close examination reveals winter buds with bud scales that are red-brown and sticky with an aromatic exudate. Root suckers stabilize stream banks and create extensive stands in river valleys, especially in western counties.
BLOOM TIME: April
LIFE ZONE: Plains, Foothills, Montane

Date _____

Where found_____

_____

Peachleaf Willow
Salix amygdaloides
The only native willow that becomes a tree; several stems, 15–30 feet tall; leaves long, slender, 2–5 inches; twigs yellowish gray. Common along streams and irrigation ditches on the eastern plains, and in moist places in the lower foothills.
BLOOM TIME: April, May
LIFE ZONE: Plains, Foothills

Date _____

Where found _____

_____

Plains Cottonwood
Populus deltoids
Massive broad-crowned tree, sometimes 100 feet tall; yellow-green, glossy trian-gular leaves with toothed margins; gray furrowed bark with thick ridges; grows along stream banks, river bottoms, and flood plains at low elevations. Glorious golden color in late fall. Plains Cotton-wood is common on the east side of the mountains, and is the only large tree native along the urban corridor at the foot of the Front Range. West of the Divide, replaced by ssp. *wislizenii*.
BLOOM TIME: April
LIFE ZONE: High Desert, Plains

Date _____

Where found _____

_____

Quaking Aspen
Populus tremuloides

Extensive groves paint the high country in lime green each spring and rich gold each autumn. Often found on moist slopes and along streams in Subalpine and upper Montane. Small to medium sized, seldom over 50–60 feet tall; small, rounded leaves with pointed tip, 1½–3 inches; bark smooth, white, or light green. Called quaking aspen because its leaves tremble in the slightest breeze, since the leaf petiole is flattened and attached at right angles to the flat leaf blade.

BLOOM TIME: April, May

LIFE ZONE: Foothills, Montane, Subalpine

Date _____

Where found _____

_____

Fendler's Barberry
Berberis fendleri

Traits generally resemble other cultivated species. Typically upright shrub, not heavily branched; leaves are simple, entire, alternate; branches with distinctive clustered thorns, especially near base of stems; flowers bright yellow, in clusters; red berries in short pendulous clusters in autumn. Often found in dappled shade of Ponderosa pines in western counties. Attractive and drought tolerant, but seldom grown and should be used more.

BLOOM TIME: June, July

LIFE ZONE: Foothills, Montane

te _____

here found _____

_____

Fremont's Mahonia
Mahonia fremontii

Rounded shrub up to 6 feet tall; evergreen compound leaves, often a rich blue-green, holly-shaped, sharply spined along margins; flowers bright yellow in clusters; fruits turning red by mid-summer. Scattered distribution in Colorado's southwest counties and throughout the Southwest. Very drought tolerant and beautiful all year. Wonderful desert shrub as a specimen or background. Wear gloves when working among pointy fallen leaves!

BLOOM TIME: April, May

LIFE ZONE: High Desert

ate _____

Where found _____

_____

Birch Family (Betulaceae)

Bog Birch
Betula glandulosa
Dwarf shrub with dark brown or gray-brown bark; short, stubby, green or brown catkins in leaf axils; leaves thick, rounded, finely toothed, turning brilliant orange to maroon in autumn; often only a few inches high at timberline but can be 5–6 feet at lower elevations. Found in all high mountain and Arctic regions of North America.
BLOOM TIME: June, July
LIFE ZONE: Subalpine, Alpine

Date _____

Where found _____

_____

Buckthorn Family (Rhamnaceae)

Common Buckthorn
Rhamnus cathartica
Large shrub or small tree to 20 feet, with smooth, deep mahogany bark when young; leaves opposite, slightly glossy, prominent parallel veins; flowers not conspicuous, followed by small black berries that are spread by birds. Formerly planted as an ornamental, now a common urban weed sometimes appearing in natural areas. Listed as a noxious weed in several states. **Non-native species.**
BLOOM TIME: June
LIFE ZONE: Plains, Foothills

Date _____

Where found _____

_____

Fendler Ceanothus
Ceanothus fendleri
Lightly spiny shrub up to 4 feet; clusters of small white flowers at stem tips, often so prolific as to nearly cover the plant; leaves small, pale beneath. Common on dry hillsides, often forms large patches.
BLOOM TIME: June, July
LIFE ZONE: Foothills

Date _____

Where found _____

_____

Mountain Balm
Ceanothus velutinus
Low shrub, 1–3 feet tall, with leathery, sticky, evergreen leaves, prominently 3-veined from base toward tip; small creamy white flowers in dense clusters. Leaves exude a pleasant fragrance similar to pipe tobacco, especially when crushed. Found on sunny slopes over a wide range. One of a handful of broadleaf evergreen natives for the xeric garden.
BLOOM TIME: June, July
LIFE ZONE: Foothills, Montane

Date _____

Where found _____
_____

Golden Currant
Ribes aureum
Shrub of medium height, up to 6 feet, with yellow, spicy clove-scented, tubular flowers, ½–¾ inch long, short petals often tipped with red; leaves wedge-shaped and 3-lobed; stems smooth, without spines; fruit a small sweet round black or red-brown berry. Common in the foothills and plains. Very drought-tolerant, and one shrub will perfume the spring garden!
BLOOM TIME: May, June
LIFE ZONE: Plains, Foothills

Date _____

Where found _____
_____

Red Prickly Currant
Ribes montigenum
Low, spreading shrub to 4 feet tall, with 3 spines at leaf base; greenish-white to purplish saucer-shaped flowers; berries red, sticky-hairy; common and found on rocky slopes.
BLOOM TIME: July
LIFE ZONE: Montane, Subalpine

Date _____

Where found _____
_____

Buckthorn Family (Rhamnaceae)

Currant or Gooseberry Family (Grossulariaceae)

Subalpine Black Currant
Ribes coloradense
Low sprawling shrub under 3 feet tall, stems lacking spines or bristles; flowers pink, tubular, with 5 lobes; leaves almost heart-shaped with 5 toothed lobes; berries black, sticky. Common in western Colorado.
BLOOM TIME: July
LIFE ZONE: Subalpine

Date _____

Where found _____

_____

Wax Currant
Ribes cereum
Low, rather sticky-hairy shrub under 6 feet tall; leaves are slightly fragrant; small, lobed, with toothed edges, flowers pinkish, tubular, in small clusters; fruit orange-red, edible but rather insipid. There are several other species of currants in the Rocky Mountains, but this is a common one. Abundant on dry sunny slopes. Sometimes called squaw currant.
BLOOM TIME: May, June
LIFE ZONE: Foothills, Montane

Date _____

Where found _____

_____

Wild Gooseberry
Ribes inerme
Branched shrub with arching stems, up to 3 feet high; sharp spines at leaf nodes; leaves small, about ¾–1½ inches broad, rounded and slightly to deeply lobed; pale yellow tubular flowers; the fruit is picked when amber and translucent for pie or preserves, but turns nearly black and unpleasant when fully ripe. Moist slopes and gulches.
BLOOM TIME: June
LIFE ZONE: Foothills, Montane

Date _____

Where found _____

_____

Date _____

Where found _____

Common Juniper
Juniperus communis
Low spreading shrub, never more than 2–3 feet high, often spreading 6 feet or more; needles sharply pointed, awl-like, green, with white line on upper surface; fruits are berrylike, blue. A circumpolar species, found over the whole northern hemisphere. Varieties of it have been selected and used in landscape planting. Dry forests and open slopes from foothills and mesas to timberline.
BLOOM TIME: May
LIFE ZONE: Foothills, Montane, Subalpine

Cypress Family (Cupressaceae)

Date _____

Where found _____

Red-Osier Dogwood
Cornus sericea ssp. *sericea*
Many bright red slender stems in a clump, up to 6 feet tall, but appearing more green than red during summer; leaves opposite, broadly lanceolate with prominent veins all turning toward the tip; small white flowers in a more or less flat-topped cluster, followed by white berries, much enjoyed by birds. Common along streams from Foothills to Subalpine. Used for winter color in the garden.
BLOOM TIME: May, June, July
LIFE ZONE: Foothills, Montane, Subalpine

Dogwood Family (Cornaceae)

Frankenia
Frankenia jamesii
Low mounded shrub, up to 18 inches; leaves tiny, almost needle-like, under ½ inch, not evergreen; flowers ¼ inch, white, 5 petals. Found only on particular soils in the Arkansas River drainage. Related *Frankenia* species have an odd discontinuous distribution over several continents that may link them to the ancient Sea of Tethys!
BLOOM TIME: June
LIFE ZONE: High Desert

Date _____

Where found _____

Frankenia Family (Frankeniaceae)

Four-Wing Saltbush

Atriplex canescens

Rangy rounded shrub, 3–8 feet tall; leaves linear, to 2 inches, silver-green, persisting into winter; flowers small, in oblong clusters; seeds enclosed in papery dry 4-winged fruits, generally soft yellow, sometimes with pink shades. Ornamental when used in xeric gardens, or as part of a mixed shrub backdrop.

BLOOM TIME: May

LIFE ZONE: High Desert, Plains

Date _____

Where found _____

_____

Winter Fat

Krascheninnikovia lanata

An attractive woolly-white shrub, 1–3 feet tall; flowers and fruiting bracts with long silky white hairs, turning rufous brown in late summer; leaves threadlike. Common on dry or sandy alkaline flats and plains, sometimes dominating large areas. Valuable as winter feed for livestock, but also attractive in a xeric or prairie garden where its fluffy silvery-white plumes are a bright contrast to the browning late-season grasses.

BLOOM TIME: July, August

LIFE ZONE: Plains

Date _____

Where found _____

_____

Manzanita

Arctostaphylos patula

Shrub up to 3 feet; leaves bright green, ovate, evergreen, and leathery; stems smooth with thin peeling layers, satiny reddish-brown; flowers small downfacing urns, rosy-pink to near-white, followed by round red or brownish berries. Widely scattered populations from western Colorado, south and west, in open dry woodlands and hillsides. Populations on the Uncompahgre Plateau include many forms and hybrids with other species. Excellent broadleaf evergreen for xeric gardens, remaining rich green all winter. Prefers sunny, warm, dry locations with good drainage. Named selections are now available from nurseries.

BLOOM TIME: March, April

LIFE ZONE: Foothills

Date _____

Where found _____

_____

Mountain Laurel
Kalmia polifolia
Low shrub 6–18 inches tall, with bright pink to rose, 5-petaled, saucer-shaped flowers, ¾-inch across; leathery ever-green leaves 1 inch long, white beneath;. Found in cold subalpine bogs and along wet margins of streams and lakes.
BLOOM TIME: July, August
LIFE ZONE: Subalpine

Date _____

Where found _____

_____

Bush Honeysuckle
Lonicera involucrata
Shrub 2–9 feet tall, with opposite, oval leaves; yellow tubular flowers, ½-inch long, in pairs, enclosed in leafy bracts that turn red as fruits ripen to black berries. Common Rocky Mountain shrub along streams and moist slopes.
BLOOM TIME: June
LIFE ZONE: Foothills, Montane, Subalpine

Date _____

Where found _____

_____

Mountain Snowberry
Symphoricarpos oreophilus
Much-branched low shrub, 1–3 feet tall, often in dense thickets; leaves round to ovate, greener above than beneath; pink tubular flowers, ½-inch long in axils of leaves; berries white spongy spheres, clusters may persist most of the winter. Common, along with three similar species: *S. albus*, *S. occidentalis* and *S. longiflorus* pictured here.
BLOOM TIME: May
LIFE ZONE: Foothills, Montane, Subalpine

Date _____

Where found _____

_____

Heath Family (Ericaceae)

Honeysuckle Family (Caprifoliaceae)

Red-Berried Elder

Sambucus racemosa

Coarse shrub up to 8 feet tall; large pinnately compound leaves with 5–7 leaflets; white, rounded flower clusters; bright red to orange-red berries. Found on slopes, roadsides and in ravines.

BLOOM TIME: July

LIFE ZONE: Montane, Subalpine

Date _____

Where found _____

_____

Cliff Fendlerbush

Fendlera rupicola

Shrub up to 6 feet, upright when young, later vase-shaped or spreading with dark branches; narrowly eliptical leaves 1–1½ inches long, edges often curled; flowers fragrant, bright white, rarely with a pink tint, 4 widely spread spatulate petals have a slight fringe; fruits a dry pointed capsule with papery red-brown seeds. Found in dry canyon sides, sandy flats with piñon and juniper, in Colorado's southwest counties and beyond. Lovely in the xeric or naturalistic garden, somewhat resembling a mock orange, with more delicate features.

BLOOM TIME: May

LIFE ZONE: High Desert

Date _____

Where found _____

_____

Little-Leaf Mock Orange

Philadelphus microphyllus

Woody, wiry shrub up to 5 feet; branches arching and dense; leaves ovate to lanceolate, lighter green on reverse, from ½ to 1¼ inches; fragrant flowers white, 4 petals, up to 1 inch. Found in woodland openings, dry hillsides, and canyons in Colorado's southwest and into the Great Basin. Fine-textured shrub provides a fresh green contrast to sage or evergreens in a xeric garden.

BLOOM TIME: May, June

LIFE ZONE: High Desert, Foothills

Date _____

Where found _____

_____

Waxflower
Jamesia americana
Stiffly branched shrub with opposite twigs and branches, up to 4 feet; bark shredding, giving a two-toned appearance; leaves opposite, dark green, deeply veined, oval with sharp teeth; flowers with 5 waxy, creamy white petals, in clusters; seed heads persistent through winter. Grows on rocky slopes, or in crevices of large boulders and canyon cliffs.
BLOOM TIME: May, June, July, August
LIFE ZONE: Foothills, Montane

Date _____
Where found _____
_____

Mormon Tea or Jointfir
Ephedra viridis
Low, much-branched shrub to four feet high, with bright green, leafless stems; short branches are whorled, in broom-like clusters. Flowers small, greenish-yellow, not individually showy, but in great quantity, followed by dry brown seeds enclosed in papery scales.   Found in dry, sandy areas in western Colorado, Arizona, New Mexico, and Utah. Early pioneers brewed a hot drink from the dried stems. Fine texture and bright green stems are a nice contrast to sage and yuccas in the xeric garden all year. Some non-native relatives produce colorful berries.
BLOOM TIME: May, June
LIFE ZONE: High Desert

Date _____
Where found _____
_____

Dwarf Leadplant
Amorpha nana
Compact and densely branched shrub up to 3 feet, usually less; flowers tightly packed in short 2-inch spikes at branch tips, pinkish-purple, fragrant. Scattered populations in eastern Colorado in open prairie and rocky outcrops along the Front Range foothills.
BLOOM TIME: June, July, August
LIFE ZONE: Plains, Foothills

Date _____
Where found _____
_____

Hydrangea Family (Hydrangeaceae)

Jointfir Family (Ephedraceae)

Legume Family (Fabaceae)

61

Legume Family (Fabaceae)

False Indigo

Amorpha fruticosa var. *angustifolia*
Sprawling shrub up to 7 feet; pinnate leaves; flowers at stem tips, dusky purple with deep yellow anthers, less showy than *A. canescens*. Widespread throughout the U.S., and found along streams, ditches, and swales in eastern Colorado.
BLOOM TIME: July, August
LIFE ZONE: High Desert, Plains, Foothills

Date _____

Where found _____

_____

Leadplant

Amorpha canescens
Rounded shrub, 2–4 feet tall, with many stems rising from a central crown. Leaves pinnate, bluish-green, with very fine hairs; flowers small but dense, each with a single petal, in branched spikes at stem tips, rich purple with orange protruding anthers. Found in sandy soils of eastern Colorado and scattered throughout the Plains states. One of the finest native shrubs for the xeric garden, prairie, or mixed border, adding welcome color to the mid-summer garden.
BLOOM TIME: July, August
LIFE ZONE: Plains

Date _____

Where found _____

_____

Mint Family (Lamiaceae)

Frosted Mint

Poliomintha incana
Spreading shrub, under 2 feet tall, twiggy; small gray-green leaves with fine silvery hairs; flowers small, bluish-white. Entire plant fragrant, resembling mint, rosemary, or lavender, depending on who is sniffing! Found in far southwest Colorado, and scattered throughout the southwest deserts, always in sandy soil or dunes. Potentially useful in difficult situations. The related species *P. maderensis* is used in warmer desert gardens.
BLOOM TIME: May, June
LIFE ZONE: High Desert

Date _____

Where found _____

_____

Shrub Live Oak
Quercus turbinella
Shrub or small multi-stemmed tree to 12 feet; leaves evergreen in all but the coldest winters, blue-green, stiff, with sharp-tipped teeth like a holly; flowers greenish-yellow in hanging racemes, male and female flowers are separate, females followed by small acorns that mature in late summer. Hybrids with other species have variable traits. Limited distribution in dry canyons and ravines in Colorado; more widespread south and west. Durable small tree for a xeric landscape, hedge, or naturalistic garden.
BLOOM TIME: May
LIFE ZONE: High Desert, Plains

ate _____
here found _____
_____

Oak Family (Fagaceae)

Canada Buffaloberry
Shepherdia canadensis
Shrub 2–4 feet tall, with opposite leaves and gray branches; dark green leaves somewhat leathery with prominent mid-vein, often curled under at the sides, buds and undersides of leaves have reddish, scurfy scales; berries translucent orange-red when ripe, edible, though very bitter. Found in open forests and rocky slopes.
BLOOM TIME: May
LIFE ZONE: Foothills, Montane

Date _____
Where found _____
_____

Oleaster Family (Elaeagnaceae)

Silver Buffaloberry
Shepherdia argentea
Tall thicket-forming shrub, up to 15 feet, with silvery, willow-like leaves and thorn-tipped twigs; bright red or orange berries, sour but edible. Common along streams, irrigation ditches, and river bottoms west of the Continental Divide.
BLOOM TIME: May
LIFE ZONE: Plains, Foothills

Date _____
Where found _____
_____

Rose Family (Rosaceae)

Antelope-Brush
Purshia tridentata
Small shrub, 2–4 feet high; leaves less than 1-inch long, widest near the tip, with three teeth, hence the Latin name *tridentata;* pale yellow flowers ½-inch across, late May or early June. A favorite browse food for deer; attracts pollinators. Dry, rocky slopes throughout the inter-mountain West. Well suited for the xeric garden.
BLOOM TIME: May, June
LIFE ZONE: Foothills, Montane

Date _____

Where found _____

_____

Apache Plume
Fallugia paradoxa
Fine textured shrub up to 4 feet; branches dense, arching, with whitish twigs; leaves firm, narrow, up to 1 inch long with deep lobes; flowers white, like a single rose, up to 1¼-inch across; seeds are fuzzy achenes, in a dense puff, silvery with pink shades. Found in Colorado's south-ern and western counties and through-out the Southwest along dry washes, canyons, and floodplains. Excellent airy shrub for a xeric garden. Can spread by root sprouts, forming small colonies.
BLOOM TIME: June, July, August
LIFE ZONE: High Desert

Date _____

Where found _____

_____

Boulder Raspberry
Rubus deliciosus
Medium shrub, up to 5 feet tall; flowers white, rose-like, 1–2 inches broad, scattered singly, not in clusters; bark light brown, shredding on older stems; leaves 1–2½ inches wide, 3–5 lobes with toothed edges; fruits flattened, salmon-colored, disappointingly insipid. Flowers showy, enough to "stop the traffic." Arching habit requires plenty of space to spread. Tolerates dry shade. Also called flowering raspberry. Found in foothills and canyons on dry rocky ground.
BLOOM TIME: June, July, August
LIFE ZONE: Foothills, Montane

Date _____

Where found _____

_____

Cliff Rose
Purshia stansburiana
Much-branched shrub, up to 5 feet tall, flowers 5-petaled, yellow or creamy, re-sembling a small yellow rose; feathery-tailed fruits; leaves small, ⅛–½-inch long, wedge-shaped, 3–5 lobed; bark pale gray-brown, shredding. A shrub of dry, rocky southwestern mesas and deserts, and very beautiful in May when in bloom. Honeybees find them irresistible. Plants acquire interesting character as they age, and are excellent specimens in a xeric planting or rock garden.
BLOOM TIME: May, June
LIFE ZONE: High Desert, Foothills

Date _____
Where found _____
_____

Mountain Mahogany
Cercocarpus montanus
Stems may be tall, up to 6 or 7 feet, erect, stiff, with gray bark; leaves gray-green with prominent veins and toothed edges; flowers in early spring are small creamy bells; fruits, persistent into winter, are 1-seeded with a fuzzy corkscrew-like style that straightens when moistened; these plant themselves by twisting and untwisting as they become dry or moist, depending upon soil moisture. A very common shrub on dry rocky slopes. Wonderful in dry gardens.
BLOOM TIME: April, May
LIFE ZONE: Foothills

Date _____
Where found _____
_____

Ninebark
Physocarpus monogynus
Shrub with limber stems 2–5 feet tall; bark shred-ding in layers, hence the name ninebark; flat clus-ters of small white flowers yield fruits that turn greenish-red to brown when seeds ripen in late summer; leaves with 3–palmate lobes, similar in shape to currant leaves. Found on rocky slopes.
BLOOM TIME: May, June
LIFE ZONE: Foothills, Montane

Date_____
Where found _____
_____

Rose Family (Rosaceae)

Rose Family (Rosaceae)

Rock Spirea
Holodiscus dumosus
Medium-sized, much-branched shrub, 3–6 feet tall; resembles garden spirea; small-toothed leaves; flowers in large, plume-like, creamy white clusters, which later turn rust-colored, remaining throughout the summer. Found on steep, rocky slopes. Vigorous and adaptable, its frothy nodding flowers blend well in conventional or naturalistic gardens. Also called mountain spray.
BLOOM TIME: June, July
LIFE ZONE: Foothills, Montane

Date _____

Where found _____

_____

Sand Cherry
Prunus pumila ssp. *besseyi*
Small rounded shrub up to 5 feet, though often less. Leaves lanceolate, alternate; flowers white, ½-inch across, and densely encircling the stems as new leaves emerge; fruits nearly black, shiny, to ¾ inch, with a large pit, edible but very tart. Scattered on ledges and rocky outcrops on Colorado's eastern plains. Low-growing forms like 'Pawnee Buttes' are especially useful in xeric gardens, draping over walls or among boulders.
BLOOM TIME: April, May
LIFE ZONE: Plains, Foothills

Date _____

Where found _____

_____

Serviceberry
Amelanchier utahensis
Low to medium-sized shrub may reach 15 feet; leaves oval to nearly round with toothed edges toward the tip; clusters of white, fragrant, 5-petaled flowers with slender petals; juicy, berry-like fruits in late summer, edible, and eaten by birds; blooms early in the spring. Widely scattered; where plentiful, entire hillsides are adrift with white clouds of spring blooms. The similar *A. alnifolia* is most common east of the Continental Divide.
BLOOM TIME: April, May
LIFE ZONE: Plains, Foothills, Montane

Date _____

Where found _____

_____

Shiny-Leaved Hawthorn
Crataegus erythropoda
Thorny shrub or small tree under 20 feet, with smooth, shiny leaves and branches; flat clusters of small white 5-petaled flowers with pink anthers; leaves diamond-shaped, toothed; pines purplish brown, 1–1½ inches long. Small black or brown fruits, called "haws." Other species of hawthorn in our area look very similar. Shiny-leaved hawthorn is common along streams in the foothills, mesas, and plains.
BLOOM TIME: May
LIFE ZONE: Plains, Foothills

ate _____

here found _____

_____

Shrubby Cinquefoil
Potentilla fruticosa ssp. *floribunda*
Small rounded shrub, 1–3 feet tall, with numerous bright yellow, 5-petaled rose-like flowers, 1–1½ inches broad; small pinnately compound leaves with 3–7 leaflets. Common in moist sunny locations. This, and related species, are colorful and much-used in gardens.
BLOOM TIME: June, July, August
LIFE ZONE: Foothills, Montane, Subalpine, Alpine

Date _____

Where found _____

_____

Squaw Apple
Peraphyllum ramosissimum
Much-branched thicket-forming shrub, up to 6 feet, with rigid gray branches and dark, leathery, simple oblong leaves; attractive 5-petaled, pale pink and white flowers, resembling small apple blossoms; fruits small, yellow to reddish brown, bitter tasting. Found on open meadows and slopes in southwestern Colorado and Utah.
BLOOM TIME: May
LIFE ZONE: Foothills

Date _____

Where found _____

_____

Thimbleberry

Rubus parviflorus

Medium shrub with few erect, pithy canes, 2–3 feet tall; bark on old stems shredding; leaves up to 5 inches broad, 3–5 lobed; 5-petaled white flowers, cup-shaped, in small clusters of 2–4. Fruits pink, edible, a favorite of birds. Widely distributed, on moist slopes and shaded canyons. More common west of the Continental Divide.

BLOOM TIME: June, July
LIFE ZONE: Montane

Date _____

Where found _____

_____

Wild Plum

Prunus americana

Small shrub or tree, forming dense thickets; generally under 15 feet in our region, but may grow larger; rigid, rather spiny branches, grayish bark; covered in May with clusters of white, 5-petaled flowers, opening before the leaves. Fruits are orange to purple plums, 1-inch long. Common along streams and irrigation ditches in foothills, on mesas, and plains.

BLOOM TIME: May
LIFE ZONE: Plains, Foothills

Date _____

Where found _____

_____

Wild Raspberry

Rubus idaeus

Low, rambling, bristly shrub; arching canes 3–5 feet long may scramble over adjacent plants; leaves compound with 3–5 leaflets, sharply toothed, white beneath; small white 5-petaled flowers; typical raspberry fruits; common on talus slopes and disturbed ground along trails and roads.

BLOOM TIME: June, July, August
LIFE ZONE: Montane, Subalpine

Date _____

Where found _____

_____

Date _____

Where found _____

_____

Wild Rose
Rosa woodsii

Shrub with prickly branched stems, may be reddish or turning silvery gray on older growth, 1–5 feet tall; leaves pinnately compound with 3–7 leaflets, winged petioles; flowers easily recognized as single, pink roses in clusters of 2–4, very fragrant; fruits red, usually persistent into winter. Found on dry hillsides, fence rows, and gravelly roadsides. Stoloniferous habit can be a challenge in the garden.

BLOOM TIME: June, July
LIFE ZONE: Plains, Foothills, Montane

Date _____

Where found _____

_____

Mountain Lover or Oregon Boxwood
Paxistima myrsinites

Low, evergreen, much-branched shrub, generally 2 feet or less; flowers 4-pointed, brownish green to dark red, in leaf axils; leaves shiny, leathery, oval, finely toothed, ½-inch long, arranged in pairs. Found in moist forests of upper Montane and lower Subalpine. This broadleaf evergreen performs well in shaded gardens.

BLOOM TIME: May, June
LIFE ZONE: Montane, Subalpine

Date _____

Where found _____

_____

Poison Ivy
Toxicodendron radicans

Low shrubs or woody vines, 6–24 inches tall, plants sometimes growing as low scrambling ground cover; flowers small, inconspicuous, yellowish white, clustered in leaf axils; fruits yellowish white berries; leaves compound with 3 bright green, oval, pointed leaflets with smooth or toothed margins, turning bright red or orange in the fall. Found in waste places, hillsides, and rocky ravines. Poisonous to the touch, causing blisters and an itching skin rash. Wash affected skin with soap and water as soon as possible after exposure. Smoke from burning poison ivy can cause severe eye irritation, or even blindness.

BLOOM TIME: May, June
LIFE ZONE: Plains, Foothills

Rose Family (Rosaceae)

Staff-tree Family (Celastraceae)

Sumac Family (Anacardiaceae)

Sumac Family (Anacardiaceae)

Smooth Sumac
Rhus glabra
Tall shrub to 10 feet, with stout stems and thick twigs; leaves pinnately compound, with 11–21 lance-shaped leaflets that turn a brilliant red in autumn; flowers small, greenish-white in cone-shaped clusters; fruits berry-like, red and velvety. Found on dry banks, roadsides of the foothills, often seen in large masses.
BLOOM TIME: May, June
LIFE ZONE: Foothills

Date _____

Where found _____

Three-Leaf Sumac
Rhus trilobata
A many-branched, dense, rounded shrub, 2–5 feet high; leaves compound with 3 leaflets, middle leaflet largest; tiny yellow-green flowers in clusters, blooming in May before the leaves; fruits red-orange, slightly sticky, sour. Found on dry, sunny slopes in the foothills throughout the Rocky Mountains. Also called skunk bush because of its strong odor.
BLOOM TIME: April
LIFE ZONE: Plains, Foothills

Date _____

Where found _____

Sunflower Family (Asteraceae)

Dwarf Rabbitbrush
Chrysothamnus viscidiflorus
Plants 10–24 inches tall; stems green, branching from base; leaves narrow, usually twisted; yellow, tubular disk flowers (no ray flowers) in small heads not over ¼-inch long in flat-topped clusters. Found on dry hillsides, common west of the Continental Divide, less common to the east. Excellent small shrub for the xeric garden with a long season of interest. Attracts native pollinators through late summer and fall.
BLOOM TIME: July, August, September
LIFE ZONE: High Desert, Foothills, Montane

Date _____

Where found _____

Rabbitbrush

Ericameria nauseosus ssp. *nauseosus* var. *nauseosus*

Spreading shrub, 2–4 feet or more tall; woody stems, silver-green branches and slender, sharp pointed silvery leaves; flower heads are massed in large rounded golden yellow clusters. Colorful and showy in late summer along road-sides, fields, and dry slopes. Excellent large shrub for gardens that can accommodate, drawing plenty of compliments all year and scores of native pollinators when in flower. In spring, trim to about 12 inches to keep habit uniform.

BLOOM TIME: August, September
LIFE ZONE: Plains, High Desert, Foothills

Date _____

Where found _____

_____

Sagebrush

Artemisia tridentata

Gray-green, rigid, many-branched shrub, commonly 1–4 feet high, but can reach 10 feet where the soil is rich and deep; 3-toothed, wedge-shaped leaves aromatic and evergreen; flowers of sages are in tiny greenish heads becoming bright yellow with abundant pollen in late summer. Sagebrush covers many square miles of dry hillsides, basins, and open range in the Rocky Mountains in lower and middle elevations. Black sage (*A. nova*) is similar, but forms a low dense shrub in poor soils in our western counties.

BLOOM TIME: August
LIFE ZONE: Plains, High Desert, Foothills, Montane

Date _____

Where found _____

_____

Sand Sage

Artemisia filifolia

Shrub up to 4 feet with arching branches, tips often nodding or swirled; leaves fine, silver-green, upper ones simple linear, but lower ones 3-parted; soft yellow flowers on short stems crowded along upper branches. Found in sandy soils in Colorado's eastern counties and adjacent states, and also in the four-corners region. Soft texture and informal habit is a beautiful contrast to yuccas and cacti in a desert landscape.

BLOOM TIME: July, August
LIFE ZONE: Plains, High Desert

Date _____

Where found _____

_____

Tamarisk or Salt Cedar

Tamarix ramosissima

Feathery shrub or small tree to 15 feet, found along waterways and ditches; leaves tiny, scale-like, resembling those of juniper; flowers in feathery light to deep pink plumes. Aggressively spreading, and the subject of much research and eradication efforts. It has displaced entire riparian plant communities and changed hydrology in areas where water is already at a premium. Very widespread, and considered a noxious weed in Colorado and many other southwestern states. **Non-native species.**

BLOOM TIME: June, July, August, September
LIFE ZONE: Plains , High Desert

Date _____

Where found _____

Alpine Thicket Willows

Salix spp.

Singly or mixed, these species form almost impenetrable thickets 2–5 feet high in drainages from well above timberline down into the Subalpine, where they grow as tall as 8 feet.

BLOOM TIME: May, June, July
LIFE ZONE: Subalpine, Alpine

Date _____

Where found _____

Arctic Willow

Salix arctica

A creeping mat-former just a few inches tall, on gravelly soil that is almost constantly wet from melting snow. Young leaves downy but older leaves shiny. Very large catkins are prominent on these tiny plants (catkins may be ¾-inch long).

BLOOM TIME: June, July
LIFE ZONE: Alpine

Date _____

Where found _____

Tamarisk Family (Tamaricaceae)

Willow Family (Salicaceae)

Diamond-Leaf Willow
Salix planifolia
Many willows are hard to identify, but this one is distinctive. Shrub 3 to 10 feet tall; leaves oblong, pointed, often upright along the stems, revealing silvery undersides; flowering catkins appear early before the leaves, releasing fluffy white seeds when mature. Common in wet meadows, along streams, often forming dense stands.
BLOOM TIME: May, June, July
LIFE ZONE: Montane, Subalpine, Alpine

Date _____

Where found _____

_____

Sandbar Willow
Salix exigua
Common shrub, up to 5 feet, with slender reddish-brown branches; very narrow grayish green leaves 2–4 inches long. Common willow bordering streams and ditch banks at lower elevations. Winter stems gold to coral orange, lending color to winter landscapes. Very aggressive, spreading via underground roots. This quality is great for erosion control in the wild, but an enduring curse in the garden!
BLOOM TIME: April, May
LIFE ZONE: Plains, Foothills

Date _____

Where found _____

_____

Scouler Willow
Salix scouleriana
Large shrub, up to 12 feet tall; leaves narrow, much longer than broad, dark green on the upper surface, pale green beneath with scattered red hairs; twigs slender, dark yellow. This willow may also be found in dense stands away from the stream bank on moist slopes.
BLOOM TIME: April, May
LIFE ZONE: Foothills, Montane

Date _____

Where found _____

_____

Snow Willow

Salix reticulata ssp. *nivalis*

Small creeping plants just an inch tall,
found among grasses in alpine areas.
Leaves, even youngest, are smooth, but
a network of veins is very prominent.
Catkins are small and not especially
conspicuous, male and female flowers
on separate plants.

BLOOM TIME: June, July

LIFE ZONE: Alpine

Date _____

Where found _____

_____

Tundra Willows

Salix ssp.

Several alpine species can be found,
and many are difficult to distinguish.
Typically tiny creeping shrubs only
2–3 inches tall; found on higher peaks
and northward into the Arctic.

BLOOM TIME: June, July

LIFE ZONE: Subalpine, Alpine

Date _____

Where found _____

_____

Herbaceous Wildflowers; Vines; and Cacti

This section includes annual and perennial herbaceous flowering plants; flowering vines; cacti; and some of the smallest shrubs, which could easily be mistaken for perennials. For clarity, perennial plants die to the ground each fall and re-emerge from their roots in spring. Annuals grow and flower quickly each spring, but survive the winter only as seed. Vines may scramble along the ground or climb high into neighboring plants or fences, and may or may not have woody stems. Small shrubs listed here have persistent woody stems, but remain just a few inches tall. Finding plants based on flower color is a subjective endeavor. The Royal Horticultural Society color guide recognizes 884 colors! We have settled on eight broad divisions based on distinctions that people commonly make. You are likely to find exceptions, or disagree on placement of some listings, but every effort has been made to be accurate in an inexact realm.

allorhiza
ulata
ısan Rubin

Alpine Sorrel
Oxyria digyna

Fleshy plant 2–8 inches tall with round or kidney-shaped leaves, found on ledges or in crevices of rock. Small greenish flowers are tinged with red in loose cluster at top of stem. Common throughout Arctic and alpine regions of North America.

BLOOM TIME: Alpine
LIFE ZONE: July, August

Date _____

Where found _____

_____

Curly Dock
Rumex crispus

Flowers small, greenish, in a long branched cylindrical cluster; seeds sometimes with a pinkish phase, turning dark brown or rust in late summer; stems slender, up to 4 feet tall; leaves large, often up to 12 inches long with crisp wavy margins. Introduced from Europe, now common throughout the U.S., in fields and waste areas at lower to middle elevations. **Non-native species.**

BLOOM TIME: July, August
LIFE ZONE: High Desert, Plains, Foothills, Montane

Date _____

Where found _____

_____

_____

Willow-Leaved Dock
Rumex salicifolius

Flowers small, greenish, in long cylindrical clusters that turn dark brown or rust in late summer; 12–30 inches tall; leaves long, narrow, pale green. A native species, most common in the Foothills and Montane Zones, but frequently found at lower elevations in moist areas along streams and roadsides.

BLOOM TIME: May, June
LIFE ZONE: Plains, Foothills, Montane

Date _____

Where found _____

_____

Winged Buckwheat

Eriogonum alatum

Flowers greenish yellow; very small and inconspicuous, arranged in a large, open inflorescence at top of stout leafless stem; leaves long in a basal rosette; stem and leaves hairy; fruits winged; plants up to 40 inches tall, standing singly. Most common in foothills, on mesas, but also found in the Montane Zone.

BLOOM TIME: July, August
LIFE ZONE: Foothills, Montane

Date _____

Where found _____

_____

Green Hedgehog Cactus

Echinocereus viridiflorus

Small ball-type cactus; spines with subtle tan or reddish banding; satin textured flowers of lime green in May. Most of the year this little cactus will be overlooked, hidden in the vegetation along the foothills and throughout the shortgrass prairies.

BLOOM TIME: May, June
LIFE ZONE: Plains, Foothills

Date _____

Where found _____

_____

Nipple or Beehive Cactus

Coryphantha missouriensis
var. *missouriensis*

Small ball-type cactus found in rocky outcrops and fissures, or tucked in among short grasses. The small bright red fruits may show up more than the plant itself; greenish yellow flowers appear in mid spring. This species usually lacks a central spine.

BLOOM TIME: June, July
LIFE ZONE: Plains, Foothills

Date _____

Where found _____

_____

Duckweed

Lemna minor
You won't notice the flowers on this tiny plant, but they are there! Very small, disk-like plant not differentiated into stems and leaves; individual disks not over ¼-inch long; thin, hair-like rootlet beneath each disk. Found in floating or slightly submerged masses in ponds and slow streams, often covering much of the water surface. Important wildlife food.

BLOOM TIME: June, July, August
LIFE ZONE: Plains, Foothills

Date _____

Where found _____

_____

Mistletoe

Arceuthobium spp.
Seen as yellowish clusters of smooth, robust stems attached to coniferous trees. Mistletoe is a common parasite on members of the pine family, each different species having its own mistletoe. *A. americanum* is found on lodgepole pine. *A. vaginatum* is seen only on ponderosa pine. The parasite can eventually cause the death of the tree.

BLOOM TIME: June, July
LIFE ZONE: Foothills, Montane

Date _____

Where found _____

_____

Bunny in the Grass
or Western Figwort

Scrophularia lanceolata
Greenish or copper colored flowers ½-inch long, with 2 rounded lobes of the upper lip standing erect (hence its common name); plant tall, 1½ to 4 feet, coarse with deeply cut lance-shaped leaves. Found on hillsides, mesas, and gulches.

BLOOM TIME: June, July
LIFE ZONE: Foothills, Montane

Date_____

Where found _____

_____

Green Gentian

Frasera speciosa

Imposing plants, 4–6 feet tall with greenish-white 4-petaled flowers spotted with purple, very numerous along a stout stem. Plant is pale green with long, smooth, strap-like leaves in a basal rosette. Found on moist hillsides and edges of meadows. This plant can live to be 50 or more years old, but dies upon flowering.

BLOOM TIME: July, August

LIFE ZONE: Foothills, Montane, Subalpine

Date_____

Where found _____

_____

Mat Saltbush

Atriplex corrugata

Shrubs very low, forming dense evenly-spaced mats on adobe hills from western Colorado into Utah, and northwest New Mexico. Leaves silver-green, oval to rounded; flowers inconspicuous, followed by papery dry fruits, often tinted soft pink.

BLOOM TIME: April, May, June

LIFE ZONE: High Desert

Date_____

Where found _____

_____

Riverbank Grape

Vitis riparia

Climbing plant with palmately lobed leaves, tendrils, and bluish-black grapes. Found along stream banks where it climbs over shrubs and into trees. Fast and drought tolerant, though it prefers riparian areas as its name suggests.

BLOOM TIME: June

LIFE ZONE: Foothills

Date_____

Where found _____

_____

Virginia Creeper

Parthenocissus vitacea

Climbing plant with compound leaves of 5 to 7 long, pointed leaflets; bears small, black, grapelike berries on red stems; scarlet-red fall color. Scrambles quickly over nearby plants, up walls, along fences, attaching itself by tendrils, which lack adhesive discs. Otherwise, easily confused with the similar but more aggressive *P. quinquefolia*, which has naturalized in towns and populated areas. Both are drought tolerant fast growing vines.

BLOOM TIME: July

LIFE ZONE: Foothills

Date _____

Where found _____

_____

Green Pyrola

Pyrola chlorantha

Flowers greenish-white with 5 rounded petals and a long, curved, protruding style; 3–10 flowers along a naked stalk, 6–8 inches tall; leaves evergreen, rounded, and in clusters at base of stem. Common in damp Subalpine forests and bogs.

BLOOM TIME: June, July

LIFE ZONE: Subalpine

Date _____

Where found _____

_____

One-Sided Wintergreen or Pyrola

Orthilia secunda

Flowers greenish-white, bowl-shaped, ¼-inch across, 5-petaled with long protruding style; flowers hang from one side of stalk; 4–8 inches tall; leaves evergreen, oval, at base of stem. Moist Subalpine and upper Montane forests.

BLOOM TIME: June, July

LIFE ZONE: Montane, Subalpine

Date _____

Where found _____

_____

Native Hops
Humulus lupulus var. *lupuloides*
Twining rough perennial with opposite, palmately lobed leaves of 3–7 divisions and resin particles on underside; papery, cone-like fruits. Dies to the ground in winter, and grows rapidly in spring, up to 20 or 30 feet tall. Common in the foothills, along fences and sunny ravines.
BLOOM TIME: July, August
LIFE ZONE: Foothills

Date_____

Where found _____

_____

Pine Drops
Pterospora andromeda
Stems single or in small groups, to 2 feet tall, reddish-brown, leafless; flowers along the upper portions of a slender spike, down-facing, urn-shaped, from rusty-pink to cream, but overall effect is of rusty flowers on rusty stems. This unusual plant grows only in the decomposing duff of pine needles on the forest floor. It lacks chlorophyll and is parasitic on the roots of conifers.
BLOOM TIME: July, August, September
LIFE ZONE: Foothills, Montane

Date _____

Where found_____

_____

Green Comet Milkweed
Asclepias viridiflora
Leaves grayish-green, broadly lanceolate and pubescent, with wavy margins; stems to 18–24 inches; flowers 5-parted, with petals sharply reflexed, soft green shades; pods are 4 inches long, pointed, smooth. Not a showy milkweed, but without the distraction of color, the complex geometry of the flower invites a closer look.
BLOOM TIME: July, August
LIFE ZONE: Plains

Date _____

Where found _____

_____

Coral-Root Orchid

Corallorhiza maculata

Flowers purple-brown, ½-inch long, with 3 sepals and 3 petals, middle petal an enlarged white lip spotted with purple; flowers in spike-like cluster at top of fleshy, purple, leafless stalk; grows in clumps, 6–24 inches tall.

Coral-root orchids are saprophytes, meaning they lack chlorophyll (the green color in most plants) and are dependent on organic matter, such as rotting wood, in the soil for food. Found in moist, shady coniferous forest.

BLOOM TIME: June, July

LIFE ZONE: Foothills, Montane

Date _____

Where found _____

_____

Green Bog Orchid

Platanthera stricta

Tiny greenish orchid flowers often tinged with purple, with small spur at base of lower lip; flowers in a rather crowded spike; 1–3 feet tall; leaves bright green. Found in swampy areas, bogs, and along stream banks.

BLOOM TIME: June, July, August

LIFE ZONE: Montane, Subalpine

Date_____

Where found _____

_____

Mitrewort or Bishop's Cap

Mitella pentandra

Very tiny greenish 5-petaled flowers, inconspicuous, resembling miniature pinwheels, along slender leafless stalk, 4–12 inches tall; leaves have rounded lobes with coarse teeth, clustered at base of stem. Found in wet places in Subalpine and Montane forests.

BLOOM TIME: July, August

LIFE ZONE: Montane, Subalpine

Date _____

Where found _____

_____

Naked Coneflower

Rudbeckia montana

Flower heads purplish black, cone- or egg-shaped; head composed of disk flowers only, no ray flowers; plants 3½ to 6 feet tall; leaves large, divided pinnately. Found along streams and wet meadows in west-central Colorado, a striking plant not easily confused with anything else.

BLOOM TIME: July, August
LIFE ZONE: Foothills, Montane

Date _____

Where found _____

_____

White, Cream

cca glauca
.ibby Kyer

Banana Yucca
Yucca baccata

Bell-shaped creamy white flowers on a thick stalk, seldom rising much above the leaves. More imposing than *Y. glauca*, with broad, thick, rigid leaves, often twisted, with coarse fibers frayed and curled along the leaf edges; fleshy edible seed pods. Found throughout southwestern arid lands. Also called datil yucca.

BLOOM TIME: April, May, June
LIFE ZONE: High Desert, Plains

Date _____

Where found _____

_____

Harriman's Yucca or Dollhouse Yucca
Yucca harrimaniae

Narrow evergreen leaves typical of the genus, 6–18 inches long, with a few to many curling white filaments along leaf edges; flowering stems rise above leaves, up to 4 feet. Flowers waxy, creamy white, pendulous, along top half or third of stem. Especially common in our western counties and into Utah, occasional in southeast Colorado, into New Mexico. Dwarf forms with tiny 4- or 5-inch rosettes are sometimes found. Nurseries propagate these as choice rock garden plants.

BLOOM TIME: May

Date _____

Where found _____

_____

Soapweed Yucca
Yucca glauca

Low evergreen plant composed of a dense cluster of narrow, needle-pointed leaves, 1 to 2½ feet long; stout flower stalk 2–3 feet high, rising from center of leaf cluster; flowers creamy to greenish white bells, 2–3 inches wide, with large apple-green pistil; fruits are dry pods containing small black seeds. Leaf fibers have been used by Native people for cordage, sandals, and mats. Mashed roots and stems yield a soapy lather. A conspicuous and abundant plant throughout the eastern plains and foothills. Most yuccas require the presence of specific moths to achieve pollination.

BLOOM TIME: June
LIFE ZONE: High Desert, Plains, Foothills

Date _____

Where found _____

_____

Miner's Candle
Cryptantha virgata
Numerous small, 5-petaled flowers on a white torch-like unbranched stem 10–24 inches tall; leaves narrow; plant stiff-hairy all over, prickly to the touch. Found on dry fields and slopes.
BLOOM TIME: May, June, July
LIFE ZONE: Foothills, Montane

Date _____

Where found _____

_____

Annual Buckwheat
Eriogonum annuum
Tiny white to rose flowers, in lacy vase-shaped or flattened clusters; felty-white stems, up to 2 feet tall, with few narrow twisted leaves, white under-neath. Frequently found on sandy soil.
BLOOM TIME: July, August, September
LIFE ZONE: Plains, Foothills

Date _____

Where found _____

_____

Bistort
Polygonum bistortoides
Flowers in dense white or pinkish spikes up to 2 inches long on rather tall stems, up to 12 inches or more. One of the most common flowers in Alpine and Subalpine meadows, occasionally the upper Montane, throughout the Rocky Mountains.
BLOOM TIME: July, August
LIFE ZONE: Subalpine, Alpine

Date _____

Where found _____

_____

James' Wild Buckwheat

Eriogonum jamesii var. *jamesii*
Small shrubby perennial. Leaves are ovate, leathery, with fine hairs; flowers on mounding branched stems, cream-colored, in papery round clusters, turning pinkish-brown as they mature. A conspicuous plant when in flower on the Plains or open pine forests of the Foothills and lower Montane. Many other species may be encountered. The eriogonums are a variable and difficult group to identify, and names seem to undergo continual review. Perhaps DNA evidence will someday sort out the mob!

BLOOM TIME: July, August, September
LIFE ZONE: Plains, Foothills, Montane

Date _____

Where found_____

_____

Prairie Baby's Breath or Spreading Buckwheat

Eriogonum effusum
Numerous tiny flowers, sometimes with a pinkish cast, in open flat-topped clusters; shrubby, much-branched plant, 8–20 inches tall. Common on plains and mesas.

BLOOM TIME: July, August, September
LIFE ZONE: Plains

Date _____

Where found_____

_____

Alpine Anemone

Anemone narcissiflora
Flowers white or creamy yellow, 2 to 4 per stem; stalks hairy, 4–16 inches tall; leaves finely cut or dissected. Found in moist meadows. As its scientific name implies, it resembles a cultivated narcissus.

BLOOM TIME: July, August
LIFE ZONE: Subalpine, Alpine

Date _____

Where found_____

_____

Baneberry
Actaea rubra
Very numerous small white flowers in an erect feathery raceme, followed by poisonous red or rarely white berries; tall plant is herbaceous but can appear shrub-like; compound leaves with three or more leaflets. Found in moist deeply shaded woods.

BLOOM TIME: May, June
LIFE ZONE: Montane

Date _____

Where found _____

_____

Globeflower
Trollius laxus ssp. *albiflorus*
Large flowers with creamy white or yellowish petal-like sepals 1 to 1½ inches broad, centers of many stamens; flowers 1 per stalk; leaves divided palmately into sharp-toothed segments; plants 10–18 inches tall, usually in large clumps. Found in marshy areas, wet meadows, and edges of streams.

BLOOM TIME: June, July, August
LIFE ZONE: Subalpine, Alpine

Date _____

Where found _____

_____

Northern Anemone
Anemone canadensis
Delicate 1-inch wide white flowers with 5 petal-like sepals and numerous stamens; borne on long stalks above the leaves; leaves deeply cut into toothed segments; plants 4–24 inches high. Fuzzy seed-heads appear in mid-summer. Found in meadows and moist places.

BLOOM TIME: May, June
LIFE ZONE: Plains, Foothills, Montane

Date _____

Where found _____

_____

Plains Larkspur

Delphinium carolinianum ssp. *virescens*
Flowers white to very pale blue with 5 sepals,
5 smaller petals, upper sepal spurred, pointing up-
wards; flowers in long spike-like clusters at top of
unbranched stems, 1–3 feet tall; leaves palmately
lobed, finely divided, at base of stem. Found on
plains and mesas, east of the Front Range.

BLOOM TIME: May, June

LIFE ZONE: Plains

Date _____

Where found _____

_____

Virgin's Bower

Clematis ligusticifolia
Numerous white flowers, about ⅓-inch across, in
large clusters, followed by masses of silky plumed
fruits conspicuous in late summer and attractive
through the fall. Leaves pinnately compound; trailing or climbing woody vines, often up to 30 feet,
nearly covering trees and shrubs over which they
grow. Found along stream banks, canyons, and
roadsides. Can spread by seed or by roots that
sprout some distance from original plant, limiting
its usefulness in all but wild settings.

BLOOM TIME: May, June, July, August

LIFE ZONE: Plains, Foothills

Date _____

Where found_____

_____

Water Crowfoot

Ranunculus trichophyllus
Flowers dainty, white, numerous, almost
½ inch broad; submerged brownish
masses of branched stems and finely
divided, threadlike leaves; stalks with a
dilated base. Found in ponds and slow
streams throughout the Rockies, extending up to 10,000 feet in Colorado.

BLOOM TIME: June, July, August,
September

LIFE ZONE: Foothills, Montane

Date _____

Where found_____

_____

White Marsh Marigold

Caltha leptosepala

Flowers white with a gold center composed of many stamens, 1 to 1½ inches broad; 5–15 petal-like sepals, often bluish beneath; plants 3–10 inches high; leaves basal, round to oval. Marshy areas, often found in large, lush patches.

BLOOM TIME: June, July, August

LIFE ZONE: Subalpine, Alpine

Date _____

Where found _____

_____

Dogbane or Indian Hemp

Apocynum cannabinum

Clusters of tiny greenish-white bell-shaped flowers hang from tips of forked branches; plants 1–3 feet tall; leaves oval, opposite and smooth; seed pods long, slender; seeds with downy tufts of hairs, similar to seeds of milkweed; plants have milky juice. Common on dry hillsides in the plains, turning a beautiful shade of yellow in autumn. Native people made cord or rope from the plant fibers.

BLOOM TIME: June, July

LIFE ZONE: Plains

ate _____

here found _____

_____

Bunchberry

Cornus canadense

Distinctive ground cover, stem just 3–6 inches tall; leaves 4 to 6 in a whorl, parallel veins; flowers small, clustered, but surrounded by 4 large white bracts resembling the familiar dogwood tree flowers; berries red, clustered at center of leaves after bracts have fallen. A plant of damp northern forests, extending south into Colorado and New Mexico where it is uncommon. Only thrives in old, rich organic soils of the undisturbed forest floor.

BLOOM TIME: July

LIFE ZONE: Montane, Subalpine

te _____

here found _____

_____

Cut-Leaf Evening Primrose

Oenothera coronopifolia

White 4-petaled flowers, round in appearance,
½ to 1¼ inches broad, in axils of upper leaves;
petals turn pink with age; upright bushy plant up
to 12 inches tall, with pinnately cut leaves. Common along roadsides and disturbed areas. Well
suited to a short-grass meadow.

BLOOM TIME: June, July

LIFE ZONE: Plains, Foothills, Montane

Date _____

Where found _____

_____

Plains Evening Primrose

Oenothera albicaulis

Striking large 4-petaled flowers becoming pink with age; leafy, whitish stems,
much-branched to form a bushy plant
to 18 inches tall. This is an annual, re-
sponding to spring moisture and often
covering large areas on barren sandy
soil on the plains.

BLOOM TIME: May, June, July

LIFE ZONE: Plains

Date _____

Where found _____

_____

White Stemless
Evening Primrose

Oenothera caespitosa

Conspicuous, large white 4-petaled
flowers turning pink with age, fragrant;
low stemless plant with elongated basal,
wavy-edged leaves at base. Grows on dry
sunny slopes, blooming throughout
summer. Dislikes wet conditions, especially in the garden, but a staple and lovely
perennial component of xeric gardens.

BLOOM TIME: May, June, July, August,
September

LIFE ZONE: Plains, High Desert, Foothills,
Montane

Date _____

Where found _____

_____

Cornhusk Lily or False Hellebore

Veratrum tenuipetalum

Robust plant found in dense patches in high mountain meadows, and recognizable whether in flower or not. Coarse leafy-stemmed plant with large "pleated" leaves, 3–6 feet tall; small, very numerous greenish-white flowers in branched cluster at top of plant. Poisonous to livestock. Sometimes referred to locally as "skunk cabbage."

BLOOM TIME: June, July, August
LIFE ZONE: Montane, Subalpine

Date _____

Where found _____

_____

Kittentails

Besseya plantaginea

Flowers greenish-white to pinkish, in crowded spike-like cluster at top of stem; flowers very small, 2-lipped, leafy bracts intermixed with flowers; leaves oblong or rounded, in basal rosette; stem and leaves woolly-gray. Found on wooded slopes.

BLOOM TIME: June, July
LIFE ZONE: Foothills, Montane

Date _____

Where found _____

_____

Parry Lousewort

Pedicularis parryi

Flowers creamy or yellowish, tube-shaped and 2-lipped, with the upper lip forming a curved beak; 4–12 inches tall; leaves long, narrow with deeply cut edges. Found on moist slopes. Louseworts derive their common name from their use in early medicine as a remedy for head lice!

BLOOM TIME: July, August
LIFE ZONE: Subalpine, Alpine

Date _____

Where found _____

_____

Ram's-Horn or Sickletop Lousewort

Pedicularis racemosa

Flowers white to creamy, 2-lipped, with upper lip arched, slightly twisted, and folded tightly lengthwise, hence its common name; leaves lance-shaped, sharply toothed; stems and leaves reddish; grows in clumps 12–24 inches tall. Found in dry forests.

BLOOM TIME: June, July

LIFE ZONE: Montane, Subalpine

Date _____

Where found _____

Snowlover

Chionophila jamesii

Cream-colored, two-lipped flowers in compact 1-sided spikes; about 4 inches tall. Found on moist gravelly slopes. Resembles a small penstemon. Widespread but not abundant.

BLOOM TIME: July, August

LIFE ZONE: Alpine

Date _____

Where found _____

White Penstemon

Penstemon albidus

Plants short, less than 14 inches; leaves lanceolate in a basal rosette; flowers in a dense spike, white with occasional hint of purple. Requires well-drained soil in the garden and can be challenging.

BLOOM TIME: June

LIFE ZONE: Plains

Date _____

Where found _____

Sand Verbena or Prairie Snowball
Abronia fragrans
White or pinkish 5-lobed fragrant tubular flowers, each lobe deeply notched, in rounded heads with papery bracts below; opposite, fleshy leaves on sticky rambling stems, 8 inches to 3 feet long; continues to bloom throughout the summer. Preferring dry sandy soils, this is a striking plant, intensely fragrant in the evening.
BLOOM TIME: May, June, July, August
LIFE ZONE: Plains

Date _____

Where found _____

_____

White Geranium
Geranium richardsonii
Flowers in pairs, 5-petaled, white with delicate pink veining; slender, branched plant, 1–3 feet tall; leaves palmately lobed. Moist shaded locations. Subtle addition to a woodland garden.
BLOOM TIME: May, June, July, August
LIFE ZONE: Foothills, Montane

Date _____

Where found _____

_____

Least Wintergreen
Pyrola minor
Flowers white (sometimes pinkish), similar to one-sided wintergreen, but flowers hang from all sides of stem; 4–8 inches tall. Moist or boggy locations in shady forests.
BLOOM TIME: June, July
LIFE ZONE: Montane, Subalpine

Date _____

Where found _____

_____

Woodnymph or Single Delight
Moneses uniflora
Flower single, white, star-like, ½- to ¾-inch across, with 4–5 petals, very fragrant; stem 3–4 inches tall rising from a rosette of oval, toothed leaves. A delightful discovery in moist, shaded, woods.
BLOOM TIME: July, August
LIFE ZONE: Subalpine

Date _____

Where found _____

_____

Bundle Flower
Desmanthus illinoensis
Bright green, fine bipinnately compound leaves give it another common name: prairie mimosa. Stout but brittle stems to 4 feet; flowers small, white, many in a tight cluster at the top of the stems, creating a rounded powder-puff appearance; seed pods green, turning brown, tightly bundled, incurved, often slightly spiraled together like an unfurling rose. Drought-tolerant, but usually found in ditches, roadsides, prairies. Fine texture is lovely in a border or meadow garden, and seed pods are ornamental. Will self-sow in moist garden conditions.
BLOOM TIME: August
LIFE ZONE: Plains

Date _____

Where found _____

_____

Drummond Milkvetch
Astragalus drummondii
Numerous dirty white to yellowish pea-like flowers with black-hairy sepals, in spike-like racemes; drooping grooved pods; stout leafy stems, 10–24 inches tall, form clumps; silky-hairy, pinnately compound leaves. Dry, open fields and slopes.
BLOOM TIME: May, June
LIFE ZONE: Plains, Foothills

Date _____

Where found _____

_____

Ground Plum

Astragalus crassicarpus

Pea-like flowers in early spring, creamy white with blue or purple tips; plants low and spreading, stems 6–12 inches long; fruits fleshy, plum-shaped, becoming hard light brown pods when dry. Common in the foothills, mesas, and plains.

BLOOM TIME: May, June

LIFE ZONE: Plains, Foothills

Date_____

Where found _____

Rocky Mountain Loco

Oxytropis sericea

Striking white (or lavender) pea-like flower with purple spot on keel, in upright spike-like racemes, 10–18 inches tall; leaves compound, silver-hairy. Often in large colonies dominating the landscape at time of bloom. May hybridize with Lamberts loco, producing flowers of various shades of pink and lavender.

BLOOM TIME: June, July

LIFE ZONE: Plains, Foothills, Montane

Date _____

Where found _____

White Clover

Trifolium repens

Small white pea-like flowers, in rounded clusters; leaves compound with 3 leaflets; stems low and creeping, rooting at nodes. Escaped from cultivation and now common from the Plains to the Montane. **Non-native species.**

BLOOM TIME: April, May, June, July, August, September, October

LIFE ZONE: Plains, Foothills, Montane

Date _____

Where found_____

White Loco

Sophora nuttaliana

Short, branched stems, 6–14 inches tall, may stand upright or lean against their neighbors or along the ground. Leaves pinnately divided, covered with minute hairs that impart the silky gray-green appearance; flowers white or creamy, pea-like, in upright racemes 3–4 inches long. Found in grasslands, ravines, and dry slopes, this plant spreads by underground runners to form extensive patches.

BLOOM TIME: May, June, July, August

LIFE ZONE: Plains

Date _____

Where found _____

_____

White Peavine

Lathyrus leucanthus

Yellowish-white pea-like flowers on few-flowered stalks; low scrambling plant; leaves pinnately compound with tendrils at tip. Often in large patches on hillsides.

BLOOM TIME: May, June, July

LIFE ZONE: Plains, Foothills, Montane

Date _____

Where found _____

_____

White Prairie Clover

Dalea candida

Small white flowers crowded in an oblong spike on slender spreading branched stems, 12–30 inches tall; leaves 3-parted, leaflets narrow. Found in sandy soils and rocky outcrops.

BLOOM TIME: May, June, July

LIFE ZONE: Plains

Date _____

Where found _____

_____

White Sweet Clover
Melilotus alba
Very small fragrant white pea-like flowers in long racemes; bushy plant up to 5 feet tall; compound leaves with 3 slender, oval leaflets. Blooms all summer along roadsides and in fields. **Non-native species**—introduced from Europe.
BLOOM TIME: June, July, August, September
LIFE ZONE: Plains, Foothills, Montane

Date _____

Where found _____

_____

Wild Licorice
Glycyrrhiza lepidota
Small, greenish-white flowers in a dense cluster near the top of the stem; 1–3 feet tall; leaves compound, with about 15 short leaflets; fruit is a brown pod with dense cover of hooked bristles. Roots have been used as flavoring and also chewed raw as a confection. Often found in large patches in waste places, along roadsides, and stream bottoms. Spreads aggressively by vigorous stolons.
BLOOM TIME: June, July
LIFE ZONE: Plains, Foothills

Date _____

Where found _____

_____

Alpine Lily or Alplily
Lloydia serotina
Small solitary flower with 6 similar white or greenish sepals and petals with purple veins; 2–6 inches tall; a slender plant with grass-like leaves. Common on high peaks.
BLOOM TIME: July, August
LIFE ZONE: Alpine

Date _____

Where found _____

Death Camas or Wand Lily

Zigadenus venenosus

Small, ½ to ¾ inch, creamy white, 6-pointed lily-like flowers in a compact cluster at top of stem; each petal and sepal with a greenish spot at base, stamens longer than the petals; leaves slender and grass-like; 8–12 inches high. Poisonous meadow plant.

BLOOM TIME: May, June

LIFE ZONE: Plains

Date_____

Where found _____

_____

Death Camas or Wand Lily

Zigadenus elegans

Flowers creamy or greenish, 6-parted with a distinctive green spot at the base of each petal and petal-like sepal, flowers in loose cluster at top of stem; 8–18 inches tall; leaves long and slender. A highly poisonous plant, no part should be eaten.

BLOOM TIME: June, July, August

LIFE ZONE: Foothills, Montane, Subalpine, Alpine

Date_____

Where found _____

_____

False Solomon's Seal

Maianthemum stellatum

Small white starlike flowers with 3 petals and 3 similar sepals, in a simple raceme at top of unbranched leafy stem; leaves lance-shaped, folded; stem 1–2 feet tall; dark-striped berries turning purplish-black when ripe. Widespread plant of moist woods and meadows. Stoloniferous, expanding to form large colonies if conditions suit it.

BLOOM TIME: May, June, July

LIFE ZONE: Plains, Foothills, Montane

Date_____

Where found _____

_____

Mariposa or Sego Lily
Calochortus gunnisonii
Open goblet-shaped, white to lavender flowers, 3 narrow sepals, 3 broad petals with greenish throat, often with dark purplish spot at base; slender stems 10–18 inches tall; narrow leaves. In aspen groves, open meadows, and slopes. Bulbs are deep with fragile stems and should not be disturbed. Many forms are now available commercially as a result of advanced tissue culture. Challenging, preferring fairly dry undisturbed areas in the garden.
BLOOM TIME: May, June, July
LIFE ZONE: Foothills, Montane

Date _____

Where found _____

_____

Sand Lily
Leucocrinum montanum
Waxy, lily-like flowers with petals united into a long tube, arising from a conspicuous clump of low-growing, grass-like leaves. Widespread in the foothills and plains. One of the earliest spring flowers. Wonderful fragrance, though a low hands and knees stance is required!
BLOOM TIME: May, June
LIFE ZONE: High Desert, Plains, Foothills

Date _____

Where found _____

_____

Sego Lily or Nuttall's Mariposa
Calochortus nuttallii
Flowers goblet-shaped, 3 broad creamy white petals tinged with lilac; dark purple or brown spot, fringed with yellow hairs, at base of petals; plants 8–15 inches tall. Found on dry slopes and flats of the northern Great Plains, Wyoming, western Colorado, and Utah. This is the state flower of Utah. The bulbs were a food source for Native peoples and early settlers.
BLOOM TIME: June, July
LIFE ZONE: High Desert, Plains, Foothills

Date _____

Where found _____

_____

Twisted Stalk

Streptopus amplexifolius

Greenish-white, bell-shaped flowers, ⅓-inch long, hang from a slender angled stalk at leaf axils; leaves oval, tapering; stems arching, and with zigzag twist, 1½ to 4 feet tall. Found in moist woods, especially along streams. Flowers, and later bright red berries, may be overlooked, as they hang beneath the leaves.

BLOOM TIME: July, August

LIFE ZONE: Foothills, Montane, Subalpine

Date _____

Where found _____

_____

Evening Star

Mentzelia decapetala

Exotic-looking large creamy-white, night-blooming flowers, 2–4 inches across, usually with 10 petals, many golden stamens; rough, much-branched, brittle-stemmed plant, 12–20 inches tall; foliage clings like Velcro® to clothes and fur because of stiff, barbed hairs on the leaves. Prefers dry sandy soil, often seen along roadsides. This plant is biennial, forming a beautiful rosette of serrated leaves its first year and tall flowering stems the next. A show-stopper in the dry, well-drained garden!

BLOOM TIME: July, August

LIFE ZONE: Plains

Date _____

Where found _____

_____

White Evening Star

Mentzelia nuda

Stems 3 or 4 from a long-lived perennial basal crown, upright or leaning, up to 3 feet; stems smooth, dull white; leaves to 4 inches, serrated edges, with many short hairs that cling to clothing as is typical of the genus. Flowers 2½ inches wide, clustered near top of stems, opening in the afternoon, creamy white with long filamentous stamens creating a cream-colored central puff nearly as wide as the petals. Seed pods in this genus cylindrical, with just the end opening at maturity; pods of this species about 1¼ inches long.

BLOOM TIME: July, August

LIFE ZONE: Plains

Date _____

Where found _____

_____

Bedstraw
Galium boreale
Numerous very small fragrant white, 4-pointed flowers in showy clusters; stems square, erect, 8–20 inches tall, narrow leaves in whorls of 4. Found on dry slopes and roadsides, very common and widespread.

BLOOM TIME: June, July, August
LIFE ZONE: Foothills, Montane

Date _____

Where found _____

_____

Cheeseweed
Malva neglecta
Small pinkish-white 5-petaled, hollyhock-like flowers in leaf axils; creeping plant with stems 4–12 inches long; round, lobed leaves. Also called cheeseweed for the edible fruits resembling little flat-wedged cheeses. **Non-native species,** common garden weed naturalized from Europe.

BLOOM TIME: May, June, July, August, September
LIFE ZONE: Plains, Foothills

Date _____

Where found _____

_____

Modest Mallow or White Checker Mallow
Sidalcea candida
Flowers white, 3/4 inch broad, with 5 delicate thin petals; stems unbranched, 1–3 feet tall, with round, coarsely toothed leaves at the base. Mountain meadows and stream banks.

BLOOM TIME: July, August
LIFE ZONE: Montane, Subalpine

Date _____

Where found _____

_____

Dwarf Milkweed
Asclepias pumila
One of the smallest milkweeds. Stems 8–12 inches; leaves plentiful, linear, very fine, flexible, and soft-textured; flowers white, in small but showy umbels typical of the genus; pods seem disproportionately large. Sweet and attractive, but running habit may be a challenge in the garden, as it spreads underground to form small patches in short grasslands.
BLOOM TIME: August
LIFE ZONE: Plains

Date_____

Where found _____

_____

Whorled Milkweed
Asclepias subverticillata
Narrow whorled leaves at regular intervals along 2-foot stems; creamy white flowers, sometimes dusky pink, clustered in typical milkweed fashion; sweet fragrance and a long period of bloom. Wonderful addition to a spacious garden where expansion is not an issue, as these will spread underground and form impressive colonies. Found along gravely roadsides and in open prairies. Delicate yet architectural in habit.
BLOOM TIME: July, August
LIFE ZONE: High Desert, Plains

Date _____

Where found _____

_____

Catnip
Nepeta cataria
Two-lipped tubular white or purple-spotted flowers in dense clusters in an interrupted spike; leaves heart-shaped with rounded teeth, green above, white woolly below; stems 20 inches to 3 feet tall, erect; strongly aromatic. Found on roadsides and waste places. Distinct from purple-flowered catmints that are so welcome in the garden. **Non-native species** introduced from Europe.
BLOOM TIME: July, August, September, October
LIFE ZONE: Plains

Date _____

Where found_____

_____

Hoarhound
Marrubium vulgare
Tiny white 2-lipped tubular flowers in rounded clusters in axils of leaves; leaves opposite, oval to round, scalloped and wrinkled; plants stout, white-woolly with square stems, 10–40 inches tall. Found in waste places, roadsides, and fields. Though this species can be weedy, other *marrubium* species are attractive and useful in the xeric garden. **Non-native species** introduced from Europe.

BLOOM TIME: July, August, September, October

LIFE ZONE: Plain

ate _____

here found _____

Field Bindweed
Convolvulus arvensis
Flowers white to pinkish morning glories, 1 inch broad; leaves arrowhead-shaped; climbs over other plants with coiling stems. It has become a noxious weed in cultivated areas and along roadsides. Deep and extensive underground root system makes it difficult to control. Blooms all summer. **Non-native species** introduced from Europe.

BLOOM TIME: May, June, July, August, September

LIFE ZONE: High Desert, Plains, Foothills

ate _____

here found _____

Bitter Cress
Cardamine cordifolia
Flowers white, 4-petaled, ½ inch broad, in rounded cluster at top of leafy stem; leaves heart-shaped and toothed; plants 10–24 inches tall. Often found in large patches along slow streams and around springs.

BLOOM TIME: June, July, August

LIFE ZONE: Montane, Subalpine

Date _____

Where found _____

Mountain Candytuft
Noccaea montanum
Flat or rounded clusters of small, 4-petaled white flowers from a rosette of short, oval to oblong leaves; plants 1–5 inches tall. Found from mesas and foothills where it is one of the earliest spring flowers, to the Alpine tundra where it blooms throughout the summer.
BLOOM TIME: April, May, June, July, August
LIFE ZONE: Plains, Foothills, Montane, Subalpine, Alpine

Date _____

Where found _____

_____

Penny Cress
Thlaspi arvense
Numerous 4-petaled white flowers in long clusters, followed by flattened, circular pods ½-inch across; pods notched at top, erect; light green leaves, oval to lance-shaped, upper ones clasping the stems; plants erect, branched, 6–24 inches tall. **Non-native species**—introduced weed common in fields, along roadsides, and around settlements.
BLOOM TIME: May, June, July
LIFE ZONE: Plains, Foothills, Montane

Date _____

Where found _____

_____

Pepperweed
Lepidium montanum
Abundant tiny greenish-white, 4-petaled flowers; leaves narrow, not clasping stems; conspicuous, branched plant, up to 18 inches tall; small, notched oval fruits. Found on arid soils.
BLOOM TIME: April, May, June
LIFE ZONE: Plains, Foothills

Date _____

Where found _____

_____

Shepherd's Purse
Capsella bursa-pastoris
Very small, white 4-petaled flowers in racemes, followed by triangular pods notched at the top—the "shepherd's purse" by which the plant is easily recognized; stems 4–16 inches tall; basal leaves in a rosette. A common roadside and garden weed. **Non-native species** introduced from Europe.
BLOOM TIME: April, May, June
LIFE ZONE: Plains

Date _____

Where found _____

_____

Watercress
Nasturtium officinale
Flowers white with 4 petals and 6 stamens, in racemes; dense, rounded, dark green leaves. Found in cool, running water. Young shoots are delicious in salads, but do not pick unless it is known that the water is not polluted.
BLOOM TIME: April, May, June
LIFE ZONE: Plains, Foothills

Date _____

Where found _____

_____

White Bottlebrush
Stanleya albescens
Plumes of cream colored 4-petaled flowers with conspicuous protruding stamens; thick pale leaves; tall desert plant of the Western Slope. Found on soil containing the poisonous element selenium. Also called White Prince's Plume.
BLOOM TIME: June, July
LIFE ZONE: High Desert

Date _____

Where found _____

_____

Whitetop
Cardaria draba
Many small 4-petaled flowers in dense flat clusters; narrow-oval leaves clasping the stem; stem 8–26 inches tall; peppery seeds in flat pods. Attractive in flower, creating large drifts along roadsides and fields. However, this noxious weed is an introduction from Eurasia and has become a serious and widespread pest, displacing natives and altering habitats. Its taller-growing relative, *Lepidium latifolium*, is similar, and both species are considered noxious weeds in Colorado. **Non-native species.**
BLOOM TIME: April, May, June
LIFE ZONE: Plains

Date_____

Where found _____

_____

Angel's Trumpet
Datura wrightii
Broad shrubby plant, wider than tall, spreading to 5 feet. Unmistakable when in flower, with large, up-facing, open trumpets to 8 inches long, white, often with a soft lavender edge, fragrant, and opening in the evening, closing by the heat of mid-day. Leaves from 3–8 inches long, broad, soft, largest on lower part of plant where they may have irregular notches; thick perennial roots; annual in colder areas. Fruits are spiny, round, nodding, splitting 4 ways to release dry brown seeds. Native in Mexico and the Southwest, but now found worldwide due to human distribution. Seen in desert washes, roadsides, and around dwellings. Beautiful in a desert garden, but be aware: all parts of the plant are deadly!

BLOOM TIME: July, August, September
LIFE ZONE: High Desert, Plains

Date_____

Where found _____

_____

Sand Onion
Allium textile
Small white flowers in an erect umbel; flower stalk 4–16 inches tall; leaves channeled and grasslike. Characteristic onion taste and odor. Common on plains and dry foothills.
BLOOM TIME: May, June
LIFE ZONE: Plains, Foothills

Date _____

Where found _____

_____

Lady's Tresses

Spiranthes romanzoffiana

Small white flowers similar to white bog orchid but without spur; flowers in a dense spike in a spirally twisted arrangement; stem slender, 8–20 inches tall; leaves lance-shaped, slender, bright green. Found in bogs, marshes, and moist woods.

BLOOM TIME: July, August

LIFE ZONE: Montane, Subalpine

Date _____

Where found _____

_____

Rattlesnake Plantain

Goodyera oblongifolia

Low-growing rosettes to 6 inches wide; 3–7 leaves, leathery, pointed, reminiscent of small bromeliads, with silvery midribs and occasional mottling or net-like pattern; flowers atop slender stems to 12 inches tall, greenish-white, barely opening. Prefers undisturbed organic soil in the shade of spruce and fir, where underground runners will form beautiful small colonies.

BLOOM TIME: June, July

LIFE ZONE: Montane

Date _____

Where found _____

_____

Ute Lady's Tresses

Spiranthes diluvialis

Highly threatened! Very rare and scattered throughout its range, found in Colorado only along the base of the Front Range, in open riparian areas and floodplains. Leaves are narrow, forming a well-camouflaged rosette among taller grasses; flowers rising on slender stems to 18 inches, spirally arranged near the top of the stem, white, lacking the hood that is seen in *S. romanzoffiana*. Only discovered in the 1980s, now federally protected. Its habitat should never be disturbed.

BLOOM TIME: July, August

LIFE ZONE: Plains, Foothills

Date _____

Where found _____

_____

White Bog Orchid

Platanthera dilatata ssp. *albiflora*

Small waxy white orchid flowers in a dense spike; middle petal with a small spur at base; very fragrant; leaves bright green, lance-shaped; stems 1–2 feet tall. Found in boggy areas and wet stream banks.

BLOOM TIME: June, July, August

LIFE ZONE: Montane, Subalpine

Date _____

Where found _____

_____

Cow Parsnip

Heracleum maximum

Large, flat-topped umbels of small white flowers; very large compound leaves with 3 coarsely toothed leaflets 4–16 inches long and wide clasping leaf-stalk; coarse plant 5–8 feet tall. Grows along streams and in wet areas. Imposing and beautiful in flower as all cow parsnips are, but should be approached or grown with caution as direct contact with skin can result in severe photo-dermatitis!

BLOOM TIME: June, July, August

LIFE ZONE: Foothills, Montane

Date _____

Where found _____

_____

Giant Angelica

Angelica ampla

Many small white flowers in large com-pound umbels that are globular rather than flat; stout plant often 5 feet or more tall, with purplish stems; large leaves 3-branched and doubly compound; ribs of fruits narrowly winged. Grows in wet meadows and along streams. The similar (usually smaller) *A. grayi* may be found growing in alpine scree.

BLOOM TIME: July, August

LIFE ZONE: Foothills, Montane

Date _____

Where found _____

_____

Poison Hemlock
Conium maculatum
Dainty white flowers in umbels; attractive tall plant, 2–10 feet or more, with fernlike, double-compound leaves; the hollow stems are spotted with purple. Found in moist places. Listed as a noxious weed in Colorado and many other states. The deadly poisonous plant of antiquity. **Non-native species** introduced from Europe.
BLOOM TIME: July, August
LIFE ZONE: Plains, Foothills

Date _____

Where found _____

_____

Salt and Pepper
Lomatium orientale
Umbels of tiny dull-white to pinkish blossoms on low grayish plant with finely divided leaves, 1–6 inches in height. One of the first plants to bloom in the spring on grassy slopes.
BLOOM TIME: April, May
LIFE ZONE: Plains, Foothills

Date _____

Where found _____

_____

Sweet Cicely
Osmorhiza depauperata
Very tiny greenish-white flowers at ends of 2–5 long spreading stalks of umbels; plants 12–30 inches tall; leaflets oval, toothed, ¾ to 2 inches long; fruits elongated, covered with bristles that cling to clothing and fur of animals, aiding in seed dispersal. This anise-flavored plant is found in moist shady woods.
BLOOM TIME: July, August
LIFE ZONE: Montane

Date _____

Where found _____

_____

Water Hemlock
Cicuta douglasii
Small white flowers in flat-topped compound umbels; fruits round, not winged; large pinnately compound leaves with leaf veins terminating at notches between teeth on leaf margins, not at tips; stout coarse plant 2–4 feet tall, resembling angelica but often standing in water. Very poisonous.
BLOOM TIME: July, August
LIFE ZONE: Foothills

Date _____

Where found _____

_____

Wild Lovage
Ligusticum porteri
Small white or pinkish flowers in a many-stalked umbel; rather stout, 18 inches to 3 feet tall; leaves fernlike; roots aromatic with a distinctive fragrance. Common in moist fertile soil. A member of the parsnip family, somewhat resembling the well-known queen anne's lace.
BLOOM TIME: June, July
LIFE ZONE: Montane

Date _____

Where found _____

_____

Alpine Phlox
Phlox caespitosa ssp. *pulvinata*
Small trumpet-shaped, 5-lobed, white or bluish flowers from a moss-like mat plant; ½- to 1-inch tall. Flowers very fragrant. Found on the rocky tundra.
BLOOM TIME: July, August
LIFE ZONE: Alpine

Date _____

Where found _____

_____

Early Moss Phlox

Phlox hoodii ssp. *canescens*
Small white 5-petaled flowers solitary at the ends of branches; early flowering dense cushion plant; crowded, small awl-shaped gray-green leaves. Found on dry sunny plains, often covering large areas of gravelly soil. A well-drained niche in the rock garden will suit it. Sometimes called carpet phlox.
BLOOM TIME: April, May
LIFE ZONE: Plains

Date _____

Where found _____

_____

Microsteris

Microsteris gracilis
Small delicate annual with minute white tubular flowers; plants 1–4 inches tall, sticky-hairy, stems usually branched; leaves narrow and opposite. Very common but inconspicuous.
BLOOM TIME: April, May
LIFE ZONE: Foothills

Date _____

Where found _____

_____

White Fairy Trumpet

Ipomopsis aggregata ssp. *candida*
Tubular cream-colored flowers resembling trumpets, 1 to 1½ inches long, arranged along an upright stem; slender, sticky plant 10–24 inches tall, with finely divided leaves. Very common along roadsides. Sometimes hybridizes with red-flowered fairy trumpet (*I. aggregata*) to produce varying shades of pink.
BLOOM TIME: July, August, September
LIFE ZONE: Foothills, Montane

Date _____

Where found _____

_____

Alpine Sandwort
Minuartia obtusiloba
Moss-like cushion plant with numerous tiny white 5-petaled star-like flowers; very small leaves. Often grows in carpets several feet in diameter. An arctic species extending southward in the mountains.
BLOOM TIME: June, July, August
LIFE ZONE: Alpine

Date _____
Where found _____

Creeping Nailwort
Paronychia sessiliflora
Leaves very small on short tight mats or cushions; flowers tiny cream to yellow stars on cushion surface. This species found at drier, lower elevations than *P. pulvinata*. Durable cushion or mat-forming plant for rock gardens, crevices, and path edges in the xeric garden.
BLOOM TIME: July, August
LIFE ZONE: High Desert, Plains

Date _____
Where found _____

Fendler's Sandwort
Arenaria fendleri
Flowers white, 5-petaled, $\frac{1}{3}$ inch broad, tips of stamens show as 10 dark red spots against petals; leaves in stiff, grass-like tufts; plants 3–10 inches tall. Found in sunny, dry locations.
BLOOM TIME: June, July
LIFE ZONE: Foothills, Montane

Date _____
Where found _____

Mouse-Ear Chickweed
Cerastium arvense
Flowers snowy white, almost ½-inch across, with 5 deeply cleft petals; plants up to 12 inches tall; leaves small, narrow, and velvety. Common, and often found in large patches.
BLOOM TIME: April, May, June, July, August, September
LIFE ZONE: Plains, Foothills, Montane, Subalpine, Alpine

Date _____

Where found _____

_____

Sandwort
Arenaria hookeri
From low mat to rounded cushion to spheres. Very tight tiny pointed leaves, flowers small, 5 petals, white, nearly obscuring the plant. On windswept prairies, eroding soil combined with mounding habit results in "bowling ball" specimens up to 10 inches tall. Excellent in a dry rock garden or stone wall.
BLOOM TIME: May, June
LIFE ZONE: High Desert, Plains

Date _____

Where found _____

_____

White Campion
Silene alba
Flowers white with 5, 2-lobed petals; male and female flowers on separate plants; calyx large, inflated, ribbed; leaves narrow, 1–4 inches long with smooth margins; stems branching, 1–2 feet tall, sticky-velvety. Found in open fields and roadsides. **Non-native species** introduced from Europe,
BLOOM TIME: June, July, August
LIFE ZONE: Plains, Foothills

Date _____

Where found _____

_____

Prickly Poppy

Argemone polyanthemos

Large white flowers up to 3 inches across, with 4–6 papery petals and bright yellow centers; plant thistle-like, silvery-gray, 15–30 inches tall, yellow sap; persistent fruits, bristly capsules. Found on roadsides and dry slopes, flowering throughout the summer. Bold texture and pure white flowers enhance any dry garden.

BLOOM TIME: June, July, August, September

LIFE ZONE: Plains, Foothills

Date _____

Where found _____

_____

Rock Jasmine

Androsace chamaejasme

Tiny 5-petaled white flowers with a yellow or pink "eye"; flowers clustered at the top of a short stem; plants ¼ to 2 inches tall; grows from a rosette of small hairy leaves. Found on rocky slopes.

BLOOM TIME: July, August

LIFE ZONE: Alpine

Date _____

Where found _____

_____

Rock Primrose

Androsace septentrionalis

White or reddish very tiny 5-petaled flowers arranged in an umbel at the top of a single stem; stems wiry, reddish, 1–2 inches tall, growing from a rosette of short leaves. Common on alpine tundra as well as in lower zones where it can be up to 12 inches tall.

BLOOM TIME: June, July, August

LIFE ZONE: Foothills, Montane, Subalpine, Alpine

Date _____

Where found _____

_____

Alpine Spring Beauty
Claytonia megarhiza
Rounded, fleshy basal leaves grow in a distinctive flat rosette, often tinted brilliant red. Flowers appear around the edges, and are white with pink veins, ½ to ⅓ inch broad, with 2 light-green sepals; 3–5 inches tall. Found among rocks and often in rocky crevices.

BLOOM TIME: July, August
LIFE ZONE: Alpine

Date _____
Where found _____
_____

Spring Beauty
Claytonia lanceolata
Small white or pinkish flowers, 5 petals veined with darker pink, 2 sepals; opposite leaves; a delicate, succulent herb, 2–6 inches tall. One of the earliest plants to bloom at lower elevations.

BLOOM TIME: April, May, June
LIFE ZONE: Foothills, Montane, Subalpine

Date _____
Where found _____
_____

Water Spring Beauty
Montia chamissoi
Flowers pinkish-white with 5 petals and 2 sepals; leaves spatula-shaped, fleshy, in pairs; long stems root at the nodes. Found in slow-moving streams, bogs, and wet meadows.

BLOOM TIME: June, July, August
LIFE ZONE: Foothills, Montane

Date _____
Where found _____
_____

Creamy Cinquefoil

Potentilla arguta
White or creamy 5-petaled flowers in clusters, turning yellowish on drying; stout, erect, sticky plant, 12–30 inches tall, with pinnately compound basal leaves of many sharply cut leaflets. A common meadow flower.
BLOOM TIME: July, August
LIFE ZONE: Montane

Date _____

Where found _____

_____

Mountain Dryad

Dryas octapetala ssp. *hookeriana*
Small, often creeping shrub, 8–10 inches tall, found on exposed gravel slopes and ridges. Its 1-inch cream-colored, 8-petaled flowers are followed by heads of white-plumed fruits. Evergreen with scalloped leaves, shiny green on top and white beneath.
BLOOM TIME: July, August
LIFE ZONE: Alpine

Date _____

Where found _____

_____

Wild Strawberry

Fragaria virginiana var. *glauca*
Small white 5-petaled flowers with many stamens; low spreading plant with runners often present; compound leaves with 3 slightly bluish, toothed leaflets; fruit miniature bright red strawberries. Commonly found in moist woods and meadows.
BLOOM TIME: June, July
LIFE ZONE: Foothills, Montane, Subalpine

Date _____

Where found _____

_____

Bastard Toadflax
Comandra umbellata
Numerous small, star-shaped, greenish-white to purplish flowers in crowded clusters; leaves narrow, oblong, pale bluish-green; smooth, rather succulent low plants, 5–10 inches tall. Common on dry sandy slopes. Partially parasitic on other plants.
BLOOM TIME: May, June, July, August
LIFE ZONE: Plains, Foothills

Date _____

Where found _____

_____

Dotted Saxifrage
Saxifraga bronchialis
White 5-petaled flowers, petals with red dots; stems slender, 3–6 inches tall; leaves small, spine-tipped, in rosettes forming a spreading mat. Common on dry, shady, rocky slopes and dry evergreen forests throughout the Rocky Mountains.
BLOOM TIME: July, August
LIFE ZONE: Montane, Subalpine

Date _____

Where found _____

_____

Front Range Alumroot
Heuchera hallii
Many low rosettes of leaves, fresh green, with scalloped edges; flowers white, bell-shaped, in slender spikes on wiry stems to 10–12 inches tall. Found clustered in groups among rocks, ledges, or on the forest floor. Endemic along the Front Range, as the name suggests. Suited to a partly shaded rock garden.
BLOOM TIME: June, July, August
LIFE ZONE: Foothills, Montane

Date _____

Where found _____

_____

Grass of Parnassus

Parnassia parviflora

Solitary delicate star-shaped 5-petaled flower with interesting stamen clusters that have prominent glands; slender 1-leaf stem, other leaves basal and stalked; 4–12 inches tall. Grows in grassy stream banks and bogs. Not a true grass.

BLOOM TIME: June, July, August

LIFE ZONE: Montane

Date _____

Where found _____

Nodding Saxifrage

Saxifraga cernua

Small single, cream to yellow, nodding flower with 5 petals at top of stem; reddish bulblets below flower in leaf axils; 2–6 inches tall; stem and leaves sticky. Found in moist rock crevices.

BLOOM TIME: June, July, August

LIFE ZONE: Alpine

Date _____

Where found _____

Small-leaved Alumroot

Heuchera parvifolia

Tiny greenish-yellow flower clusters along slender, leafless stem, 6–20 inches tall; leaves with rounded lobes, long petioles, in a basal rosette. Shady rock outcrops and cliffs. Common throughout the Rocky Mountains.

BLOOM TIME: June, July, August

LIFE ZONE: Montane, Subalpine, Alpine

Date _____

Where found _____

Snowball Saxifrage
Saxifraga rhomboidea
Small white flowers in a single ball or scattered clusters at top of leafless stem, 3–12 inches tall; stalk rises from a flat rosette of toothed, roughly diamond-shaped leaves. Common in early spring.
BLOOM TIME: June, July
LIFE ZONE: Foothills, Montane, Subalpine

Date _____

Where found _____

_____

Saxifrage Family (Saxifragaceae)

Croton
Croton texensis
Tiny flowers, inconspicuous but numerous, male and female on separate plants. Aromatic plant is much-branched near the top, 8–24 inches, covered with star-shaped hairs, giving it a silvery look; leaves narrow.
BLOOM TIME: May, June, July, August
LIFE ZONE: Plains

Date _____

Where found _____

_____

Spurge Family (Euphorbiaceae)

Snow on the Mountain
Euphorbia marginata
Small inconspicuous flowers surrounded by numerous showy, white-margined leaves; 1–2 feet high; single stem at base, branching and flat-topped or umbrella shaped at the top; milky sap. Common in low spots on the plains. Striking annual can self-sow in the garden, but sap from many euphorbias can cause allergic skin reactions.
BLOOM TIME: May, June, July, August, September
LIFE ZONE: Plains

Date _____

Where found _____

_____

Black-Headed Daisy

Erigeron melanocephalus

Single flower head of many white rays surrounding a yellow disk of tiny tubular flowers; small leaf-like bracts beneath the head are covered with long, dark, woolly hairs, giving this flower its common name; 2–5 inches tall. A common dwarf daisy on alpine slopes.

BLOOM TIME: July, August

LIFE ZONE: Alpine

Date _____

Where found _____

_____

Cream Tips

Hymenopappus filifolius

Small creamy white to light yellow flower heads composed only of disk flowers; plants 10–20 inches tall, covered with tufts of cottony hairs; leaves mainly at base of stem and divided into fine segments. Common on dry plains, hills, and mesas.

BLOOM TIME: May, June, July, August

LIFE ZONE: Plains

Date _____

Where found _____

_____

Creamy Thistle

Cirsium canescens

Flower heads dull white, ¾ inch broad, 1 or 2 at ends of stem and branches; stems 1–3 feet tall, hairy-cobwebby; leaves spiny, lance-shaped, with wavy, often deeply cut margins, leaf bases extending down the stem. A common thistle.

BLOOM TIME: June, July

LIFE ZONE: Plains, Foothills

Date _____

Where found _____

_____

Easter Daisy
Townsendia hookeri

White to purple-tinged large flower heads with yellow disks, ¾ to 1 inch broad, in clusters close to the ground; leaves ashy-gray. One of the earliest flowers of plains and foothills. Small stature lends itself well to the rock garden or short prairie.

BLOOM TIME: April, May, June
LIFE ZONE: Plains, Foothills

Date _____

Where found _____

_____

Elk Thistle
Cirsium scariosum

Large flower heads, dull white (sometimes purplish), clustered at top of thick, sturdy stem up to 4 feet tall; leaves gray-green, toothed, spiny. A stemless form of this thistle (shown here) with a flat rosette of large leaves and 1 to several flower heads in the center is found in wet subalpine meadows and aspen groves.

BLOOM TIME: July, August
LIFE ZONE: Subalpine

Date _____

Where found _____

_____

Heather Daisy
Chaetopappa ericoides

Small flower heads with white or pinkish rays and yellow centers; stems low, up to 4 inches; bushy branched plant, rough-hairy and sticky; numerous small, narrow leaves. Common in sandy or rocky soil. Also called sand aster.

BLOOM TIME: May, June, July, August
LIFE ZONE: Plains

Date _____

Where found _____

_____

Knapweed

Centaurea diffusa

Flower heads small, ⅛ to ½ inch, pale lavender to white (resembles a small, old-fashioned corn flower); stiff, much-branched plants, 1–3 feet tall; leaves and young stems covered with short grayish hairs. Common along roadsides, cultivated fields, and ditch banks. A **non-native species** from Eurasia, now a troublesome invasive weed, forming monocultures as it displaces native vegetation.

BLOOM TIME: June, July, August, September

LIFE ZONE: High Desert, Plains, Foothills

Date _____

Where found _____

_____

Large-Flowered or Showy Townsendia

Townsendia grandiflora

Flower heads 1 to 1½ inches broad; creamy white petals with yellow centers; plants 2–8 inches tall, branching from base, leaves narrow. Flower heads seem disproportionately large for the size of the plant, 1 flower head per stem. Found on dry slopes of foothills and mesas. Needs good drainage in the garden, but a showpiece when successful.

BLOOM TIME: April, May, June, July

Date _____

Where found _____

_____

Many-Flowered Aster

Symphyotrichum ericoides

Numerous small white flower heads with yellow centers; small rough leaves; a bushy plant 1–2 feet tall. Usually found on dry ground and along roadsides blooming in early fall.

BLOOM TIME: September, October

LIFE ZONE: Plains, Foothills

Date _____

Where found _____

_____

One-Flowered Daisy

Erigeron simplex

Flowers often nearly white, but closer inspection reveals hints of blue or violet, sometimes darker, with bright yellow disks; heads solitary, 1 inch broad; leaf-like bracts with woolly white or grayish hairs beneath flower heads; 2–8 inches tall; stems and leaves woolly. Common on alpine tundra.

BLOOM TIME: June, July, August

LIFE ZONE: Alpine

Date _____

Where found _____

_____

Oxeye Daisy

Leucanthemum vulgare

Flower heads with white rays and golden yellow centers; heads borne singly on nearly leafless stalks, 10–24 inches tall; leaves narrow, with wavy or toothed margins, forming a basal rosette. Found in meadows and along roadsides. **Non-native species**—an early introduction from Europe into the eastern U.S., now invasive in the Rocky Mountains.

BLOOM TIME: June, July, August

LIFE ZONE: Foothills, Montane

Date _____

Where found _____

_____

Pearly Everlasting

Anaphalis margaritacea

Numerous small white heads without rays but surrounded by papery bracts and clustered at top of stem; 12–18 inches tall; leaves lance-shaped, greenish above, cottony beneath. Common along disturbed roadsides and trails. Performs well in the garden, and flowers are, as the name suggests, "everlasting" when dried.

BLOOM TIME: July, August

LIFE ZONE: Montane, Subalpine

Date _____

Where found _____

_____

Porters Aster

Symphyotrichum porteri

Small white flower heads about ½- to ⅝-inch across, yellow centers turning brownish pink in age; leaves narrow, smooth; low much-branched plant 8–16 inches tall. Endemic along the Front Range, yet very common in open fields and along roadsides; brilliant white among the browning grasses of late summer.

BLOOM TIME: July, August, September
LIFE ZONE: Foothills, Montane

Date _____

Where found _____

_____

Spreading Daisy

Erigeron divergens

Much-branched plant with numerous small, white to light bluish-lavender flowers; heads with numerous, very narrow rays and yellow disks; basal leaves spatula-shaped; plants softly hairy, 10–24 inches tall. Grows on sandy ground and rocky slopes.

BLOOM TIME: June, July, August
LIFE ZONE: Plains, Foothills

Date _____

Where found _____

_____

Sun-Loving Pussytoes

Antennaria parvifolia

Small rounded flower heads white or pale pink, ¼- to ½-inch across, each stem bearing a cluster of 3 to10 heads; stems up to 6 inches tall, rising from a spreading groundcover of gray-green, woolly leaves. Common and abundant in dry meadows and on hillsides. Though the flowers come and go, the wonderful silver mats are invaluable in the rock garden all year. Pistillate and staminate flowers are distinctively different, and on separate plants.

BLOOM TIME: July, August
LIFE ZONE: Foothills, Montane, Subalpine

Date _____

Where found _____

_____

Tasselflower
Brickellia grandiflora
Yellowish-white rayless flower heads in nodding clusters; plants branching, 12–30 inches tall; triangular leaves with toothed edges. Found on dry rocky slopes. Several other brickellias may be seen, and all are similar in appearance.
BLOOM TIME: July, August
LIFE ZONE: Plains, Foothills, Montane

Date _____

Where found _____

_____

Western Fleabane
Erigeron belidiastrum
Widespread and fast-growing annual: small in poor conditions, up to 16 inches with plentiful moisture. Typical 1-inch white to pale pink daisies. Fast and easy in the garden, but reseeds prolifically!
BLOOM TIME: May, June, July, August
LIFE ZONE: Plains

Date _____

Where found _____

_____

Whiplash Daisy
Erigeron flagellaris
Small daisy with numerous, very narrow white rays, pinkish beneath, pink nodding buds, stems 4–10 inches tall; narrow leaves; plant forms numerous runners in the summer. One of the most common low daisies. Can spread to form a xeric ground cover since running habit will cover ground quickly.
BLOOM TIME: June, July
LIFE ZONE: High Desert, Plains, Foothills, Montane

Date _____

Where found _____

_____

White Paper Flower or Blackfoot Daisy

Melampodium leucanthum

Plant with numerous flower heads at ends of stems; 5–9 white to pinkish ray flowers, yellow centers; stems 4–12 inches; narrow opposite leaves. Low much-branched prairie plant of the southeastern plains. Also called black-footed daisy because of the small curved "seed" at the base of each ray. Delightful in the dry garden, requiring good drainage.

BLOOM TIME: April, May, June, July, August, September, October
LIFE ZONE: Plains

Date _____

Where found _____

_____

Woolly Thistle or Frosty Ball

Cirsium scopulorum

A giant among alpines! Flowers rise in dense woolly or cobwebby clusters, forming nodding white heads on a stout stem; 8–24 inches tall; leaves spiny. A common but dramatic thistle of rocky slopes.

BLOOM TIME: July, August
LIFE ZONE: Subalpine, Alpine

Date _____

Where found _____

_____

Yarrow

Achillea millefolium

Flat-topped clusters of small, white flower heads on stems 6–10 inches tall; grayish leaves finely divided, fern-like, and aromatic. Used as a cure for fever by Native Americans and early settlers. Many garden cultivars exist.

BLOOM TIME: May, June, July, August
LIFE ZONE: Plains, Foothills, Montane, Subalpine, Alpine

Date _____

Where found _____

Trillium
Trillium ovatum
Pure white flowers with 3 reflexed petals; 3 large leaves in whorled arrangement. Slow to reproduce, and dependant upon very specific conditions. An encounter with trilliums is a rare occurrence in Colorado. Found only in rich soils of moist woodlands in our northern mountains, their habitats should never be disturbed.

BLOOM TIME: June, July

LIFE ZONE: Montane, Subalpine

Date _____

Where found _____

_____

Tall Valerian
Valeriana edulis
Fragrant white flowers in a branching inflorescence; 12–24 inches tall; leaves thick, pale green, growing from the base of stem. Common throughout the Rocky Mountains in moist meadows and on hillsides. The stout root has been cooked and used by Native Americans for food, and as tobacco when dried and ground. Sometimes called tobacco root.

BLOOM TIME: June, July

LIFE ZONE: Montane, Subalpine, Alpine

Date _____

Where found _____

_____

Canada Violet
Viola canadensis
White flowers with lavender veins, 5-petaled, irregular, with the lower petal spurred; leafy stems with heart-shaped, long pointed leaves; plants 6–12 inches tall. Found in moist, shady locations. In the garden, tolerates relatively dry shade.

BLOOM TIME: May, June, July

LIFE ZONE: Foothills, Montane

Date _____

Where found _____

_____

Arrowhead

Sagittaria latifolia

Flowers with 3 white petals and 3 green sepals, in whorls of 3 along a central axis; leaves shaped like an arrowhead. Attractive plants found along margins of lakes, ponds, and irrigation ditches. The starchy roots were used as food by Native peoples and early settlers.

BLOOM TIME: June, July, August, September

LIFE ZONE: Plains

Date _____

Where found _____

_____

Scorpion Weed

Phacelia heterophylla

Small bluish-white flowers in coiled clusters; plant stiff-hairy, 10–24 inches tall; most leaves simple, some with small lobes at the base. Common on disturbed soil.

BLOOM TIME: May, June, July

LIFE ZONE: Foothills, Montane

Date _____

Where found _____

_____

Silver Scorpionweed

Phacelia hastata

Short-lived perennial or biennial, forming an attractive rosette when young; leaves lanceolate, silver-green with dense silky hairs, veins nearly parallel and conspicuous; flowers on upright or decumbent stems, racemes branched and curled tightly downward, unfurling as the white flowers open. Found at middle and higher elevations, especially in dry pine forests, or disturbed gritty soils. Rosettes are pretty in the garden, but can become floppy in flower.

BLOOM TIME: June, July, August

LIFE ZONE: Montane, Subalpine

Date _____

Where found _____

_____

Waterleaf
Hydrophyllum fendleri
Small flowers in ball-shaped clusters with stamens protruding; leaves long-stalked, pinnately divided, hairy and with 9–13 irregular lobes; plants 1–3 feet tall. Common in moist, shaded locations.

BLOOM TIME: May, June, July

LIFE ZONE: Foothills, Montane

Date _____

Where found _____

_____

Yellow

...ysaria bellii
Constance Sayas

Oregon Grape

Berberis repens

Sometimes shrub-like but more often low and spreading; small yellow flowers in clusters, 6 petals and 6 sepals; sweet fragrance similar to garden hyacinths; short or reclining woody stems up to 15 inches; leaves compound with 3–7 leathery, holly-like evergreen leaflets, turning bright red in autumn; fruits dark blue berries; spreads by underground stems, often occurring in large patches. Found on dry open hillsides and rocky slopes. Commonly used in landscaping, and excellent for dry shade.

BLOOM TIME: March, April, May

LIFE ZONE: Foothills, Montane

Date _____

Where found _____

_____

Many-Flowered Puccoon

Lithospermum multiflorum

Bright yellow tubular flowers, 1 to 1½ inches long, expanding into 5 spreading, slightly toothed lobes; stems leafy with stiff, short hairs, many stems in a clump, 10–14 inches tall; fruits divided into 4 shiny white nutlets. Found in dry meadows and hillsides.

BLOOM TIME: May, June, July

LIFE ZONE: Foothills, Montane, Subalpine

Date _____

Where found _____

_____

Narrow-Leaf Puccoon

Lithospermum incisum

Flower a slender tube 1½ to 3 inches long, expanding into 5 spreading, bright yellow, slightly fringed lobes; stems leafy with stiff short hairs, several stems in a clump, 3–12 inches tall; fruit composed of 4 shiny white nutlets. Found in dry meadows and hillsides.

BLOOM TIME: May, June, July

LIFE ZONE: Plains, Foothills

Date _____

Where found _____

_____

Alpine Golden Buckwheat

Eriogonum arcuatum var. *xanthum*
Tiny golden yellow flowers in clusters on branched stems; leaves densely matted with grayish, woolly hairs; 1–3 inches tall; found in gravelly areas in Alpine tundra. Nice addition to a rock garden.

BLOOM TIME: July, August
LIFE ZONE: Subalpine, Alpine

Date _____

Where found _____

Desert Trumpet

Eriogonum inflatum
Flowers yellow, very tiny, inconspicuous at tips of delicate branches; plants 1–2 feet tall, with unusual inflated stems; leaves all basal, oval or heart-shaped. Found on dry plains and hills, west of the Continental Divide and southward. The dry inflated stems persist in open desert country long after the plants have died.

BLOOM TIME: June, July, August
LIFE ZONE: High Desert

Date _____

Where found _____

James' Golden Buckwheat

Eriogonum arcuatum var. *arcuatum*
Small shrubby perennial; leaves ovate, leathery, with fine hairs; flowers on mounding branched stems, lemon-yellow, in papery round clusters, turning brown as they mature. This is sometimes viewed as a yellow-flowered variant of the James' wild buckwheat, found along the Front Range foothills, with scattered distribution elsewhere in the southern Rockies at low to middle elevations.

BLOOM TIME: July, August, September
LIFE ZONE: Foothills, Montane

Date _____

Where found _____

Sulphur Flower

Eriogonum umbellatum

Very small bright yellow flowers in umbels, turning orange to red in autumn; drooping leafy bracts at base of umbel; leafless, woolly-hairy stems, 4–12 inches tall; leaves oval, woolly white beneath, forming a mat. Common and widespread in the montane and foothills. Many subspecies exist throughout the West. Excellent in the rock garden or dry border.

BLOOM TIME: June, July, August

LIFE ZONE: Foothills, Montane

Date _____

Where found _____

Golden Columbine

Aquilegia chrysantha

Flowers cream to deep yellow, 5 rounded petals elongated into spurs, pointed sepals; compound leaves with rounded lobes, bluish-green, emerging from a basal crown. Found rarely in some Eastern Slope canyons, and listed as a protected species. Variations of this are widely scattered in sheltered canyons and seeps throughout the Southwest. All columbine hybridize easily and with so many forms in cultivation, encountering the pure species is unlikely in towns and gardens. Selections of the plain species are available in nurseries; long-flowering and adaptable, even in dry shade.

BLOOM TIME: May, June, July, August, September

LIFE ZONE: High Desert, Foothills

Date _____

Where found _____

_____

Meadow-Rue

Thalictrum fendleri

Small yellowish-green tassels of stamens, or clusters of small green fruits found on separate plants; 12–24 inches tall; leaves bluish-green, divided into small rounded leaflets resembling leaves of columbine. Forms dense patches in forests and shady ravines.

BLOOM TIME: May, June

LIFE ZONE: Foothills, Montane

Date _____

Where found_____

_____

Sagebrush Buttercup

Ranunculus glaberrimus var. *ellipticus*
Flowers bright shiny yellow, ½ to ¾ inch broad, 5 petals, 5 sepals, many stamens; 2–6 inches tall; basal leaves oval, stem leaves 3-lobed. Found on open moist hillsides and sagebrush flats. One of the earliest spring-blooming flowers, common in its favored habitats throughout the Rocky Mountains.
BLOOM TIME: March, April, May, June
LIFE ZONE: Plains, Foothills, Montane

Date _____

Where found _____

_____

Snow Buttercup

Ranunculus adoneus
Large bright yellow poppy-like flowers, 1 to 1½ inches across; leaves finely cut, segments threadlike. Most often found at the edge of snow banks above timberline, sometimes coming through the snow.
BLOOM TIME: June, July
LIFE ZONE: Alpine

Date _____

Where found _____

_____

Yellow Clematis

Clematis orientalis
Flowers numerous, yellow, nodding, with 4 petals, borne singly or in small clusters; silvery seed plumes; leafy, trailing plant; resembles virgin's bower except for flower color. Vines scramble over nearby vegetation. Reseeds readily. Quite common near Idaho Springs, where it was introduced during mining days, now spreading widely and listed as an invasive weed. **Non-native species.**
BLOOM TIME: June, July, August, September
LIFE ZONE: Foothills

ate _____

here found _____

_____

Dwarf Prickly Pear

Opuntia fragilis

Pads nearly smooth to heavily spined, small but not quite cylindrical; flowers soft yellow, small and scattered, each lasting just 2 or 3 days. The plants lay flat and weave among short grasses or spill over rock ledges or onto open ground. Prickly pears are highly variable, and this species is no exception.

BLOOM TIME: June

LIFE ZONE: High Desert, Plains, Foothills

Date _____

Where found _____

_____

Hair-Spine Prickly Pear

Opuntia heacockiae

Small variable pads are rounded to flat, very much like *Opuntia fragilis*; flowers sparse, pale yellow, small. Found occasionally in the Arkansas valley. Its status as a species is disputed, (now also listed as *O. polyacantha* var. *polyacantha*) yet it seems unique in that even the roots will produce glochids when exposed, and new pads can sprout directly from the roots, even some distance from the original plant—interesting, but perhaps not a desirable trait for the garden!

BLOOM TIME: June

LIFE ZONE: Plains

Date _____

Where found _____

_____

Hunger Cactus or Plains Prickly Pear

Opuntia polyacantha

Widespread throughout the arid West, and the most common species on the plains, with variable flowers in shades of yellow, orange, or pink. Spination is variable and often heavy; fruits of this cactus are dry, not fleshy. Spines are formidable, but beware the fine hair-like glochids found at their base: difficult to see, but very irritating. A classic and sculptural plant for any dry Western garden.

BLOOM TIME: May, June

LIFE ZONE: High Desert, Plains, Foothills

Date _____

Where found _____

_____

New Mexican Prickly Pear
Opuntia phaeacantha

Robust spreading shrub up to 18 inches with upright new growth, later reclining and rooting to form large patches. Pads may reach 8 inches across, well-armed with reddish-brown to tan spines clustered with plentiful glochids; flowers typically bright yellow with red flares near the base, but shades of pink to orange occur; fruits distinctive, plump, juicy, cherry-red, with depressed tan flower scar at the top. Found in dry open country, canyons, ledges, or among short grasses. Beautiful all year in the garden, and easy in sunny, dry, well-drained settings.

BLOOM TIME: June
LIFE ZONE: High Desert, Plains

Date _____

Where found _____

Prickly Pear
Opuntia macrorhiza

Opuntias hybridize easily and species are sometimes hard to distinguish. *O. macrorhiza* is primarily a midwestern U.S. species with sporadic populations in the western Great Plains and Rockies. Showy yellow flowers 1½ to 3 inches broad, many petals; numerous stamens clustered around a large green style. Flowers are on edges of fleshy pads that are often sparingly spined compared to our other species. The fruits are fleshy and make delicious jelly. Scattered on Colorado's eastern plains and mesas.

BLOOM TIME: May, June
LIFE ZONE: Plains

te _____

here found _____

Puncture Vine
Tribulus terrestris

Mat-forming plant with trailing stems 1–6 feet long; flowers yellow, ⅙ to ⅓ inch broad, 5 petals; leaves divided pinnately into 4–8 pairs of small leaflets; fruit a hard spiny bur, injurious, can puncture bicycle tires. A weedy plant now found widely in the U.S. in cultivated fields and disturbed roadsides. **Non-native species** introduced from Europe.

BLOOM TIME: May, June, July, August
LIFE ZONE: High Desert, Plains

te _____

ere found _____

Yellow Bee Plant
Cleome lutea

Light yellow flowers in a dense cluster along top of stem, 4 petals, with 6 long protruding stamens; long slender, maturing seed pods usually stand out at an angle below the flower cluster; leaves divided into 5–7 leaflets; coarse, branching plant, up to 3 feet tall. Often seen in large patches in western Colorado, Utah, and New Mexico on dry hills and plains. Similar to Rocky Mountain bee plant.

BLOOM TIME: July, August

LIFE ZONE: High Desert, Foothills

Date _____

Where found _____

_____

Common Evening Primrose
Oenothera villosa

Tall coarse plant, up to 3 feet, with pale yellow 4-petaled flowers, $\frac{2}{3}$ to 1 inch broad; leaves lance-shaped, gray-hairy; seed capsules cylindrical, in upper leaf axils, often quite conspicuous, 1 to $1\frac{1}{2}$ inches long. Common on plains, mesas, lower foothills; can be weedy in the garden.

BLOOM TIME: July, August, September

LIFE ZONE: Plains, Foothills

Date_____

Where found _____

_____

Dainty Sundrops
Calylophus serrulatus

Small light yellow, delicate 4-petaled flowers, $\frac{1}{2}$ to $\frac{3}{4}$ inch broad; on bushy plant, 6–12 inches high; leaves narrow, toothed. Found on sandy or gravelly soil of the lower foothills, mesas, and plains mainly east of the Continental Divide. Cheerful, long-blooming plant for a dry border or rock garden.

BLOOM TIME: May, June, July

LIFE ZONE: Plains, Foothills

Date _____

Where found _____

_____

Golden Evening Primrose

Oenothera flava
Flowers golden yellow, turning pink in age, 4-petaled; plants stemless, deeply cut narrow leaves form a basal rosette. Found on dry rocky slopes, ridges and sandy banks in the lower foothills, mesas, and plains.

BLOOM TIME: May, June, July
LIFE ZONE: Plains, Foothills

Date _____

Where found _____

_____

Sundrops

Calylophys lavandulifolius
Long-lived perennial, forming low mounds 6–8 inches tall; leaves linear to 2 inches, alternate; flower buds appear yellow, shading to reddish pink in a striped pattern, opening wide during the day (despite the family name) to 4-petaled bright yellow blooms with wavy edges, fading to dull orange; long flowering season. Often found in evenly spaced clumps on dry flats, hillsides, and roadcuts. A treasure for the desert garden or dry border.

BLOOM TIME: June, July, August, September
LIFE ZONE: High Desert, Plains

te _____

ere found _____

_____

Yellow Stemless Evening Primrose

Oenothera brachycarpa
Large 4-petaled, golden yellow fragrant flowers nestled in basal rosette of long narrow leaves, opening late in the day, fading to orange-red. Locally common on dry slopes at lower elevations throughout our area. Well suited and showy in a xeric or rock garden with good drainage. The species *howardii* is nearly identical, and many believe it to be the same species.

BLOOM TIME: May, June, July
LIFE ZONE: Plains

e _____

ere found _____

_____

Bracted Lousewort

Pedicularis bracteosa

Flowers pale yellow, 1 inch long, tubular with 2 lips, upper lip arched downwards; flowers in a dense spike-like arrangement at top of stem, 1–3 feet tall; basal leaves fernlike. Found in moist woods and meadows.

BLOOM TIME: July, August

LIFE ZONE: Montane, Subalpine

Date_____

Where found _____

_____

Butter and Eggs

Linaria vulgaris

Snapdragon-like yellow flowers ¾ to 1 inch long, 2-lipped with orange spot on lower lip, long spur at base of flower; stems upright, 10–24 inches tall; leaves narrow, crowded, pale green. Common along roadsides and waste places. Blooms all summer. Spreads by seed and aggressive stolons underground, and is listed as a noxious weed in many areas. Avoid "wildflower" seed mixes that include this weedy **non-native species!**

BLOOM TIME: June, July, August, September

LIFE ZONE: Plains, Foothills, Montane

Date_____

Where found_____

_____

Dalmation Toadflax

Linaria dalmatica ssp. *dalmatica*

Pale yellow flowers, snapdragon-like, 2-lipped, with long spur at base, bright orange spot in the throat; flowers clustered along top of stem; plants sturdy, 2½ to 4 feet tall; leaves bluish-green, clasping. A native of southeastern Europe, now commonly found on roadsides and open slopes in large patches. Its range is expanding, and it is now listed as a noxious weed. **Non-native species.**

BLOOM TIME: July, August

LIFE ZONE: Plains, Foothills

Date_____

Where found _____

_____

Mullein

Verbascum thapsus

Tall, unbranched plant with a long spike of bright yellow, 5-lobed flowers, ½ to ¾ inch across; basal leaves often up to 14 inches long; plant covered with soft mat of woolly hairs. Mullein is a biennial, forming a rosette of light green leaves the first year; a flowering stalk, which may be up to 6 feet tall, develops the second season; the dead, brown flower stalks may stand for several years. Found over much of the U.S. in dry sandy or gravelly areas, fields, and along roadsides. Though this species is listed as an invasive weed, there are many other verbascums that are well behaved and beautiful in the garden. **Non-native species** introduced from Europe.

BLOOM TIME: June, July, August, September

LIFE ZONE: Plains, Foothills, Montane

Date _____

Where found _____

_____

Owl Clover

Orthocarpus luteus

Tiny yellow 2-lipped snapdragon-like flowers in terminal, club-shaped inflorescences almost hidden by 3-cleft green bracts; stems erect, 4–12 inches tall; leaves narrow, usually with smooth margins and no leaf stalks. Not a true clover. Common in dry fields and hillsides.

BLOOM TIME: June, July, August

LIFE ZONE: Foothills, Montane

Date _____

Where found _____

_____

Plains Monkeyflower

Mimulus glabratus

Flowers bright yellow, snapdragon-like, with short flower tube expanded into five short lobes, forming two lips; flowers few, in loose clusters; plants low or creeping, leaves opposite. Found in marshy places or along irrigation ditches in the plains and lower valleys.

BLOOM TIME: June, July, August

LIFE ZONE: Plains

Date _____

Where found _____

_____

Western Yellow Paintbrush
Castilleja occidentalis
Hairy greenish-yellow bracts below each small, greenish-yellow tubular flower give this plant a rounded paintbrush-like appearance; stems 5–10 inches tall; grows in clumps. Common plant in alpine tundra and on subalpine slopes.
BLOOM TIME: July, August
LIFE ZONE: Subalpine, Alpine

Date _____

Where found _____

_____

Yellow Monkeyflower
Mimulus guttatus
Flowers bright yellow, snapdragon-like, ¾ to 1½ inches long, with red spots in throat; stems square, leaves opposite, oval, toothed edges; plants 4–18 inches tall. Found along wet streambanks, springs, and lakes.
BLOOM TIME: June, July, August
LIFE ZONE: Foothills, Montane, Subalpine

Date _____

Where found _____

_____

Golden Smoke
Corydalis aurea
Pale yellow, delicate flowers, ¾ inch long, with 2 tiny sepals and 4 petals, in racemes; outer 2 petals spreading, 1 with a ¼-inch spur, inner 2 petals joined at tips enclose the stamens; spreading plant in low clumps; leaves delicately cut, fern-like, bluish-green. Found in moist areas and disturbed soils of ravines and road banks.
BLOOM TIME: May, June, July, August
LIFE ZONE: Plains, Foothills, Montane

Date _____

Where found _____

_____

Buffalo Gourd
Cucurbita foetidissima
Flowers large, yellow, bell-shaped, 1 to over 2 inches long; baseball-like striped gourds, turning yellowish after frost; leaves large, triangular, grayish, pointing upward; coarse trailing plant with large roots. Plant has an unpleasant odor. Found on dry plains, roadsides, and ravines.
BLOOM TIME: June, July, August
LIFE ZONE: Plains

Date _____

Where found _____

Mock Cucumber
Echinocystis lobata
Flowers light greenish-yellow, both staminate and pistillate flowers in leaf axils; fruits are egg-shaped, spiny, papery seed pods containing large, flat black seeds when ripe; leaves thin and palmately lobed into 3–7 divisions; tall climbing annual with angular stems and 3-forked tendrils. Found on high plains and lower foothills.
BLOOM TIME: June, July
LIFE ZONE: Plains, Foothills

Date _____

Where found _____

Mountain Golden Banner
Thermopsis montana
Flowers golden-yellow, pea-like, resembling lupines, ½ to ¾ inch long, loosely clustered at top of stem; stems 12–24 inches tall, leafy; leaves compound with 3 leaflets; pods long, straight and erect or slightly curved. One of the showiest and most widespread mountain flowers, often seen in large patches along roadsides, forming sheets of lemon yellow—a fitting complement to the fresh lime green of emerging aspen leaves. The spread-fruit golden banner is similar in most respects, but less widespread, with pods curved and widely spreading. Excellent in a "wild" garden, but stoloniferous habit is a challenge in gardens with more structure.
BLOOM TIME: May, June
LIFE ZONE: Foothills, Montane

Date _____

Where found _____

Prairie Golden Banner

Thermopsis rhombifolia
Similar in many respects to *T. montana*—some authorities group them as one species—but this species is found at lower elevations. Leaves tend to be more broad and rounded, and seed pods are more curved. This species is probably more tolerant of poor soils and drier conditions than *T. montana*.
BLOOM TIME: May, June
LIFE ZONE: High Desert, Plains, Foothill

Date _____

Where found _____

_____

Yellow Sweet Clover

Melilotus officinalis
Several stems emerge from the crown of a deep perennial taproot. Stems much-branched, reaching to 5 feet where conditions favor it; clover-like 3-parted leaves, leaflets slender; flowers small but many, pea-like, in short loose racemes to 3 inches long. This weed is highly adaptable, now found throughout North America in almost every habitat. Though it does create an impressive show of flowers, it aggressively colonizes roadsides and moist meadows, likely displacing natives that could be creating a show of their own. **Non-native species.**
BLOOM TIME: June, July, August, September
LIFE ZONE: High Desert, Plains, Foothills, Montane

Date _____

Where found _____

_____

Avalanche Lily

Erythronium grandiflorum
Bright yellow drooping flowers with turned-back petals and sepals; slender stalks 6–18 inches tall; leaves long, narrow, shiny green. Found on moist, rich soil in meadows, often growing in large patches where snowdrifts have melted.
BLOOM TIME: July, August
LIFE ZONE: Subalpine, Alpine

Date _____

Where found _____

_____

Small-Flowered Stickleaf or Evening Star
Mentzelia albicaulis
Small 5-petaled light yellow flowers open during the day; plants 8–15 inches tall with white, shining stems; leaf margins toothed; leaves, stems, and fruits with stiff, short, curved hairs that cling like Velcro® to fur and clothing, thus aiding seed dispersal. Found on dry slopes and banks, often sandy soil.
BLOOM TIME: June, July, August
LIFE ZONE: Plains, Foothills

te _____

here found_____

_____

Yellow Evening Star
Mentzelia multiflora
Bright yellow flowers, 1½ to 2 inches broad, on branching plant, 1–2 feet tall; leaves toothed; stems, fruit, and leaves with stiff, curved hairs rough to the touch. Flowers of this plant open in late afternoon or early evening. Found on dry banks, roadsides, and fields of the foothills and mesas.
BLOOM TIME: June, July, August
LIFE ZONE: Foothills

Date _____

Where found _____

_____

Bell's Bladderpod
Physaria bellii
Leathery, silver, spatulate leaves in a rosette 4–6 inches in diameter; bright yellow flowers on horizontal stems that extend past the leaves, forming a ring of gold. This beautiful endemic plant has a very limited distribution along the Front Range in northern Colorado, where it finds footing in exposed shale outcrops. Can be purchased at specialty nurseries. Though rare in habitat, it does seem adaptable to cultivation and is lovely in a well-drained rock garden.
BLOOM TIME: May
LIFE ZONE: Plains

te _____

ere found_____

_____

Bladderpod
Lesquerella montana
Pale yellow 4-petaled flowers in clusters at ends of S-shaped pedicels; pods becoming inflated or bladder-like with age; leaves oval with smooth or toothed margins, in a basal rosette; stems hairy, grayish, 4–8 inches tall. Found on dry, sandy soil and along roadsides.
BLOOM TIME: May, June
LIFE ZONE: Foothills, Montane

Date _____

Where found _____

_____

Fiddle-Leaf Twin Pod
Physaria vitulifera
Flowers yellow, about ¾ inch broad, 4-petaled; fruits are deeply divided (double) inflated papery pods; low, compact grayish plant with spreading stems and small, fiddle-shaped leaves. Found on sandy or gravelly foothill slopes.
BLOOM TIME: May, June, July
LIFE ZONE: Foothills

Date _____

Where found _____

Golden Draba
Draba aurea
Small bright yellow 4-petaled flowers in cluster at top of 2–6 inch stem; leaves small, spatula-shaped, in basal rosette; stem and leaves with long hairs. Common in open coniferous forests, and also on the tundra.
BLOOM TIME: July, August
LIFE ZONE: Montane, Subalpine, Alpine

Date _____

Where found _____

_____

Plains Bladderpod
Lesquerella ludoviciana
Small light yellow 4-petaled flowers; plants 6–12 inches tall; silver-hairy linear leaves in basal rosette; stems elongate as fruits ripen; fruits round, inflated, thus a "bladderpod." Common on dry gravelly or sandy slopes.

BLOOM TIME: March, April, May

LIFE ZONE: Plains

Date _____

Where found _____

_____

Prince's Plume
Stanleya pinnata
Bright yellow flowers in tall showy spike-like racemes, 4 narrow petals and long stamens give spikes a feathery appearance; seed in long slender pods; plants tall, up to 5 feet. Common in plains, mesas, and arid lands. Found on soil containing the poisonous mineral selenium, but succeeds in most well-drained soils. Displayed at its finest against the red rock walls of our western canyons.

BLOOM TIME: April, May, June, July, August

LIFE ZONE: High Desert, Plains

Date _____

Where found _____

_____

Twisted-Pod Draba
Draba streptocarpa
Small golden-yellow 4-petaled flowers in a cluster at the top of the stem, rising from a rosette of silky-hairy leaves; pods twisted; plants 2–6 inches tall. Found on open gravelly slopes.

BLOOM TIME: July, August

LIFE ZONE: Montane, Subalpine, Alpine

Date _____

Where found _____

_____

Western Wallflower

Erysimum asperum

Flowers fragrant, bright yellow or orange, 4-petaled, sometimes light brown on backs of petals, ½ inch broad, in loose clusters at top of stem; 8–24 inches tall; leaves narrow, seed pods long, narrow. Very common. Self-sows easily in the garden. Very similar to *Erysimum capitatum*.

BLOOM TIME: July, August

LIFE ZONE: Plains, Foothills, Montane

Date _____

Where found _____

Wild Alyssum

Alyssum parviflorum

Very tiny pale yellow, 4-petaled flowers; plants 2–10 inches tall; leaves oblong, ½ to 1 inch long; leaves and stems rough with star-shaped hairs (use a hand lens). One of the most common early spring weeds, blooming in masses on open hillsides, fields, and along roadsides in the lower foothills, mesas, and plains. **Non-native species** introduced from Europe.

BLOOM TIME: March, April, May, June

LIFE ZONE: High Desert, Plains, Foothills

Date _____

Where found _____

Winter Cress

Barbarea orthoceras

Clusters of bright yellow 4-petaled flowers at top of stout stalk, 12–20 inches tall; plants smooth, bright green, leaves deeply cut. A bright, showy weedy plant of wet places in fields, pastures, and roadsides on the plains and lower foothills.

BLOOM TIME: June, July, August

LIFE ZONE: Plains, Foothills

Date _____

Where found _____

Buffalo Bur or Star Thistle
Solanum rostratum
Saucer-shaped bright yellow flowers, 1 to 1¼ inches wide; plant branched, covered with straw-colored slender spines; leaves deeply cut with rounded lobes; fruit a bur with long sharp spines. An introduced weed of fields, meadows, roadsides, disturbed areas. **Non-native species.**
BLOOM TIME: May, June, July, August, September
LIFE ZONE: High Desert, Plains

Date _____

Where found _____

_____

Yellow Ladyslipper
Cypripedium parviflorum var. *pubescens*
Rare member of the orchid family, and protected throughout most of its range, with a large, bright yellow sac-like lower lip; 2 upper petals are narrow, twisted and greenish; leaves lance-shaped, clasping the stem; plant 8–12 inches tall. Grows in moist open woods. This beautiful plant is in danger of extinction and should never be picked, nor its habitat disturbed. Please help protect it.
BLOOM TIME: June, July
LIFE ZONE: Foothills, Montane

Date _____

Where found _____

_____

Alpine Parsley
Oreoxis alpina
Tiny umbels of small yellow flowers; finely divided leaves; low mat-forming plant, 1–4 inches tall; found on gravelly alpine slopes. Related to the much taller mountain parsley found at lower elevations.
BLOOM TIME: July, August
LIFE ZONE: Alpine

Date _____

Where found _____

_____

Whiskbroom Parsley

Harbouria trachypleura

Flowers tiny, yellow, in flat-topped umbels; leaves very finely divided; stems in tufts, plants 3–20 inches tall. Common in dry meadows and hillsides along the eastern slope of the Front Range.

BLOOM TIME: May, June, July

LIFE ZONE: Foothills, Montane

Date_____

Where found _____

_____

Yellow Mountain Parsley

Pseudocymopterus montanus

Flowers very tiny, bright yellow, in flattish umbels, attached at tip of slender stem, 10–18 inches tall; leaves deeply cut, parsley-like. A variable plant found in aspen groves and moist meadows.

BLOOM TIME: July, August

LIFE ZONE: Foothills, Montane, Subalpine

Date_____

Where found _____

_____

Nailwort

Paronychia pulvinata

Forms dense cushion-like mats, leaves short, crowded, light green; flowers tiny, pale yellow stars, inconspicuous among the leaves. Common on dry, rocky alpine tundra.

BLOOM TIME: June, July, August

LIFE ZONE: Alpine

Date _____

Where found _____

_____

Common Purslane

Portulaca oleraceae

Succulent obovate leaves on low spreading succulent stems; flowers with 5 notched petals, yellow, to ½ inch across; seeds tiny, round, and black. Very common introduced weed of gardens, roadsides, and abandoned fields. Annual, but persistent in the garden, seeding prolifically; broken pieces re-root and continue to grow. Edible? Yes. Delicious? No. **Non-native species.**

BLOOM TIME: June, July, August, September

LIFE ZONE: High Desert, Plains, Foothills

Date _____

Where found _____

Alpine Avens

Geum rossii

Flowers bright yellow, 5-petaled; leaves dark green, finely divided; plants 3–10 inches tall; often forms dense clumps. One of the most abundant flowers above timberline. Leaves turn bronze to deep red in late summer.

BLOOM TIME: June, July, August

LIFE ZONE: Alpine

Date _____

Where found _____

Bur Avens

Geum macrophyllum

Flowers bright yellow, 5-petaled, ½ inch across; 5 sepals, droop after bud opens; styles persistent, jointed and bent, fruits becoming a bur; stems erect with bristly hairs, 1–3 feet tall; leaves compound of 3–7 leaflets, with rounded terminal leaflet larger than others. Grows in meadows and wet areas. Attractive plant, but hooked seeds can be a nuisance; becomes weedy in the garden.

BLOOM TIME: June, July

LIFE ZONE: Montane

Date _____

Where found _____

Glaucous Cinquefoil

Potentilla diversifolia and other species
Flowers yellow, 1/2 inch broad, with 5 rounded petals and 5 sepals plus 5 small, sepal-like bracts, stems 10–12 inches tall, spreading; leaves bluish-green, palmately compound with 5–7 leaflets. A common flower of moist meadows. The potentillas, or cinquefoils, comprise a very large group of plants in the rose family and are found in a wide variety of habitats. All have 5 petals and 10 calyx parts, and most of them have an orange spot at the base of each yellow or creamy petal.
BLOOM TIME: May, June, July, August
LIFE ZONE: Subalpine, Alpine

Date _____

Where found_____

_____

Leafy Cinquefoil

Potentilla fissa
Flowers creamy to light yellow, 5-petaled, up to 1 inch broad, resemble buttercups, in clusters on leafy erect stems, 8–12 inches tall; leaves compound with 9–13 broad leaflets, sharply toothed; stems and foliage with brown, sticky hairs. Common on rocky slopes and roadsides.
BLOOM TIME: May, June, July, August
LIFE ZONE: Foothills, Montane

Date _____

Where found _____

_____

Sibbaldia

Sibbaldia procumbens
Inconspicuous 5-petaled, very tiny yellow flowers; blue-green clover-like leaves; a low mat plant often found near patches of late-lying snow in gravelly tundra. An interesting, often overlooked plant found throughout the Northern Hemisphere in Alpine locations.
BLOOM TIME: June, July
LIFE ZONE: Alpine

Date _____

Where found _____

_____

Silver Cinquefoil
Potentilla hippiana
Pinnately divided leaves; silky hairs that give an elegant silver sheen. Wiry flowering stems rise 8–12 inches above low mounding foliage; delicate lemon yellow five-petaled flowers. This potentilla would be a desirable plant for gardens even if it did not flower.
BLOOM TIME: June, July, August
LIFE ZONE: Plains, Foothills, Montane, Subalpine

Date _____

Where found _____

_____

Fairy or Golden Saxifrage
Saxifraga chrysantha
Golden flowers with 5 orange-dotted petals; yellow seed pods turn red when ripe; very small plant, 2–3 inches tall, growing from a leafy rosette; found on rocky ridges, often forming mats. There are a number of saxifrages in the alpine and subalpine zones, and most are very small plants. Fairy saxifrage is one of the easiest to recognize.
BLOOM TIME: July, August
LIFE ZONE: Alpine

Date _____

Where found _____

_____

Whiplash Saxifrage
Saxifraga flagellaris
Bright yellow 5-petaled flowers; leaves and stems with sticky hairs growing from a leafy rosette; stems 1–3 inches tall; often abundant on Alpine ridges. This plant sends out runners that root at the tips, forming new plants as strawberries do.
BLOOM TIME: July, August
LIFE ZONE: Alpine

Date _____

Where found _____

_____

Donkeytail Spurge

Euphorbia myrsinites

Low, gray-green stems radiate from a central crown; evergreen leaves have a succulent appearance, leathery, with milky sap, ovate, neatly arranged in spiraling rows. Flowers are small, greenish, surrounded by showy yellow bracts. This escapee from gardens produces abundant seed and is known to spread into some natural areas, thus its listing as a noxious weed. Related *E. rigida* is distinct with narrower leaves, and is much more restrained in the garden. **Non-native species.**

BLOOM TIME: April, May, June
LIFE ZONE: High Desert, Plains, Foothills

Date _____

Where found_____

Leafy Spurge

Euphorbia esula

What appear to be yellowish-green flowers in clusters of small umbels at the top of the plant are whorls of leaf-like bracts enclosing small inconspicuous flowers; plants 15–30 inches tall, leafy; in dense patches along moist roadsides, fields, and pastures. Introduced from Europe, it has become a noxious weed, spreading by seed and aggressive underground stems. **Non-native species.**

BLOOM TIME: June, July, August
LIFE ZONE: Plains, Foothills

Date_____

Where found _____

St. Johnswort or Klamath Weed

Hypericum perforatum

Bright yellow 5-petaled flower, ¾ inch across, with many stamens; flowers very numerous in broad cluster at top of bushy plant, 1–2 feet tall; leaves with black dots near the margins make this plant easy to identify. Found in moist pastures, roadsides and fields, this introduced European weed is particularly poisonous to sheep. It has been controlled (not eliminated) by the introduction of a specific beetle for which this plant is its only food. **Non-native species.**

BLOOM TIME: July, August
LIFE ZONE: Plains, Foothills

Date_____

Where found _____

Yellow Stonecrop
Sedum lanceolatum
Bright yellow star-shaped flowers on succulent stems, 2–5 inches tall. Small fleshy leaves form rosettes, often tinted red in chilly or stressed conditions. Found in stony, dry ground and rocky ledges, and is a close relative of rock garden sedums.

BLOOM TIME: June, July, August

LIFE ZONE: Foothills, Montane, Subalpine, Alpine

Date _____

Where found _____

_____

Actinea or Perky Sue
Tetraneuris acaulis
Flower heads bright yellow, ¾ to 1 inch across, solitary at top of leafless stalk, ray flowers 3-toothed; leaves narrow, woolly or silky-gray, in tuft at base of stem, usually 8–20 inches tall. Found in dry, often rocky areas. Durable plant in the xeric border or rock garden, requiring good drainage and full sun. Several similar varieties are found throughout the West.

BLOOM TIME: June, July, August, September

LIFE ZONE: Plains, High Desert, Foothills

Date_____

Where found _____

_____

Aspen Sunflower
Helianthella quinquenervis
Flower heads 3–4 inches across with light yellow rays, darker yellow disk, usually one head per stem; leaves leathery, shiny, with 5 main veins (as the name indicates); basal leaves may be a foot or more long; stems erect, 1–4 feet tall, un-branched, bent at top with flower head facing to the side. Found in damp open woods and aspen groves.

BLOOM TIME: July, August

LIFE ZONE: Montane

Date _____

Where found _____

_____

Balsam Root
Balsamorhiza sagittata
Flower heads large, 2–3 inches broad, both ray flowers and disk flowers bright yellow; flower heads usually solitary at tips of leafless stalks, 10–20 inches tall; leaves arrow-shaped, gray-green, up to 12 inches long. More common west of the Continental Divide, often covers dry hillsides with bright yellow. Sometimes roots, shoots, and seeds used as food; roots have a balsam flavor.
BLOOM TIME: June, July, August
LIFE ZONE: Foothills, Montane

Date _____

Where found_____

_____

Beggar's Tick or Bur Marigold
Bidens cernua
Flower heads bright yellow with short, stubby rays, resembling small sunflowers; plants stout, 10–30 inches tall, leaves lance-shaped, with toothed edges; fruits with 2 or 4 barbed spines at top, an easy plant to identify if fruits are found, or if they find you! Common along streams, irrigation ditches, and boggy areas.
BLOOM TIME: August, September
LIFE ZONE: Plains, Foothills

Date _____

Where found _____

_____

Black-Eyed Susan
Rudbeckia hirta
Flower heads large, 2–3 inches broad, orange-yellow rays with pointed or slightly notched tips, disk oval, dark brown to nearly black; plants 12–20 inches tall, stem often purple-dotted; basal leaves oval, upper leaves narrow, rough and alternate. A showy wild-flower, common in meadows and aspen groves. Many cultivars and hybrids are used in cultivation, though the simple species is lovely and bright in any garden.
BLOOM TIME: June, July, August
LIFE ZONE: Foothills, Montane

Date _____

Where found _____

_____

Black-Tipped Senecio

Senecio atratus

Numerous small yellow flower heads, ½ inch broad; conspicuously black-tipped narrow bracts at base of each head; stems stout; leaves oblong; stem and foliage silver-gray, woolly. A handsome plant forming large clumps, 12–30 inches high, along roadsides and gravelly banks.

BLOOM TIME: July, August
LIFE ZONE: Subalpine

Date_____

Where found _____

_____

Broom Senecio

Senecio spartioides

Numerous small yellow flower heads; bushy plants 10–24 inches tall; leaves linear, slender, light green. A very common *Senecio*, conspicuous along roadsides in late summer with bright masses of yellow flowers. In the dry garden or prairie, creates clouds of lemon-yellow in time to complement the purple spires of *Liatris punctata*.

BLOOM TIME: July, August
LIFE ZONE: Plains, Foothills, Montane

ate _____

here found_____

_____

Chocolate Flower

Berlandiera lyrata

Perennial with slender gray-green stems and leaves, irregular pinnate lobes, with those near the tip more broad than those near the base, up to 2 feet tall; flowers yellow, daisy-like, to 1¼ inches, usually 8 clear yellow ray flowers, reddish reverse, with notched tips, centers dark brown, chocolate-scented on warm mornings. As seeds mature, green cup-like calyces turn papery and tan. Found in southeast Colorado along roadsides and dry slopes; more common in the southern plains and into the Chihuahuan Desert. A delight in a xeric border or meadow.

BLOOM TIME: June, July, August, September
LIFE ZONE: Plains

te _____

ere found_____

_____

161

Colorado Rubber Plant

Hymenoxys richardsonii

Numerous yellow flower heads, ½ to ¾ inch broad, in flat clusters; rays usually 8, with 3-toothed tips, drooping upon aging; leaves divided into 3–7 narrow segments, with tufts of woolly hairs in the leaf axils; plants much-branched, with several stems from a woody base, 4–18 inches tall. Found on sunny, dry plains and rocky slopes. Was considered at one time as a possible alternate source of rubber.

BLOOM TIME: June, July, August

LIFE ZONE: Foothills, Montane

Date _____

Where found _____

_____

Common Dandelion

Taraxacum officinale

Dense, rounded flower heads composed of many yellow strap-shaped flowers, about 1 inch broad, on leafless, hollow stems; leaves lance-shaped, lobed, sharply toothed, in a basal rosette; contains milky juice. A **non-native species** from Eurasia, now found throughout most of the world.

BLOOM TIME: April, May, June, July, August, September, October

LIFE ZONE: High Desert, Plains, Foothills, Montane, Subalpine, Alpine

Date _____

Where found _____

_____

Common Groundsel

Senecio vulgaris

Single or branched stems to 12 inches, leaves to 1½ inches, pinnately lobed with irregular short teeth; many small yellow flowers that appear never to fully open; white fluff on seeds carries them far and wide on every breeze. A pest in gardens and nurseries everywhere. **Non-native species**—a common annual weed from Eurasia, now found world-wide.

BLOOM TIME: March, April, May, June, July, August, September, October

LIFE ZONE: High Desert, Plains, Foothills, Montane

Date _____

Where found _____

_____

Cut-Leaf Gaillardia

Gaillardia pinnatifida

Flower heads 1½ inches across, usually solitary, rays yellow-orange, 3-lobed, often reddish at base; disk dark red; plants 8–20 inches tall, leaves pinnately cut, ash-gray and primarily at the base of the stems; resembles a small cultivated Gaillardia. Found in dry hills and plains in southern and southwestern Colorado, and beyond.

BLOOM TIME: July, August
LIFE ZONE: Plains, High Desert

ate _____

here found_____

_____

Dwarf Goldenrod

Solidago simplex var. *nana*

Flowers in small, roundish yellow heads composed of up to 15 or 20 small "daisies," but ray petals are few, so does not typically form a symmetrical "daisy" shaped flower. Alternate, smooth leaves on a reddish stem 4–6 inches tall. Found on rocky slopes. There are many species of goldenrods from the plains to highest peaks; this is one of the smallest.

BLOOM TIME: June, July, August
LIFE ZONE: Subalpine, Alpine

te _____

here found_____

_____

Dwarf Sunflower

Helianthus pumilus

Long-lived perennial; under 2 feet tall; oblong leaves, rough sandpapery texture; 2 inch yellow sunflowers. At 60 mph, other sunflowers are more noticeable, but this is common along roadsides on the prairie, and along banks and road-cuts as you climb into the foothills. This is a delightful but underused native. Its small stature and deep-lemony blooms from early summer till frost make it well suited for xeric gardens and naturalistic landscapes.

BLOOM TIME: July, August, September
LIFE ZONE: Plains, Foothills

te _____

ere found_____

_____

Early Spring Senecio

Senecio integerrimus

Flower heads yellow, ⅔ to ¾ inch across, in loose clusters; plants 10–24 inches tall, stems stout, grayish, hairy-cobwebby especially when young; leaves lance-shaped. Common, and one of the earliest spring flowers at lower elevations.

BLOOM TIME: April, May, June, July

LIFE ZONE: Plains, Foothills, Montane

Date _____

Where found _____

_____

Engelmann Daisy

Engelmannia peristenia

Perennial with basal rosette of erect light green leaves to 8 inches, coarse pinnate lobes, hairy, becoming smaller and alternately spaced along flowering stems; plants up to 2 feet tall; upper stems branched; flowers bright lemon to golden yellow daisies over a long season. Found in Colorado's southeastern prairies along roadsides. Long-lived and colorful in the xeric garden; stout lobed leaves contrast nicely with grasses and finer plants.

BLOOM TIME: June, July, August

LIFE ZONE: Plains

Date _____

Where found _____

_____

Fendler's Senecio

Packera fendleri

Yellow flower heads, ⅔ to ¾ inch across in loose clusters; leaves grayish, linear, folded lengthwise, toothed along margins (teeth often rounded); plants 10–20 inches tall. Found on gravelly slopes and dry pine forests.

BLOOM TIME: May, June, July

LIFE ZONE: Foothills, Montane

Date _____

Where found _____

_____

Fetid Marigold
Dyssodia papposa
Pinnately divided leaves are deep green; golden flowers, small and tight with tiny ray petals, stems to 12 inches; found along roadsides or on disturbed sites. This annual will self sow in gravelly soils or mulch. Essentially a small wild marigold, though it's the scent of the plant, not the flowers, that will convince you, which completely lack the flash of their highly hybridized garden cousins.
BLOOM TIME: June, July, August, September
LIFE ZONE: High Desert, Plains

Date _____

Where found _____

_____

Flat-Spine Bur Ragweed
Ambrosia acanthicarpa
Perennial with stems to 2 feet, spreading widely by underground runners; leaves irregularly lobed with silver hairs, alternate; flowers in terminal spikes, greenish-yellow, producing large amounts of pollen; seeds are spiny sharp burs. Widespread throughout the West, along roads, abandoned fields, and in prairies.
BLOOM TIME: August, September
LIFE ZONE: High Desert, Plains

Date _____

Where found _____

_____

Fringed Sage
Artemisia frigida
Silver-gray, finely cut foliage is the most noticeable feature of this plant; grows in tufts 4–8 inches tall; small yellow nodding flower heads; plants have a pungent sage odor, similar to other artemisias. Common on dry gravelly slopes. Naturalizes well in a wild garden or short meadow planting.
BLOOM TIME: August, September
LIFE ZONE: Plains, Foothills, Montane

Date _____

Where found _____

_____

Gaillardia or Blanket Flower

Gaillardia aristata

Large showy flower heads, 2–3 inches across, orange-yellow rays, though native variants often pure yellow, with 3-toothed tips; disk flowers maroon; plants 10–24 inches tall; leaves lance-shaped, foliage and stems with stiff hairs. Found on dry meadows and slopes. This beautiful wild-flower is widely cultivated.

BLOOM TIME: June, July, August

LIFE ZONE: Foothills, Montane

Date _____

Where found _____

_____

Golden Aster

Heterotheca fulcrata

Flower heads bright yellow, 1 inch broad; several leafy bracts at base of each head; heads 1 to several, at ends of leafy, spreading stems and branches; 8–24 inches tall. Common on dry hill-sides and meadows.

BLOOM TIME: July, August

LIFE ZONE: Montane, Subalpine

Date _____

Where found _____

_____

Golden Aster

Heterotheca villosa

Flower heads golden yellow, 1 inch broad, near tips of branches; usually several spreading stems in a cluster, leaves and stems gray-green, covered with short, stiff hairs, 10–20 inches tall. Common on dry slopes and open ground. Long season of bloom makes this attractive in a low border, but self-sows prolifically.

BLOOM TIME: July, August, September

LIFE ZONE: Plains, Foothills

Date _____

Where found _____

_____

Goldweed
Verbesina encelioides
Felty, rank-smelling annual with golden-yellow to orange-yellow flower heads, about 1 inch broad; leaves broad with toothed edges; fruits flattened, with corky wings. Common in pastures and disturbed areas, plains.
BLOOM TIME: July, August, September
LIFE ZONE: Plains

Date _____
Where found _____
_____

Greenthread
Thelesperma filifolium
Bright yellow flower heads with few rays, on branching plant, 1 to 2½ feet tall; leaves finely divided, slender, thread-like, bright green; inner row of leaf-like bracts at base of flower head form a unique cuplike structure, making this plant easy to identify. Found on dry eastern plains and mesas. Similar to garden coreopsis, but prefers dry conditions even in the garden.
BLOOM TIME: June, July, August
LIFE ZONE: Plain

ate _____
here found_____
_____

Gumweed
Grindelia squarrosa
Numerous yellow flower heads, ¾ to 1 inch across, on a bushy, much-branched plant; sticky bracts at base of flower heads curl downwards; buds with white, sticky covering; leaves stiff, often toothed. Common along dry roadsides and fields where soil has been disturbed.
BLOOM TIME: August, September
LIFE ZONE: Plains, Foothills

Date _____
Where found _____
_____

Heart-Leaved Arnica
Arnica cordifolia
Flower heads bright yellow, 1 to 2½ inches broad; plants with a single stem and 1 flower head; leaves opposite, in 2–3 pairs, roughly heart-shaped. Common on the forest floor in open forests in late summer.
BLOOM TIME: July, August
LIFE ZONE: Montane, Subalpine

Date _____

Where found _____

_____

Kansas Sunflower or Common Sunflower
Helianthus annuus
Flower heads 2–4 inches broad, rays bright yellow, disks dark brown or black; leaves alternate; plants branching, rough and hairy, often up to 6 feet tall. The common sunflower of the plains and lower foothills, making a showy display along roadsides and in fields in late summer. Abundant flowers over a long season attract many native pollinators when in bloom, and songbirds when in seed.
BLOOM TIME: July, August, September
LIFE ZONE: Plains, Foothills

Date _____

Where found _____

_____

Maximillion's Sunflower
Helianthus maximilian's
Tall, bold plants up to 8 feet, perennial and long-lived. Leaves lanceolate, to 8 inches long, downward-curving, sand-papery surface; flowers outward-facing sunflowers to 3 inches across, on upper half of stems, often closely set in spike-like arrangement, though leaning stems appear more branched as flowers try to re-orient themselves. Widespread through the Midwest; spotty in Colorado's eastern prairies. Bold effect in the late-summer and fall garden, and a verita-ble buffet for native insects and birds.
BLOOM TIME: August, September, October
LIFE ZONE: Plains

Date _____

Where found _____

_____

Meadow Arnica

Arnica fulgens

Bright golden flower heads with darker disk, 1 to 2½ inches across; each flower stalk usually with a single head; leaves opposite, narrow; stems and foliage sticky-hairy, with strong odor. Common in grassy mountain meadows and pastures.

BLOOM TIME: May, June

LIFE ZONE: Foothills, Montane

Date_____

Where found _____

_____

Mountain Gumweed

Grindelia subalpina

Flowers with yellow rays and centers, heads 1 to 1½ inches broad; buds very sticky, white-gummy, and aromatic, bracts beneath flower heads curl downwards; leaves thick, clasping, sharp-toothed to pinnately lobed; coarse, much-branched plants 8–18 inches tall. Found in open fields and hillsides, common along roadsides and in disturbed soil.

BLOOM TIME: July, August, September

LIFE ZONE: Montane

Date _____

Where found _____

_____

Mule's Ears

Wyethia arizonica

Large yellow flower heads, 3–5 inches broad, both ray flowers and disk flowers yellow; coarse plant with large hairy leaves. Found west of the Continental Divide. Mule's ears often grow in large patches, covering whole hillsides.

BLOOM TIME: May, June, July

LIFE ZONE: Foothills

Date _____

Where found _____

_____

Northern Mule's Ears
Wyethia amplexicaulis
Tough, long-lived perennial. Upright lanceolate leaves, smooth, bright green, to 12 or more inches tall; flowers large golden sunflowers 4–6 inches across. Found in open meadows, forest openings among pine, aspen, and sagebrush. From north-western Colorado into Utah and the northern Great Basin.

BLOOM TIME: May, June
LIFE ZONE: Foothills, Montane

Date_____

Where found _____

_____

Old Man of the Mountain or Rydbergia
Hymenoxys grandiflora
Showiest and most easily recognized Alpine plant. Bright yellow heads 2–4 inches broad, tips of rays 3-notched; stout woolly stems and foliage; common on alpine slopes and ridges. Heads usually face away from the prevailing winds.

BLOOM TIME: June, July, August
LIFE ZONE: Alpine

Date _____

Where found _____

_____

Orange Sneezeweed
Hymenoxys hoopesii
Orange-yellow flowers in large heads with a mound-shaped disk, nearly 1 inch across, rays drooping; leaves thick, oval to lance-shaped, 5–10 inches long near base of plant, smaller near top; plants stout, erect, up to 3½ feet. Found in meadows and open areas, more com-mon west of the Continental Divide. A poisonous plant of major concern to sheep raisers, but bold and bright in the garden.

BLOOM TIME: June, July, August
LIFE ZONE: Montane

Date _____

Where found_____

_____

Paperflower
Psilostrophe bakeri

Tidy dome-shaped perennial, densely branched and mounding, 1–2 feet. Leaves linear to 1 inch, grayish, slightly wooly; flowers rich golden-yellow, 3–5 ray flowers, each 3-lobed. Widely scattered in eastern Colorado, but more common farther south. Long blooming but seldom long-lived. Requires a sunny, warm niche with good drainage.

BLOOM TIME: June, July, August
LIFE ZONE: High Desert, Plains

Date _____

Where found _____

_____

Plains Coreopsis
Coreopsis tinctoria

Annual plant, can range from 1–3 feet tall, depending on conditions. Leaves fine, bright green, bipinnately divided, especially on lower stems; smooth round green buds; flowers with showy red and yellow overlapping ray petals, each with two notches, center lobe extending beyond the outer two. Widespread in fields, along roadsides nationwide; at lower elevations in Colorado. Cheerful, fast-growing annual in the garden.

BLOOM TIME: July, August, September
LIFE ZONE: Plains

Date _____

Where found_____

_____

Prairie Coneflower
Ratibida columnifera

Drooping bright yellow rays (sometimes orange or burgundy) to 1½ inches long, surrounding a tall grayish-yellow cylindrical cone of disk flowers, ½ to 2½ inches high; flower heads solitary at tips of branches; plants leafy, leaves deeply dissected; plants 10–30 inches tall. Common on dry plains and mesas. Cheerful and long-blooming in dry borders or mixed prairie gardens. Seed heads attractive into winter.

BLOOM TIME: July, August, September
LIFE ZONE: Plains

Date_____

Where found _____

_____

Prairie Sage
Artemisia ludoviciana
Most often noticed for its silvery white to greenish foliage and stems, covered with a dense mat of woolly hairs; plants 10–30 inches tall; leaves usually linear, but vary; bears a spike with clusters of small yellow disk flowers in late summer. Common on dry plains. Foliage pleasantly aromatic, as are most of the artemisias. Several horticultural selections have been made, and the silver foliage is welcome in the garden. Plants increase by runners.

BLOOM TIME: August, September
LIFE ZONE: Plains, Foothills

Date_____

Where found _____

_____

Prairie Sunflower
Helianthus petiolaris
Flower heads 2–3 inches broad, with bright yellow ray flowers and dark brown disk flowers; leaves narrow, alternate, stems and foliage rough; plants 10–36 inches tall. Common along roadsides and in fields. Sometimes called narrowleaf sunflower. Similar to common or Kansas sunflower (*H. annuus*), and sometimes grows with it. Smaller habit is better suited to smaller gardens.

BLOOM TIME: July, August, September
LIFE ZONE: Plains, Foothills

Date _____

Where found _____

_____

Rayless Senecio
Senecio bigelovii
Tiny, yellowish disk flowers enclosed in a large, fleshy, nodding turban-shaped head with purplish bracts; ½ to ¾ inch long; plant stout, 1–3 feet tall; leaves 8–15 inches long. Aspen groves and moist meadows.

BLOOM TIME: July, August
LIFE ZONE: Subalpine

Date _____

Where found _____

_____

Rock Ragwort
Senecio fremontii var. *blitoides*
Flower heads 1 to 1½ inches broad, bright yellow; leaves short, broad, and coarsely toothed; plant spreading, branched at base, 6–20 inches tall; grows in alpine rock slides and crevices. A showy, rounded plant, often seen along road cuts above timberline.
BLOOM TIME: July, August
LIFE ZONE: Alpine

Date _____

Where found _____

Salsify or Oyster-Plant
Tragopogon dubius
Flower heads pale yellow, 1 to 1½ inches broad, composed of narrow ray flowers and much longer, narrow green phyllaries; stems hollow, 12–18 inches tall; leaves long, slender; plants have milky juice. The huge round, white or buff dandelion-like seedheads, 3–4 inches across, are more conspicuous than the flowers in late summer. Found in mountain meadows, waste places, and along roadsides. **A non-native species** introduced from Europe.
BLOOM TIME: June, July, August, September
LIFE ZONE: High Desert, Plains, Foothills, Montane

te _____

here found _____

Skeleton Bur Ragweed
Ambrosia tomentosa
Perennial with stems rising from creeping roots; leaves green above and gray beneath, pinnately lobed, somewhat irregular; flowers small, nodding greenish-yellow, at tops of stems; seeds in a small spiney bur. Common along roads, in fields, grasslands, and a persistent nuisance in gardens!
BLOOM TIME: August, September
LIFE ZONE: Plains

Date _____

Where found _____

(sidebar, vertical) **Sunflower Family (Asteraceae)**

Sleepyhead

Encelia nutans

Single large, greenish-yellow head with no ray flowers, 1 to 1½ inches across, nodding, at top of leafless stem, 6–12 inches tall; leaves large, oval, at base of plant. Locally common west of the Continental Divide on clay soils of the mesas.

BLOOM TIME: May, June

LIFE ZONE: High Desert

Date _____

Where found _____

Smooth Goldenrod

Solidago missouriensis

Very small yellow flower heads in clusters, inflorescence along top of stem usually contains numerous clusters; leaves smooth, rather leathery in texture; plant 10–15 inches tall. The most common low goldenrod of the plains and foothills, often along streams and ditch banks.

BLOOM TIME: July, August, September

LIFE ZONE: Plains, Foothills

Date _____

Where found _____

Snakeweed

Gutierrezia sarothrae

Many very small yellow flower heads, ⅛ inch broad, clustered at end of branches; many small slender leaves; plants rather bushy, 6–20 inches tall, resembling rabbitbrush but greener, and all parts much smaller. Found in dry soil in open areas, abundant. Forms perfect domes of chartreuse, then gold, along highways and roadcuts. To maintain shape in the garden, trim to 4–6 inches tall each spring.

BLOOM TIME: August, September

LIFE ZONE: Plains, Foothills

Date _____

Where found _____

Stiff Sunflower
Helianthus pauciflorus ssp. *pauciflorus*
Flower heads 1½ to 2½ inches broad, bright yellow ray flowers (sometimes streaked with darker lines); center disk brownish purple; leaves stiff, rough, usually opposite, stems stout, upright 10–20 inches tall. Common on dry slopes and open ground.
BLOOM TIME: July, August, September
LIFE ZONE: Plains, Foothills

Date _____

Where found _____

_____

Sunspots or Goldeneye
Heliomeris multiflora
Golden yellow flower heads, resembling small sunflowers; plants much-branched, stems slender, 10–24 inches tall; leaves lance-shaped, rough, usually in pairs. Very common along roadsides. Attractive in the wild garden; self-sows abundantly.
BLOOM TIME: August, September
LIFE ZONE: Foothills

Date _____

Where found _____

_____

Tall Coneflower
Rudbeckia laciniata var. *ampla*
Large flower heads with deep yellow drooping rays, disk cone-shaped, greenish-brown; plant tall, up to 6 feet; leaves palmately lobed or cut. Common along stream banks. Stately plant for the back of the border, or naturalized in partial shade.
BLOOM TIME: July, August
LIFE ZONE: Foothills, Montane

Date _____

Where found _____

_____

Tall False Dandelion

Agoseris glauca

Yellow flower heads resembling common dandelion with strap-like ray flowers; leafless flowering stalks 6–20 inches tall, milky juice; leaves basal, lance-shaped, pale green. Found on grassy open hillsides and dry meadows.

BLOOM TIME: June, July, August
LIFE ZONE: Foothills, Montane

Date _____

Where found _____

_____

Tall Goldenrod

Solidago gigantea

Clusters of very small yellow flower heads in a large pyramid-shaped inflorescence at top of stout, leafy, tall stalk, up to 6 feet; flower-bearing branches curve downward, usually with flowers along one side; leaves lance-shaped, toothed. A common goldenrod of wet areas in the plains and lower valleys, standing out in the late summer landscape.

BLOOM TIME: August, September
LIFE ZONE: Plains

Date _____

Where found _____

_____

Tall Marsh Sunflower

Helianthus nuttallii

Bright yellow flower heads, 2 to 3½ inches broad, at top of un-branched stems, often up to 8 feet tall. Found along ditch banks, sloughs, and marshy places, but adaptable to ordinary garden conditions.

BLOOM TIME: July, August, September
LIFE ZONE: Plains, Foothills

Date _____

Where found _____

_____

Triangle-Leaved Ragwort
Senecio triangularis
Bright yellow flower heads, 1 inch broad, in loose cluster at top of tall un-branched stems up to 3 feet; leaves narrowly triangular, coarsely toothed. Forms large clumps along wet stream banks, very common.
BLOOM TIME: July, August
LIFE ZONE: Montane, Subalpine

Date _____

Where found _____

_____

Wavy-Leaf False Dandelion
Nothocalais cuspidata
Pale yellow single flower head on leafless stem, resembling a common dandelion, 3–8 inches tall; leaves basal, long and narrow, with wavy margins bordered by white hairs. A very common early spring flower of mesas and plains.
BLOOM TIME: April, May, June
LIFE ZONE: Plains, Foothills

Date _____

Where found _____

_____

Western Golden Ragwort
Senecio eremophilus
Numerous small bright yellow flower heads, ½ to ⅔ inch; bushy, purplish stems 1–2 feet tall; leaves toothed and deeply cut, dark green. Common along roadsides and on gravelly slopes. *Senecio* means "old man," in reference to the rounded, fuzzy seed heads, suggesting white hair.
BLOOM TIME: July, August
LIFE ZONE: Foothills, Montane

Date _____

Where found _____

_____

Wild Chrysanthemum
Bahia dissecta
Bright yellow flower heads, 1 inch broad, with short, wide rays, and yellow disks; flowers on long stalks and scattered at top of plant, 10–30 inches tall; leaves in a basal rosette, gray-green, divided into several segments. Found in dry gravelly soil.
BLOOM TIME: July, August, September
LIFE ZONE: Foothills

Date _____

Where found _____

_____

Wild Zinnia
Zinnia grandiflora
Showy yellow flower heads, 1 to 1½ inches broad, with orange center disk; low linear-leaved plants, 6–8 inches tall; rays 4–5, becoming papery with age, often whitish. Sometimes called golden paperflower. Common in southeastern Colorado. This is an excellent ground-cover for dry Western gardens, carpeted in gold over much of the summer.
BLOOM TIME: July, August
LIFE ZONE: Plains

Date _____

Where found _____

_____

Woolly Actinella
Tetraneuris acaulis var. *caespitosa*
Bright yellow heads with 3-toothed rays; woolly leaves; 2–4 inches tall; Found in rocky places. Resembles old man of the mountain, but much smaller.
BLOOM TIME: June, July
LIFE ZONE: Alpine

Date _____

Where found _____

_____

Yellow Violet
Viola nuttallii
Perennial, under 6 inches; leaves rise from a central crown, lanceolate with petiole as long as the blade; flowers typical violet shape, yellow, lowest petal having numerous dark stripes. Found in short grasslands, forest openings, widespread throughout Colorado, but easily overlooked where grasses and showier plants compete. Useful in a rock garden or short prairie planting.
BLOOM TIME: April, May, June
LIFE ZONE: Plains, Foothills

ate _____
here found_____
_____

Yellow Pond Lily
Nuphar luteum
Flowers yellow, cup-like, 3–5 inches across, at the end of strong stalks, lying on or just beneath the water surface; conspicuous flower parts are waxy yellow sepals, often tinged with red; the petals are smaller and mostly concealed by the stamens; leaves large and oblong, heart shaped, resting on the water surface. The only native water lily of mountain lakes, blooming in midsummer. Prefers the cold still waters of subalpine lakes. Native peoples roasted the seeds and ate them like popcorn.
BLOOM TIME: July, August
LIFE ZONE: Montane, Subalpine

ate _____
here found_____

Wood-Sorrel
Oxalis stricta
Flowers 2 or 3 at top of plant, ½ inch across, pale yellow, 5 petals, dainty low plant with erect or curving stems; bright green compound leaves with 3 leaflets, clover-like, with pleasantly sour taste. Found in open fields and woods, also a common weed in gardens. **Non-native species.**
BLOOM TIME: May, June, July, August, September, October
LIFE ZONE: Plains, Foothills

Date _____
Where found _____
_____

Orange

ium philadelphicum
Mary Clark

Claret Cup
Echinocereus triglochidiatus
Stems solitary when young, becoming large multi-stemmed dome-shaped clumps with age. Up to 10 distinct ribs; spines up to 2 inches, usually shorter, curved, in clusters of 3; flowers intense reddish-orange to salmon, green stigma at the center. Found in grasslands, rock ledges, piñon-juniper forests, over a wide range. Subspecies *inermis* is often entirely spineless and has spotty distribution in Colorado's western counties.
BLOOM TIME: May
LIFE ZONE: High Desert, Foothills

Date _____

Where found _____

Wood Lily
Lilium philadelphicum
Very striking large red-orange flowers with dark spots at inner base of petals and sepals, dark purple anthers; stems erect, 1–2 feet tall; leaves whorled, broadly linear. Found in moist, open woods. Because of past collecting, wood lily is rare and its habitat should never be disturbed.
BLOOM TIME: July, August
LIFE ZONE: Foothills, Montane

Date _____

Where found _____

Cowboy's Delight
Sphaeralcea coccinea
Flowers a warm salmon-orange, 5-petaled, saucer-shaped, in dense cluster at top of stem, 8–12 inches tall; leaves deeply palmately lobed or cut, stems and leaves silver-gray. Abundant along roadsides, dry plains, and mesas, spreading slowly underground to form small colonies. The rich color is unique and welcome in the garden.
BLOOM TIME: July, August
LIFE ZONE: Plains, Foothills

Date _____

Where found _____

Butterfly Weed
Asclepias tuberosa
Leaves rich green, lanceolate; stems rise from a central crown, 10–16 inches tall, sometimes arching slightly near the top where flowers are clustered. Flowers typical of milkweeds: 5 reflexed petals around a starry corona; commonly orange throughout its range, though Colorado forms are often more yellow. Pods in late summer and fall are slender, upright, splitting to release parachute-type seeds. This species has little or no milky sap. Found in grasslands and roadsides. Very colorful and durable perennial for the average or xeric garden, and a useful plant to native insects.
BLOOM TIME: June, July
LIFE ZONE: Plains

Date _____

here found _____
_____

Wallflower
Erysimum capitatum
Flowers 4-petaled, ½ to ¾ inch broad, in rounded clusters. Color varies widely, flowers most commonly orange to yellow, especially in the Montane Zone, but can be yellow or lavender to maroon in the Alpine and Subalpine. Leaves narrow, grayish; plants 4–20 inches tall depending on altitude and local conditions; fruits are narrow pods, 1 to 2½ inches long. Found on open slopes and roadsides.
BLOOM TIME: June, July
LIFE ZONE: Montane, Subalpine, Alpine

Date _____

Where found _____
_____

Burnt-Orange Dandelion
Agoseris aurantiaca
Flower heads deep orange, solitary, at top of leafless stalk, 5–20 inches tall; heads composed of strap-shaped ray flowers, as in dandelions; leaves lance-shaped, in a basal rosette. Found on dry, grassy meadows and slopes.
BLOOM TIME: July, August
LIFE ZONE: Montane, Subalpine

Date _____

Where found _____
_____

Red, **Maroon**

lleja miniata
Boyd

Cardinal Flower

Lobelia cardinalis ssp. *graminea*

Vivid red flowers on a tall narrow spike; 2 spreading upright petals, 3 lower petals fused and forming a notched lower lip, protruding upright pistil is white-tipped; leaves narrow, linear. In Colorado, restricted to hospitable canyon bottoms and valleys in the eastern counties where moisture persists year-round, mostly on private lands. At the right time of year, its presence will be unmistakable with its hot red flower spikes highlighting small streams. Many color forms and cultivars of lobelia are available in the nursery trade.

BLOOM TIME: July, August

LIFE ZONE: Plains

Date_____

Where found _____

_____

Sheep Sorrel

Rumex acetosella

Most noticeable are the very slender, smooth, reddish-brown stems, 8–18 inches tall; flowers tiny, in narrow panicles; leaves narrow, arrowhead-shaped. An abundant weed in the plains and foothills. Found along roadsides, abandoned fields and disturbed areas throughout temperate North America and Europe. **Non-native species.**

BLOOM TIME: July, August

LIFE ZONE: High Desert, Plains, Foothills, Montane

Date_____

Where found _____

_____

Western Red Columbine

Aquilegia elegantula

Flowers red and yellow, nodding, 1 inch broad; 5 yellow petals elongated into straight red spurs, 5 red sepals; leaves mostly at base, compound leaflets with rounded lobes. Smaller than its relative, blue Colorado columbine, 10–12 inches tall. Common in moist rocky or wooded areas west of the Continental Divide. A hummingbird favorite!

BLOOM TIME: July, August

LIFE ZONE: Montane, Subalpine

Date _____

Where found _____

_____

Bridges' Penstemon
Penstemon rostriflorus
Sub-shrub up to 18 inches, leaves tough, linear, evergreen, up to 3 inches long; flowers over a long season, tubular, red to coral, similar to those of *P. barbatus*. Found in our southwest counties and throughout the Southwest. Excellent and long-lived in the xeric or rock garden, and irresistible to hummingbirds!
BLOOM TIME: June, July
LIFE ZONE: High Desert

Date_____

Where found _____
_____

Desert Paintbrush
Castilleja chromosa
Flowers in red or orange-red rounded paintbrush-like spikes; brilliant color due to deeply cut, leaf-like bracts at the base of the small greenish-yellow, tubular flowers; foliage and stem bristly; plants 6–30 inches tall. A common Indian paintbrush in western Wyoming, western Colorado, and Utah. Found in dry plains, mesas, piñon-juniper woodlands, often an associate of sagebrush.
BLOOM TIME: June, July
LIFE ZONE: High Desert, Foothills

Date_____

Where found _____
_____

Firecracker Penstemon
Penstemon eatonii
Plants up to 3 feet; basal leaves shiny rich green, wider than many penstemon species, narrower on the flowering stems; flowers hot red and unmistakable in the landscape, among the earliest of our desert penstemons to flower. Found only in our southwestern counties and widely distributed throughout the desert Southwest. Requires good drainage, and not always long-lived in the garden, but worth the effort for its electric spring display.
BLOOM TIME: May
LIFE ZONE: High Desert

Date _____

Where found _____
_____

Figwort Family (Scrophulariaceae)

187

Indian Paintbrush

Castilleja linariaefolia

Green, red-edged tubular flowers, 1 inch long, protrude noticeably from brilliant red bracts; inflorescence a dense, rounded paintbrush-like spike on upper part of stem; branched plants, up to 2 feet or more tall, with very narrow leaves. Found on dry ground, often among shrubs. State flower of Wyoming and often called Wyoming paintbrush.

BLOOM TIME: June, July

LIFE ZONE: Foothills, Montane

Date _____

Where found _____

_____

Orange Paintbrush

Castilleja integra

Flowers in red-orange, rounded, paintbrush-like spikes, leaf-like bracts at base of the small greenish flowers are broad and rounded (some with 2 small side appendages); plants usually in clumps, 4–16 inches tall. Found in dry hills, mesas, and plains on rocky or gravelly soil. Long-flowering in a dry prairie garden, though tricky to get established. Most *castillejas* are believed to be hemiparasitic on the roots of other plants.

BLOOM TIME: June, July, August

LIFE ZONE: Plains, Foothills

Date _____

Where found _____

_____

Scarlet Paintbrush

Castilleja miniata

Small reddish tinged tubular flowers protrude slightly from scarlet bracts; flowers in dense rounded paintbrush-like spikes on upper part of stems, 1–2 feet tall; leaves narrow, lanceolate to ovate. Common in open woods and aspen groves.

BLOOM TIME: June, July, August

LIFE ZONE: Montane

Date _____

Where found _____

_____

Scarlet Penstemon
Penstemon barbatus
Narrow, bright red tubular flowers somewhat resembling fairy-trumpet, but 2-lipped and hanging; 15 inches to 3 feet tall; leaves entire, oblong to spatulate. Found on open rocky or gravelly soils. Generally restricted to southern and western parts of Colorado, and northern New Mexico and Arizona. Irresistible to hummingbirds and excellent in xeric gardens. Can reach 5 feet in cultivation.
BLOOM TIME: July, August, September, October
LIFE ZONE: High Desert, Foothills

Date _____

Where found _____

_____

Strawberry Blite
Chenopodium capitatum
Flowers not conspicuous, but dark red berry-like fruiting clusters characterize this plant; usually low growing, 6–10 inches tall, but may reach a height of 2 feet; triangular, coarsely toothed leaves. Found on roadsides, burned forest openings, and rich moist soil around old barnyards, fruiting in late summer. **Non-native species.**
BLOOM TIME: August
LIFE ZONE: Foothills, Montane

ate_____

here found _____

_____

Antelope Horns
Asclepias cryptocerus
Stout plants under 12 inches with leathery blue-green leaves on decumbent stems. Flowers large and very showy, creamy petals reflexed, and central parts dull maroon to rich wine-red or magenta. Found from Colorado's western counties throughout the Great Basin along roadsides, in adobe hills, and other well-drained habitats.
BLOOM TIME: July, August
LIFE ZONE: High Desert

ate_____

here found _____

_____

Fairy Trumpet or Scarlet Gilia
Ipomopsis aggregata
Many slender, tubular 1 to 2 inch flowers with flared petals arranged along slender, sometimes branched stems 1–3 feet tall. Most common color is bright red but hybrids can range through pink to white shades. This biennial forms a small tight rosette of lacey leaves the first year, and flower spikes the next, after which it dies. Common and widespread on dry, sunny slopes, and naturalizes well in xeric gardens.

BLOOM TIME: July, August
LIFE ZONE: Foothills, Montane

Date_____
Where found _____

King's Crown
Rhodiola integrifolia
Succulent sedum-like plant 4–12 inches tall with dark red to maroon flowers in tight, flat-topped clusters at the top of fleshy stems. Leaves resemble those of its many common garden relatives. Found on moist slopes.

BLOOM TIME: June, July, August
LIFE ZONE: Subalpine, Alpine

Date_____
Where found _____

Short-Rayed Coneflower
Ratibida tagetes
Perennial plant up to 18 inches tall; leaves fine, pinnately lobed; flowers with dark, short thimble-like cones; ray petals at base of cone, very short, dusky red to yellow, as shown here. Widespread in shortgrass prairies, rocky slopes, and roadsides. Attractive in a prairie garden, and beneficial to native insects.

BLOOM TIME: July, August
LIFE ZONE: Plains

Date_____
Where found _____

Reddish-Purple

irabilis rotundifolius
Marjorie Joy

Houndstongue
Cynoglossum officinale
Reddish-purple flowers, ⅓ inch long, with 5 rounded petals, clustered along top of stout stem, 1–3 feet tall; leaves numerous, lance-shaped, covered with soft white hairs; fruit divided into 4 flattened, prickly nutlets. Found in waste places, along roadsides, and in sandy areas. **Non-native species** introduced from Europe.
BLOOM TIME: June, July, August
LIFE ZONE: Foothills

Date _____

Where found _____

_____

Red Anemone
Anemone multifida var. *multifida*
Deep reddish-purple flowers, ½ to ¾ inch broad, without petals (but the red sepals look like petals); many bright yellow stamens; stem 10–12 inches tall; leaves cut in narrow segments, both leaves and stem grayish, silky-hairy. Common meadow flower and an attractive addition to a meadow garden.
BLOOM TIME: June, July
LIFE ZONE: Montane, Subalpine

Date _____

Where found _____

_____

Candelabra Cactus or Cholla
Cylindropuntia imbricata
Shrubby plant with cylindrical woody green stems covered with sharp barbed spines, 3–6 feet tall; flowers maroon to rose-pink, rarely white, 2–3 inches broad; fruits small, yellow, persistent, covered with spiny hairs. Found on dry plains and hillsides from southeastern Colorado to Texas and Mexico. The lacy skeletons of dead plants are sometimes used in crafts. Architectural form is classic for a "southwestern" or desert garden.
BLOOM TIME: June, July
LIFE ZONE: Plains

Date _____

Where found _____

_____

Fendler's Hedgehog
Echinocereus fendleri
Small and often solitary cylindrical cactus; some-times forming clumps; spines stout, creamy white or tan; robust appearance; flowers large and brilliant, typically a rich reddish-purple. Found only in lower elevations of southwest Colorado, and an isolated group on the Eastern Slope. Wonderful plant for dry rock gardens. These are readily available from local nurseries, but slow to reproduce in the wild, and their habitats should be left undisturbed.
BLOOM TIME: June
LIFE ZONE: High Desert, Plains

Date _____

Where found _____

_____

Cactus Family (Cactaceae)

Rocky Mountain Bee Plant
Cleome serrulata
Flowers deep reddish-purple to soft lavender-pink, 4 petals, stamens extend beyond petals; plants much-branched, 1–3 feet tall; flowers clustered along tops of stems; long, slender pendant seed pods below flowers; leaves compound with 3 lance-shaped leaflets. Found in sandy areas, along roads, and on overgrazed land. Colorful annual: will self-sow in the garden if soil suits it.
BLOOM TIME: July, August
LIFE ZONE: High Desert, Plains, Foothills

Date _____

Where found _____

_____

Caper Family (Capparidaceae)

Fireweed
Chamerion angustifolium
Brilliant rose-purple, 4-petaled flowers, 1 to 1½ inches across, in an elongated raceme on stems 1–5 feet tall; leaves lance-shaped or willow-like. Likes moist, rich ground, often found in masses in burned over areas and along disturbed roadsides. Wonderful in wild settings, but stoloniferous habit makes it hard to contain in a garden.
BLOOM TIME: July, August
LIFE ZONE: Montane, Subalpine

Date _____

Where found _____

_____

Evening Primrose Family (Onagraceae)

Desert Four-O'clock
Mirabilis multiflora
Flowers rich magenta-purple, funnel-shaped, 1–2 inches long, opening in late afternoon and fading mid-morning. Flower clusters surrounded by large bracts; plants leafy, in rounded clumps. A very showy plant, common in piñon-juniper woodlands in western Colorado and Utah. Thrives un-irrigated in dry gardens, spreading to a 3- or 4-foot wide mound. Best if not pampered—any water or shade will produce an impressive but floppy 8-foot wide giant!
BLOOM TIME: July, August, September
LIFE ZONE: High Desert, Plains, Foothills

Date _____

Where found _____

_____

Round-Leaf Four-O'clock
Mirabilis rotundifolia
Similar to *M. multiflora*. Stems usually under 12 inches tall, reclining along the ground or against other plants; leaves opposite, rubbery texture, widely spaced along stems; flowers purplish-pink, smaller, less showy than *M. multiflora*. Endemic, with very limited distribution in south-central Colorado. Considered critically endangered in Colorado and imperiled globally.
BLOOM TIME: July, August, September
LIFE ZONE: Plains

Date _____

Where found _____

_____

Fremont's Geranium
Geranium caespitosum var. *fremontii*
Lavender-pink 5-petaled flowers with darker veins; leaves deeply palmately lobed, leaf stalks hairy, stems branched and leafy, up to 2 feet tall. Found in open dry meadows. Most geraniums have bright red to orange fall color. *G. viscosissimum* is quite similar, flowers sometimes verging on deep purple.
BLOOM TIME: June, July, August
LIFE ZONE: Foothills

Date _____

Where found _____

_____

Lambert Loco
Oxytropis lambertii
Reddish-purple pea-like flowers arranged in a many-flowered upright raceme on a leafless stalk; pinnately compound silvery, hairy leaves; plants 4–12 inches high. The most conspicuous early loco, often in large patches and common along roadsides. Light colored specimens may be hybrids.
BLOOM TIME: May, June, July, August
LIFE ZONE: Plains, Foothills, Montane

Date _____

Where found _____

_____

Leather-Pod Loco
Astragalus shortianus
Flowers rose-purple to violet, pea-like, in crowded clusters; pods curved, thick, fleshy, becoming leathery with age, 1–2 inches long; leaves pinnately compound with 11–15 oval, silky-hairy leaflets; plants low, stems about 4 inches tall. Common in dry areas. Also called early purple milkvetch.
BLOOM TIME: May, June
LIFE ZONE: Plains, Foothills

Date _____

Where found _____

_____

Purple Peavine
Lathyrus eucosmos
Pea-like flowers, rose-purple and sometimes bi-colored with white, in few-flowered clusters; leaves compound with linear leaflets, upper leaves ending in tendrils. Stems angular, climbing, or trailing, to 12 inches tall. Found in gulches and canyons.
BLOOM TIME: May, June, July
LIFE ZONE: Plains, Foothills

Date _____

Where found _____

_____

Whorl-Leaf Loco

Oxytropis splendens

Small rose-purple to dark purple pea-like flowers in a woolly, many-flowered spike-like raceme; silvery, silky leaves with leaflets arranged in whorls; plants 4–12 inches tall. Found on open dry soil.

BLOOM TIME: June, July

LIFE ZONE: Montane

Date _____

Where found _____

_____

Wild Hollyhock

Sidalcea neomexicana

Rose-purple flowers resemble miniature hollyhocks; upright stems 1–3 feet tall, often branched; upper leaves deeply cut, lower leaves round, scalloped, and hairy. Found in moist meadows and on stream banks.

BLOOM TIME: July, August, September

LIFE ZONE: Montane

Date _____

Where found _____

_____

Winecups

Callirhoe involucrata

Stems from a central crown, trailing in all directions along the ground to 6 feet wide, or clambering over nearby vegetation; leaves palmately divided into 5–7 lobes; flowers upright, bright magenta with a lighter or white eye, 5 petals forming a cup, produced over a long season. Found in grasslands of eastern Colorado and throughout the High Plains. Excellent plant for a dry border, trailing over walls, or in a short meadow, and widely available from nurseries.

BLOOM TIME: June, July, August, September

LIFE ZONE: Plains

Date _____

Where found _____

_____

Henbit
Lamium amplexicaule
Low weedy annual, usually among other plants; stems square, straggling or mounded, to 8 inches; leaves opposite, rounded and deeply lobed; flowers in whorls at leaf nodes and clustered at stem tips, hooded, purple with paler lower lip. Germinates in cool weather and can be among the earliest weeds to flower and set seed. Large patches are showy, but it is a weedy nuisance in the garden, and naturalized widely, robbing wildflowers of spring moisture. **Non-native species.**
BLOOM TIME: March, April, May, June, July, August, September, October, November
LIFE ZONE: High Desert, Plains, Foothills, Montane

Date _____

Where found _____

Self-Heal
Prunella vulgaris
Purple flowers in short dense spikes with broad pointed purplish leaf-like bracts interspersed; flowers small, tubular with 2 lips; stems leafy, leaves opposite; plants 4–12 inches tall. Common in moist woods and canyons.
BLOOM TIME: June, July, August
LIFE ZONE: Foothills

Date _____

Where found _____

Dame's Rocket
Hesperus matronalis
Biennial or perennial plants 2–4 feet tall, leaves alternate, soft, oblanceolate, toothed; flowers in shades of purple, sometimes white, fragrant, clustered at the top of the stem, resembling garden phlox, but with 4 petals. Found in sun or partial shade. **Non-native species,** but naturalized in some areas and seems to be spreading: now listed as a noxious weed in Colorado and several other states.
BLOOM TIME: May, June, July, August
LIFE ZONE: Plains, Foothills

Date _____

ere found _____

Purple Mustard
Chorispora tenella
Purple to rose 4-petaled flowers in crowded racemes; long, narrow fruits with long beak; upright low annual 8–20 inches tall. A common weed along roadsides and in fields and vacant lots, often covering large areas, and among the first species to flower each spring. **Non-native species** introduced from Asia.
BLOOM TIME: April, May, June
LIFE ZONE: High Desert, Plains

Date _____

Where found _____

_____

Telesonix
Telesonix jamesii
Basal rosettes of rounded palmate leaves up to 1½ inches across, irregularly notched edges; flowers bright magenta with 5 spatulate petals, on a spike up to 6 inches tall. Limited distribution on higher terrain of Colorado's Front Range. Charming addition to the rock garden, preferring cool crevices; a challenge at low elevations, but worth the effort.
BLOOM TIME: July, August
LIFE ZONE: Subalpine, Alpine

Date _____

Where found _____

_____

Canada Thistle
Cirsium arvense
Flower heads rose to light purple, numerous, small, ¾ inch across; heads cone-like with sharp bracts, only disk flowers present; leaves very spiny; plants 1–3 feet tall. Because this thistle spreads by creeping rootstocks, it can be found in dense patches of several acres, taking over moist fields and roadsides. Despite the name, this is an aggressive Eurasian species, now one of our most noxious weeds. **Non-native species.**
BLOOM TIME: June, July, August
LIFE ZONE: High Desert, Plains, Foothills

Date _____

Where found _____

_____

Dotted Gay Feather or Blazing Star
Liatris punctata

Bright rose-purple flower heads in a crowded spike; 2 long twisted style branches of each disk flower give flower heads a feathery appearance; leaves linear; plants usually in clumps, 8–24 inches tall, found in dry open areas on the eastern side of the Continental Divide. A striking late-summer wildflower, and a drought tolerant replacement for the thirsty garden varieties of Midwestern *liatris*.

BLOOM TIME: August, September
LIFE ZONE: Plains, Foothills

Date _____

Where found _____

_____

Musk Thistle
Carduus nutans

Flower head pink to light purple, 1 to 1½ inches broad; stiff, sharp-pointed, flattened bracts at base of heads; usually solitary and nodding at end of stem; leaves spiny, deeply lobed or cut; plants 2–5 feet tall. A **non-native species** from Europe, found abundantly along roadsides and on overgrazed lands where it has become a noxious weed.

BLOOM TIME: June, July, August
LIFE ZONE: High Desert, Plains, Foothills

te _____

ere found _____

_____

Scotch Thistle
Onopordum acanthium

Large coarse plant reaching 8 feet or taller, up to 6 feet wide. Stout, leafy, much-branched stems; flower heads pale purple with spine-tipped bracts at base of head; leaves oblong, woolly-white with long spines, leaf bases extend down the stems. A **non-native species** of Eurasia, now spreading, and listed as a noxious weed.

BLOOM TIME: July, August
LIFE ZONE: Plains, Foothills

Date _____

Where found _____

_____

Tansy Aster
Machaeranthera bigelovii
Flower heads with reddish-purple rays and bright orange centers, 1 to 1½ inches across; leaf-like, sticky bracts beneath flower heads curl downward; plants 1–3 feet tall. A common and showy signature plant of late summer and fall, creating drifts of rich purple along roadsides. Re-seeds readily in the garden.

BLOOM TIME: August, September, October
LIFE ZONE: Plains, Foothills, Montane, Subalpine

Date _____

Where found _____

Prairie Verbena
Glandularia bipinnatifida
Annual or short-lived perennial, under 6 inches tall, but spreading as wide as 2 feet; leaves bipinnately lobed, deep green, opposite; flowers soft pink through bright purple, in rounded clusters at stem tips, elongating as old flowers fade, and flowering over a long season. Found in sandy or gravelly soils along roadsides, scattered in Colorado's eastern counties, and wide-ranging on the plains beyond. Useful for its long season of color in a xeric garden; it declines if kept too moist, especially during winter.

BLOOM TIME: June, July, August, September
LIFE ZONE: High Desert, Plains

Date _____

Where found _____

Pink

Dodecatheon pulchellum
by: Karen Cleaver

Showy Dock or Wild Begonia
Rumex venosus
Stems usually relaxed along the ground, under 12 inches tall. Brilliant pink to orange-red papery-winged, heart-shaped fruits are 1–2 inches wide and account for the common name wild begonia. These are prominent against fleshy low leaves in late spring. Common in sandy ground, waste places, and roadsides, often forming patches. Long shoe-string roots help to stabilize sandy soils.
BLOOM TIME: May, June
LIFE ZONE: Plains

Date _____

Where found _____

_____

Smartweed
Polygonum pensylvanicum
Very small rose-colored flowers in short erect spike-like clusters; leaves lance-shaped; sheathed at stem joints, 12–30 inches tall. Common in marshy places.
BLOOM TIME: July, August, September
LIFE ZONE: Plains

Date _____

Where found _____

_____

Water Buckwheat
Polygonum amphibium
Small bright pink to red flowers, in erect spike-like clusters; leaves oval, thick and shiny, floating on the water surface. Found in ponds.
BLOOM TIME: July, August, September
LIFE ZONE: Plains, Foothills, Montane

Date _____

Where found _____

_____

Beehive Cactus
Coryphantha vivipara var. *vivipara*
Common ball cactus, with a wide range throughout the western plains and into the Great Basin. Stems 1 to 5 inches in diameter, partially submerged, especially during drought, solitary or in small clumps; flowers at top of stems, pink with pointed petals; fleshy fruits greenish turning brown. Choice and colorful in the rock garden. Several subspecies may be encountered.

BLOOM TIME: May, June, July
LIFE ZONE: High Desert, Plains, Foothills

Date_____

Where found _____

_____

Fishhook or Devil Claw Cactus
Sclerocactus parviflorus
One of Colorado's larger barrel-form cacti. Stems blue-green, solitary or in small groups, up to a foot tall, distinct ribs and tubercles, diameter up to 5–6 inches in the largest specimens. Flowers usually pink; central spines dark, an inch or longer, hooked; radial spines lighter, shorter. Several *Sclerocactus* species and subspecies occur. All are uncommon, and several are classified as threatened. Their habitats should never be disturbed.

BLOOM TIME: May
LIFE ZONE: High Desert

Date _____

Where found _____

Hedgehog Prickly Pear
Opuntia polyacantha var. *erinacea*
Pads medium green covered with distinct long white to tan flexible spines; flowers pink or light yellow. As with most cold-hardy prickly pears, stems recline and spread horizontally as plant grows, never attaining any height above 12–18 inches. Seen in canyons of western Colorado and throughout the Southwest's high deserts. Sometimes listed as a subspecies of *polyacantha*. Long spines make this especially attractive in the garden.

BLOOM TIME: June
LIFE ZONE: High Desert

Date _____

Where found_____

Lace Cactus

Echinocereus reichenbachii var. *perbellus*

Cylindrical plant; slender white to tan spines may be dense, can obscure any glimpse of the green plant beneath; late spring flowers generally clear rich pink with green and white center; offsets can produce small clumps. Like many cacti, this species has very limited distribution and only occurs in a few locations in the Arkansas Valley of eastern Colorado. It is available to gardeners through local nurseries.

BLOOM TIME: June, July

LIFE ZONE: Plains

Date _____

Where found _____

_____

Mountain Ball Cactus

Pediocactus simpsonii

Fragrant, satiny rose-colored flowers centered on the top of a small slightly flattened ball that may reach 5 inches wide; stout radiating spines. Several subspecies exist. Common on dry open ground and slopes. Available from nurseries and wonderful in a well-drained rock garden.

BLOOM TIME: May, June

LIFE ZONE: Foothills, Montane

Date _____

Where found _____

_____

Clammy Weed

Polanisia dodecandra

Flowers pale pink to white, in crowded, slender clusters at top of stem, 4-petaled, with conspicuous long purplish stamens; leaves compound with 3 oval leaflets; coarse sticky hairy plant with a foul odor, 20–40 inches tall. Plants resemble *Cleome*, but seed pods are upright, not hanging. Usually found along roadsides. Unusual and attractive in a dry garden.

BLOOM TIME: May, June, July

LIFE ZONE: Plains

Date _____

Where found _____

_____

Dogbane

Apocynum androsaemifolium

Small pink bell-shaped flowers in few to several flowered clusters; branching plant with milky sap, 8–20 inches tall; opposite leaves drooping and shiny, dark green above and pale beneath, turning golden in fall. Slender bean-like pods in twos, unusual in that they are typically joined at both ends. Common on gravelly slopes and along roadsides.

BLOOM TIME: June, July

LIFE ZONE: Foothills, Montane

ate _____

here found _____

_____

Scarlet Gaura

Gaura coccinea

Spidery light pink flowers darken as they age, 4-petaled, in clusters at ends of stems; leaves lance-shaped with wavy teeth; plants branching from base, up to 14 inches tall. Dry locations, often along roadsides. Delicate-looking addition to shortgrass prairie gardens.

BLOOM TIME: May, June, July

LIFE ZONE: Plains

Date _____

Where found _____

_____

Spotted Evening Primrose

Oenothera canescens

Relaxed stems to 8 inches tall, in small colonies as it spreads via underground runners; leaves linear, an inch or less, slightly scalloped; flowers soft pink, generously speckled with deep rose pink. In habitat, found among short grasses in Colorado's northeastern counties. In the garden, can spread widely, forming a dense groundcover lightly sprinkled with blooms over a long season.

BLOOM TIME: June, July, August

LIFE ZONE: Plains

ate _____

here found _____

_____

Willow-Herb

Epilobium ssp.

Several species may be encountered, all with similar characteristics. Tiny pinkish to lavender flowers with 4 petals and 8 stamens, rarely wide open, atop 4-angled developing seed pods, ½ to 2½ inches long; seeds bear tufts of white hairs, like willow seeds; leaves small, oval, usually opposite; slender plants, branched or unbranched, 4–24 inches tall. Common and widespread, especially in moist soil.

BLOOM TIME: July, August

LIFE ZONE: Plains, Foothills, Montane, Subalpine, Alpine

Date _____

Where found _____

Alpine Lousewort

Pedicularis sudetica

Rose colored flowers with 2 lips, upper lip short, curved, beaklike; flowers in crowded spikes at top of short stem, 4–8 inches tall; leaves lance-shaped with comb-like divisions. Found in wet meadows and along lakeshores. Uncommon.

BLOOM TIME: July, August

LIFE ZONE: Subalpine, Alpine

Date _____

Where found _____

Elephant Heads

Pedicularis groenlandica

Distinctive flowers are small, light to deep pink, resembling elephant heads with curving trunks; flowers tightly clustered in dense spike, 6–14 inches tall; leaves fern-like, green, or deep wine-colored in full sun. Found in wet meadows and along stream banks, often occurring in large masses.

BLOOM TIME: June, July, August

LIFE ZONE: Subalpine, Alpine

Date _____

Where found _____

Rosy Paintbrush
Castilleja rhexifolia
A beautiful species found in subalpine meadows and on moist tundra. Flowers in brilliant rose to bright purple; rounded, paintbrush-like spikes; color is due to a broad, leaf-like bract below each small, pointed, yellow-green flower; leaves narrow, plants 7–15 inches tall.
BLOOM TIME: July, August
LIFE ZONE: Subalpine, Alpine

Date _____

Where found _____

_____

Shell-Leaf Penstemon
Penstemon grandiflorus
Leathery blue-green leaves, sturdy rosettes; 2-foot stems of large trumpet flowers; large brown seed capsules persist throughout the winter. Plants usually live for 3 or 4 years, but self-sow easily. Found in open prairies of far eastern Colorado and beyond. One of the great prairie plants. In the selection 'Prairie Jewels', colors range from white through shades of rich pink, lavender, and purple.
BLOOM TIME: May, June, July
LIFE ZONE: Plains

te _____

here found _____

_____

Pineywoods Geranium
Geranium caespitosum
Flowers soft pink to rose-purple; ¾ to 1 inch broad, 5 petals with dark veins, 5 sepals, 10 stamens; plants in clumps 1–2 feet high; leaves deeply cut into 5–7 palmate lobes, tips slightly rounded compared to other species. Common in foothills, meadows, and open ponderosa pine forests.
BLOOM TIME: May, June, July, August
LIFE ZONE: Montane

Date _____

Where found _____

_____

Storksbill

Erodium cicutarium

Small bright pink flowers with 5 petals, 5 sepals; upright flower stalks grow from flat rosettes of pinnately compound, toothed leaves; fruits long and pointed, resembling a stork's head. Very common in disturbed areas, overgrazed fields, and roadsides. A **non-native species** introduced from Europe, now found over most of the U.S. Also known as fillaree.

BLOOM TIME: April, May, June, July, August, September

LIFE ZONE: High Desert, Plains, Foothills

Date _____

Where found _____

_____

Bog Wintergreen

Pyrola asarifolia

Small flowers are pink, waxy, hanging singly along a leafless stalk, 8–12 inches tall; round or oval leathery evergreen leaves at base of stem. Found in shaded, moist locations in coniferous forests.

BLOOM TIME: July, August

LIFE ZONE: Montane, Subalpine

Date _____

Where found _____

_____

Kinnikinnick

Arctostaphylos uva-ursi

Trailing ground cover with woody stems and glossy evergreen leaves; small flowers, pinkish white, urn-shaped; fruits are bright red berries. Important food for wildlife. Found in open coniferous forests; often forms large mats in lodgepole pine forests. Though sometimes a challenge to establish in the garden, this is one of the most widespread plants in the world, with circumpolar distribution in the northern hemisphere. Its various forms are found in such far-flung habitats as Greenland, Siberia, Spain, Greece, and the Himalayas!

BLOOM TIME: March, April

LIFE ZONE: Foothills, Montane

Date _____

Where found _____

_____

Mountain Blueberry
Vaccinum myrtillus
Technically a low spreading shrub,
4–12 inches tall, but often dwarfed by
its herbaceous neighbors. Small, pink,
urn-shaped flowers, hanging singly or
in clusters beneath small oval leaves;
berries blue-black. Common in rocky
locations; a favorite food of black bears,
small mammals, and birds.
BLOOM TIME: June, July
LIFE ZONE: Montane, Subalpine

Date _____

Where found _____

_____

Twinflower
Linnaea borealis
Flowers pink, bell-shaped, in pairs at the top of
2 short stalks, 2–4 inches tall. Low mat-forming
plants trail beneath conifers in moist shady forest
soils, with shiny oval notched evergreen leaves ½
inch long. The favorite flower of Carolus Linnaeus,
the great Swedish botanist.
BLOOM TIME: July, August
LIFE ZONE: Montane, Subalpine

Date _____

Where found _____

_____

Alpine Clover
Trifolium dasyphyllum
Two-toned, purplish-pink, pea-like
flowers ½ inch long; small cushion plant
1–5 inches tall; leaves have 3 narrow,
pointed leaflets. Grows in gravelly areas;
the most common dwarf clover at high
altitudes throughout the southern
Rocky Mountains.
BLOOM TIME: June, July, August
LIFE ZONE: Alpine

Date _____

Where found _____

_____

Alsike Clover
Trifolium hybridum
Flowers pale pink or white, ¼ inch long, pea-like, grouped in round heads at the ends of erect leafy stems; leaves with 3 leaflets. Common in fields, meadows and along roadsides. **Non-native species** that escaped from cultivation,
BLOOM TIME: May, June, July, August, September
LIFE ZONE: Plains, Foothills

Date _____

Where found _____

Common Sweet Pea
Lathyrus latifolius
The common perennial "sweet pea" of old-fashioned gardens. Scrambling stems have thin wings that run lengthwise between the leaves; plant clings with tendrils; flowers are classic pea-shape, deep pink to white; seed pods hanging, to 4 inches. A **non-native species,** but long-lived, persisting around old homesites, and naturalized in some Front Range canyons, and along roadsides.
BLOOM TIME: July, August
LIFE ZONE: Plains, Foothills

Date _____

Where found _____

Dwarf Clover
Trifolium nanum
Pink, pea-like flowers in clusters of 2 or 3 at the tips of short stems; flowers ½ to ¾ inch long; 3 leaflets, strongly veined. A compact, mat-forming plant; not as common as alpine clover, but found in the same locations.
BLOOM TIME: June, July
LIFE ZONE: Alpine

Date _____

Where found _____

Limber Vetch
Astragalus flexuosus
Small, pink pea-like flowers in racemes; calyx covered with short, sometimes black, hairs; fruits slender, cylindric pods up to 1 inch long; compound leaves with narrow leaflets; low spreading plant with stems 6–20 inches long. Common in dry fields and hillsides.
BLOOM TIME: May
LIFE ZONE: Foothills, Montane

Date _____

Where found _____

_____

Prairie Clover
Dalea purpurea
Small rich pink, pea-like flowers in short dense spike-like cluster, 1–2 inches long, at top of stem; leaves compound with 3–5 leaflets, small resinous dots on lower surface; plants 10–20 inches tall. Plant shape is a distinctive stout vase shape, very ornamental, with attractive seed heads persisting into winter. Common east of the Continental Divide.
BLOOM TIME: May, June
LIFE ZONE: Plains, Foothills

ate _____

here found _____

_____

Rose Clover or Parry's Clover
Trifolium parryi
The tallest and showiest of the alpine clovers. Small rose-pink pea-like flowers ½ to ¾ inch long, in compact, round heads; 1–6 inches tall; compound leaves of 3 leaflets. Common on the tundra and in moist subalpine areas.
BLOOM TIME: June, July
LIFE ZONE: Subalpine, Alpine

Date _____

Where found _____

_____

Wild Sweet Pea

Lathyrus polymorphus
Showy bicolored flowers are clear deep pink and white, resembling garden sweet peas, fragrant; trailing angular stems; pinnately compound leaves with or without tendrils. Low growing, along roadsides.

BLOOM TIME: May, June, July
LIFE ZONE: Plains

Date _____

Where found _____

_____

Showy Milkweed

Asclepias speciosa
Flowers pink to whitish, ¾ inch broad, 5 petals, 5 reflexed sepals, and an unusual hooded arrangement between stamens and pistil, fragrant, in drooping round clusters; leaves thick, oblong, in pairs on stout stem 1½ to 5 feet tall; forms clumps along roadsides, streams, irrigation ditches. Common throughout the Rocky Mountains. Best suited to the "wild" garden where its tendency to spread is not problematic. Excellent for native pollinators, and is the host plant of the fabled Monarch butterfly.

BLOOM TIME: July, August
LIFE ZONE: Plains, Foothills

Date _____

Where found _____

_____

Swamp Milkweed

Asclepias incarnata
Tall plants where moisture is plentiful, reaching 5 feet; leaves smooth, linear, opposite; flowers showy in several umbels at top of stem, rich pink, other shades including white occasionally seen. Usually found along ditches, pond margins, marshy areas, mainly in northeast Colorado, but with a wide range throughout the U.S. Adaptable to garden conditions, and several horticultural selections have been made. One of our finest wildflowers, and an important food source for many insects.

BLOOM TIME: July, August
LIFE ZONE: Plains

Date _____

Where found _____

_____

Horsemint

Monarda fistulosa var. *menthaefolia*

Flowers rose pink, tightly clustered in rounded heads, 1–3 inches broad; individual flowers slender, tube-shaped, 1 to 1½ inches long, with 2 lips, lower lip with 3 lobes; stems 1–2 feet tall; leaves opposite, oval, with sharp teeth. Common in the foothills along roadsides and in meadows. Often grows in large clumps.

BLOOM TIME: June, July, August
LIFE ZONE: Plains, Foothills

Date _____

Where found _____

_____

Bush Morning Glory

Ipomoea leptophylla

Large pink funnel-shaped flowers have typical morning glory shape, 2 to 2½ inches across. Coarse bushy plant with much-branched stems, 1–4 feet tall; vertical narrow leaves. Entire plant dries and breaks free in winter winds, dispersing large seeds from its satiny brown pods. Turnip-shaped roots of enormous size, growing deep in dry, sandy plains. Spectacular in a dry garden.

BLOOM TIME: June, July, August
LIFE ZONE: Plains

Date _____

Where found _____

_____

Shaggy Dwarf Morning Glory

Evolvulus nuttalianus

Purple to rose morning glory–like flowers, ½ inch across; 4–8 inches tall; inconspicuous plant with hairy leaves. Common in Colorado's eastern counties and adjacent states on sandy plains and hills.

BLOOM TIME: May, June, July
LIFE ZONE: Plains

Date _____

Where found _____

_____

Geyer Onion
Allium geyeri

Small, deep pink flowers in upright umbels are distinct, on stems 4–24 inches tall; 3 or more slender leaves; characteristic onion odor. This plant is dwarfed on the tundra, taller in lower zones.

BLOOM TIME: June, July, August
LIFE ZONE: Foothills, Montane, Subalpine, Alpine

Date _____

Where found _____

_____

Nodding Onion
Allium cernuum

Small pale pink flowers in a nodding cluster; long, narrow leaves and typical onion odor; 4–12 inches tall. Found in fields and meadows in early summer. Used as food by Native peoples, trappers, and early settlers.

BLOOM TIME: May, June
LIFE ZONE: Foothills, Montane

Date _____

Where found _____

_____

Fairy Slipper
Calypso bulbosa

One of the high country's true gems. Flower pink or rose, 1 inch broad, orchid flowers with 3 sepals, 3 petals, middle petal sac-like resembling a delicate slipper; plant 3–8 inches high, with single broad leaf at the base; grows in shady, moist coniferous forests. Very uncommon and not well suited for the garden. Please do not disturb its habitat.

BLOOM TIME: June, July, August
LIFE ZONE: Montane, Subalpine

Date _____

Where found _____

_____

Pungent Gilia

Leptodactylon pungens

Numerous small yellowish- or pinkish-white phlox-like blossoms, pungent odor; low woody plant, 4–12 inches tall, with short sharp-pointed stiff leaves; dry rocky or sandy soil.

BLOOM TIME: May, June, July

LIFE ZONE: Plains, Foothills

Date _____

Where found _____

_____

Rocky Mountain Phlox

Phlox multiflora

A low mat-forming plant with numerous light pink to lavender, sometimes white or blue, flowers, tubular with 5 spreading lobes; leaves linear. Abundant on shrubby slopes in the foothills. One of the most common and widespread phlox.

BLOOM TIME: May, June, July

LIFE ZONE: Plains, Foothills

Date _____

Where found _____

_____

Tiny Trumpet or Collomia

Collomia linearis

Small trumpet-shaped pink flowers, ¼ inch across; in dense clusters in leaf axils of the upper leaves; leaves narrow, lance-shaped; plants 2–12 inches tall. Common, often in large patches on hillsides and along roads.

BLOOM TIME: May, June, July, August

LIFE ZONE: Plains, Foothills, Montane

Date _____

Where found _____

_____

Bouncing Bet or Soapwort

Saponaria officinalis

Pale pink to lavender flowers, usually 5 petals, though often double, sepals united into a cylindrical tube; 12–18 inches tall. The leaves make a lather when crushed and rubbed in water. Blooms all summer. A **non-native species** introduced from Europe, this plant is a garden escapee, established widely in dense stands along roadsides in the foothills.

BLOOM TIME: May, June, July, August, September

LIFE ZONE: Plains, Foothills

Date _____

Where found _____

_____

Moss Campion or Cushion Pink

Silene acaulis var. *subacaulescens*

Moss-like mat plant with numerous rose or pink 5-petaled flowers, the petals narrow and slightly notched; leaves are small; grows in mats, ½ to 1 inch tall; found in exposed rocky or gravelly areas. One of the most colorful and common tundra plants.

BLOOM TIME: June, July, August

LIFE ZONE: Alpine

Date _____

Where found _____

_____

Fairy Primrose

Primula angustifolia

Small, 5-petaled, rose-colored flower, ½ inch across, with a bright yellow center, or "eye"; only 2–3 inches tall; leaves broadest towards the tip. Found in rocky alpine tundra and subalpine meadows.

BLOOM TIME: June, July, August

LIFE ZONE: Subalpine, Alpine

Date _____

Where found _____

_____

Parry Primrose
Primula parryi
Dazzling pink to rose-purple flowers with bright yellow centers in loose clusters at the top of a stout, smooth, light green stem; leaves broadest towards the tip. Strikingly beautiful, it resembles its close relative, fairy primrose, but is much taller, 10–15 inches. Widespread along streams, and all but impossible in cultivation—it needs its feet in icy flowing water!
BLOOM TIME: July, August
LIFE ZONE: Subalpine, Alpine

Date _____
Where found _____
_____

Shooting Star
Dodecatheon pulchellum
Distinctive rose-pink flowers with reflexed petals; resembles cyclamen, to which it is related. Petals flare back, 1 to 1½ inches long; anthers fused, forming a dark beak; several flowers on a wiry stem in drooping umbels; stalks leafless, 6–16 inches tall; leaves spatula-shaped in basal rosette. Wet meadows and stream banks.
BLOOM TIME: June, July
LIFE ZONE: Foothills, Montane, Subalpine

Date _____
Where found _____
_____

Bitterroot
Lewisia rediviva
Clustered thin, cylindrical, succulent leaves 1–2 inches, from a deep fleshy taproot; leaves visible during cool seasons, but shriveling away as weather warms; flowers pale to deep pink, up to 1½ inches across, appearing to sit on bare ground. Found on gravelly slopes and sage flats in Colorado's northern counties. A gem for well-drained rock gardens, preferring dry summer conditions.
BLOOM TIME: June, July
LIFE ZONE: Montane

Date _____
Where found _____
_____

Large Flowered Rock Pink

Talinum calycinum

Narrow succulent leaves crowd the base; wiry 8-inch stems; hot pink flowers to ¾ inch, fading by late in the day. Uncommon, in scattered locations in northeast Colorado. Above-ground portions disappear by mid autumn, leaving small carrot-like roots that regrow in the spring. *Talinums* prefer sandy soils, and will self-sow nicely in the garden if the soil suits them.

BLOOM TIME: July, August

LIFE ZONE: Plains

Date _____

Where found _____

_____

Prairie Fameflower

Talinum parviflorum

Slender cylindrical leaves are succulent, to 2 inches long, clustered above a small perennial taproot; flowers small, 5-petaled, pink, to ½ inch. Found in scattered locations in eastern Colorado in sandy soils and on rock ledges. Delicate-looking plant for a dry rock garden.

BLOOM TIME: July, August

LIFE ZONE: Plains, Foothills

Date _____

Where found _____

_____

Pygmy Bitterroot

Lewisia pygmaea

Flowers pale pink to rose, 5-petaled, ½ inch across with striking star-shaped pistils; plant just ½ to 2 inches tall, with small rosettes of linear, flattened, succulent leaves. Found at higher elevations over a wide range, meadows and gravelly slopes, to above treeline.

BLOOM TIME: May, June, July, August

LIFE ZONE: Montane, Subalpine, Alpine

Date _____

Where found _____

_____

Prairie Smoke
Geum triflorum
Urn-shaped dusty-pink flowers have a superficial resemblance to columbines. Sepals and small bracts tightly enclose small petals; usually 3 nodding heads on a stalk; leaves fern-like. Fluffy seed heads inspire the common name. Common in meadows and aspen groves.
BLOOM TIME: June, July
LIFE ZONE: Foothills, Montane, Subalpine

Date _____

Where found _____

_____

Rose Crown or Queen's Crown
Rhodiola rhodantha
Succulent plant similar to king's crown but with delicate pink flowers held in oblong clusters on the upper part of stem, 3–10 inches tall. Usually found in clumps in wet places and along small streams in open meadows.
BLOOM TIME: June, July, August
LIFE ZONE: Subalpine, Alpine

Date _____

Where found _____

_____

Palafoxia
Palafoxia sphacelata
Small, branched annual plant 6–8 inches tall. Leaves lanceolate, to 1½ inches; flowers soft purplish-pink, petals 3-lobed, central flower parts curled. Scattered populations in sandy flats and along roadsides on Colorado's eastern plains. Favorable conditions can produce massive displays.
BLOOM TIME: June, July
LIFE ZONE: Plains

Date _____

Where found _____

_____

Pussytoes
Antennaria rosea

Mat-forming plant with grayish-green stems and leaves; 2–8 inches high. Found in moist meadows, often in large patches. Clusters of small, round, velvety flower heads, ¾ inch across, pink to rose-colored (sometimes white). Well-behaved ground cover or rock garden plant.

BLOOM TIME: July, August

LIFE ZONE: Foothills, Montane, Subalpine

Date _____

Where found _____

_____

Skeleton Plant
Lygodesmia juncea

Pink flower heads composed of strap-shaped ray flowers, usually 5, at tips of branches, resembling a dianthus flower. Plant easily overlooked unless in bloom, with few stem-like leaves on relatively bare green stems, much-branched and stiff, often full of galls, 6–18 inches tall. Found on barren gravelly soil.

BLOOM TIME: June, July, August

LIFE ZONE: Plains

Date _____

Where found _____

_____

Subalpine Daisy
Erigeron peregrinus

Flower heads with ⅛-inch wide pale pink or lavender rays and bright yellow disk; leaf-like bracts beneath heads curl downwards; heads usually solitary on stem, 1 to 1½ feet tall. A showy species in subalpine meadows.

BLOOM TIME: June, July, August

LIFE ZONE: Subalpine

Date _____

Where found _____

_____

Phyla or Fog-Fruit, Frog Fruit
Phyla cuneifolia

Lavender-pink globe-like heads of 4-lobed, small, 2-lipped flowers; trailing plant with wedge-shaped, rough leaves; spreads by stolons and by long above-ground runners that will root and form large patches. Found along stream and pond shores, roadside ditches, and damp swales.

BLOOM TIME: June, July, August
LIFE ZONE: Plains

Date _____

Where found _____

_____

Blue, Bluish-Purple

adescantia occidentalis
Mervi Hjelmroos-Koski

Great Blue Lobelia

Lobelia syphilitica var. *ludoviciana*

Very showy wetland plant; flowers in narrow spike, up to 2 feet; rich blue to purplish, 3 lower lobes typical of the genus, fine white striping; leaves narrow, linear, crisp green, irregularly serrated along edges. Wide ranging on the plains and reaching westward along the foot of the mountains, but nowhere common, preferring pond margins, stream sides and damp meadows and swales with constant moisture. Excellent in the home bog garden or at water's edge.

BLOOM TIME: July, August

LIFE ZONE: Plains

Date _____

Where found _____

_____

Harebell or Bluebell

Campanula rotundifolia

Lavender-blue (sometimes white), bell-shaped, 5-lobed flowers hanging from slender stems; 4–12 inches tall. Lower leaves somewhat rounded; those along the upright stems are narrow; grows in clumps. Found from foothills to tundra throughout the Northern Hemisphere. The true "Scottish bluebell" and an easy, long-flowering addition to any garden.

BLOOM TIME: May, June, July, August, September, October

LIFE ZONE: Foothills, Montane, Subalpine, Alpine

Date _____

Where found _____

_____

Parry Harebell

Campanula parryi

Flowers purple, bell-shaped with 5 lobes; usually only 1 flower at tip of slender stem; flower upright and open, not nodding like *C. rotundifolia*. Found in moist meadows and aspen groves. Not often cultivated, but could be charming in a rock garden.

BLOOM TIME: July, August

LIFE ZONE: Montane, Subalpine

Date _____

Where found _____

_____

Alpine Chiming Bells

Mertensia viridis

Bright blue, tubular flowers, ½ inch long, hanging in clusters; plants 6–12 inches tall with thick, bluish leaves. Common on Alpine slopes; other species of *Mertensia* are found in lower zones.

BLOOM TIME: June, July, August

LIFE ZONE: Alpine

Date _____

Where found _____

_____

Alpine Forget-Me-Not

Eritrichium nanum var. *elongatum*

Like small fragments of sky, mats of tiny brilliant blue flowers (occasionally white) fill the gaps between lichen-covered granite on mountaintops and rocky slopes. Flowers have 5-petals, with a yellow center or "eye" on short stems, rising from a dense mat of tiny, hairy, silver-white leaves. Don't forget to crouch down and smell its delicate fragrance!

BLOOM TIME: July, August

LIFE ZONE: Alpine

Date _____

Where found _____

_____

False Forget-Me-Not

Hackelia floribunda

Flowers small, light blue with yellow "eye"; fruit composed of 4 small nutlets with hooked prickles; leaves long with smooth margins; plant erect, 1–3 feet tall. Found in open meadows, hillsides, aspen groves, and roadsides. Barbed nutlets cling to fur and clothing, hence often called stickseed.

BLOOM TIME: June, July

LIFE ZONE: Foothills

Date _____

Where found _____

_____

Lanceleaf Chiming Bells

Mertensia lanceolata

Small, light blue bell-shaped flowers (buds pink) hanging from a slanting stem, up to 15 inches tall; leaves rather narrowly lance-shaped, gray-green to bluish in color. Found in early spring in dry soil, on fields and slopes.

BLOOM TIME: April, May

LIFE ZONE: Plains, Foothills, Montane

Date _____

Where found _____

_____

Tall Chiming Bells

Mertensia ciliata

Flowers light blue, bell-shaped, hanging in clusters, buds pinkish; plants branching and leafy, leaves bluish green; 1½ to 3 feet tall. Usually in large clumps along streams.

BLOOM TIME: June, July, August

LIFE ZONE: Montane, Subalpine

Date _____

Where found _____

_____

American Monkshood

Aconitum columbianum

Deep purple flowers, 1 inch long, in loose spike-like arrangement at the tops of 2–5 foot tall stems; one of the sepals forms a hood covering other flower parts; leaves rounded in outline, deeply divided. Found in wet meadows and along streams. White variants are sometimes found. All parts of the plant are poisonous!

BLOOM TIME: June, July, August, September

LIFE ZONE: Montane, Subalpine

Date _____

Where found _____

_____

Colorado Columbine

Aquilegia coerulea

Large showy blue or lavender-blue and white flowers, 2–4 inches across; 5 white or creamy petals with bases elongated into slender spurs holding nectar; 5 blue, petal-like sepals. Common in aspen groves and on moist rocky slopes. The state flower of Colorado. Familiar in gardens along with many other species; hybrids are readily produced with a wide range of characteristics and colors.

BLOOM TIME: July, August

LIFE ZONE: Foothills, Montane, Subalpine

Date _____

Where found _____

_____

Dwarf Columbine

Aquilegia saximontana

This alpine gem is the envy of many a rock gardener. A miniature blue columbine with short hooked spurs (slender, tube-like extensions of the petals); 5–6 inches tall. Found infrequently, only among rocks on the high peaks.

BLOOM TIME: July, August

LIFE ZONE: Alpine

Date _____

Where found _____

_____

Leather Flower or Sugarbowls

Clematis hirsutissima

Deep blue leathery urn-shaped flowers hanging down from bushy upright stems, 1–2 feet high; silky seed clusters; compound gray hairy leaves. Found on dry open slopes. Stout constitution with elegant flowers makes this a showpiece in the garden. *C. scottii* is similar in habit, and more common in southern Colorado.

BLOOM TIME: June

LIFE ZONE: Foothills

Date _____

Where found _____

_____

Pasque Flower

Pulsatilla patens

Flowers cup-shaped, resembling the common crocus of spring gardens; pale blue, lavender to nearly white, cups enclosing very numerous conspicuous gold stamens; buds and early flowers nearly enclosed in slender furry bracts; appear in early spring, often through melting snow; fruits in a shaggy, silvery head, each with a long feathery tail; palmately divided, hairy leaves appear after the flowers. Common and widespread on open slopes. Asian and European species are similar and more common in nurseries.

BLOOM TIME: April, May

LIFE ZONE: Foothills, Montane

Date _____

Where found _____

_____

Rock Clematis

Clematis columbiana

Low-growing, semi-woody vine, scrambles only a short ways on the open forest floor, among rocks, or cool ledges. Leaves pinnately compound; flowers nodding, soft to bright lavender-blue, 4 petals, to 1¼ inches long; seeds in fuzzy round tufts. Beautiful, available from specialty nurseries, and excellent in a cool well-drained spot in the rock garden.

BLOOM TIME: May, June

LIFE ZONE: Foothills, Montane

Date _____

Where found _____

_____

Subalpine Larkspur

Delphinium barbeyi

Dark bluish-purple flowers in spike-like cluster at top of stout stems 3–6 feet tall; flowers with 4 small petals, upper petals edged with white, 5 showy petal-like sepals, upper sepal with a long spur. Similar to cultivated larkspur. Grows in large clumps in meadows and bogs.

BLOOM TIME: July, August

LIFE ZONE: Subalpine

Date _____

Where found _____

_____

Tall Larkspur

Delphinium glaucum

Flowers grayish-blue in unbranched elongated clusters; spurs prominent, slender, nearly straight, about ½ inch long; plants tall, up to 60 inches; leaves palmately divided, lobes also cleft, nearly to the base. Common in aspen groves.

BLOOM TIME: July, August

LIFE ZONE: Montane

Date_____

Where found _____

_____

Two-Lobe Larkspur

Delphinium nuttallianum

Flowers pale to deep purplish-blue, occasionally white, in short clusters of 6–10; 5 showy sepals, one forming a conspicuous spur; plants up to 15 inches high; leaves deeply palmately divided into narrow segments. Poisonous to livestock.

BLOOM TIME: May, June

LIFE ZONE: Foothills, Montane

Date_____

Where found _____

_____

Alpine Kittentails

Besseya alpina

Flowers bluish-purple, in short spikes; protruding stamens give a fuzzy appearance; 2–6 inches tall; leaves at base of plant are thick, rounded, and rather woolly. Found on rocky slopes. A tiny relative of the kittentails of the foothills.

BLOOM TIME: July, August

LIFE ZONE: Alpine

Date_____

Where found_____

_____

Alpine Penstemon

Penstemon glaber var. *alpinus*
Flowers sky-blue flushed with lavender,
growing on one side of stem; flower
tube-shaped with 2 lips; stems stout, 4–
24 inches tall; leaves opposite, smooth.
Common, and often seen in masses in
gravelly or disturbed soil on roadsides
east of the Continental Divide from
Wyoming to New Mexico. Wonderful
in the garden.
BLOOM TIME: June, July, August
LIFE ZONE: Foothills, Montane, Subalpine

Date _____

Where found _____

_____

Blue-Eyed Mary

Collinsia parviflora
Flowers tiny, 2-lipped, less than ½ inch
long, pale blue to white, in whorls near
the top of the stem or borne singly
below; stems weak, 2½ to 10 inches
high; leaves narrow, usually reddish-
purple on the underside. Generally
found in damp, shaded ground.
BLOOM TIME: April, May, June, July
LIFE ZONE: Foothills, Montane

Date _____

Where found _____

_____

Blue Mist Penstemon

Penstemon virens
Flowers bright blue, small, ½ inch long,
tube-shaped with 2 lips, clustered at top
of 6–10 inch stems; stems numerous, rising from mats of bright green leaves. A
common penstemon east of the Continental Divide, often blanketing entire
slopes.
BLOOM TIME: June, July
LIFE ZONE: Foothills, Montane, Subalpine

Date _____

Where found _____

_____

Dusky Beardtongue
Penstemon whippleanus
Flowers smoky purple or wine-colored, 1½ inches long; tube-shaped with 2-lips; flowers grouped in nodding clusters at top of stem; plants slender, 4–18 inches tall; leaves opposite and pointed. Found on alpine slopes and along trails and open areas in subalpine forests. Often found growing with its dusky white-flowered form.
BLOOM TIME: July, August
LIFE ZONE: Subalpine, Alpine

Date _____

Where found _____

_____

Hall's Penstemon
Penstemon hallii
Striking alpine plant, under 12 inches, sometimes forming a mat; leaves linear, mostly basal, deep green; flowers usually on one side of their compact stems, soft lavender or rich sky-blue to deep-blue. At its best on gravelly decomposed granite soils, often perched on near-vertical ledges among boulders in spectacular natural rock gardens. Endemic to the central and southern mountains of Colorado. A true gem of the high country, and surprisingly adaptable in the rock garden, though not always long-lived.
BLOOM TIME: June, July, August
LIFE ZONE: Subalpine, Alpine

Date _____

Where found _____

_____

Mat Penstemon
Penstemon caespitosus
A variable species, generally low and creeping, forming a deep green mat under 2 inches tall; leaves ½ inch; flowers soft lavender-blue on short upright stems or very near the ground. Found in our central and western counties, and scattered through Wyoming, Utah, and northern Arizona. Requires excellent drainage in a xeric border or rock garden.
BLOOM TIME: May, June, July
LIFE ZONE: High Desert, Foothills

Date _____

Where found _____

_____

Narrow-Leaf Penstemon

Penstemon angustifolius

Striking sky-blue flowers, crowded in a raceme, 4–10 inches tall; flowers tubular and 2-lipped; basal leaves narrow, upper stem's leaves are wider than basal leaves. Found frequently on sandy soil of plains and foothills. Replaced by variety *vernalis* in northwest Colorado. Most penstemons are lovely in the garden, but this clear bright-blue species is spectacular in the rock garden or dry border.

BLOOM TIME: May, June

LIFE ZONE: Plains, Foothills

Date _____

Where found _____

_____

One-Side Penstemon

Penstemon virgatus ssp. *asa-grayi*

Blue to purple narrow tube-shaped flowers, abruptly widening into open throat, 2-lipped flowers in a one-sided raceme. A conspicuous penstemon up to 3 feet tall, with upright stout stem; narrow leaves. Abundant on slopes in the foothills.

BLOOM TIME: June, July

LIFE ZONE: Plains, Foothills

Date _____

Where found _____

_____

Rocky Mountain Penstemon

Penstemon strictus

Tall, large-flowered blue penstemon with lighter blue to violet throat; anthers hairy; plants stout, 10–28 inches tall. A common penstemon west of the Continental Divide. Found on gravelly or sandy soil of mesas and hillsides, often with sagebrush. Showy and well adapted to cultivation, it tolerates more moisture than most penstemons and reseeds readily.

BLOOM TIME: June, July

LIFE ZONE: Foothills, Montane

Date _____

Where found _____

_____

Side-Bells Penstemon
Penstemon secundiflorus
Flowers orchid to bluish-lavender, tubular and 2-lipped, clustered loosely along one side of stem; smooth, thick, grayish leaves, opposite and clasping the stem; plants 8–20 inches tall. A very showy penstemon, abundant in the foothills and mesas in early spring and well suited to a prairie or rock garden. Sometimes called orchid penstemon.
BLOOM TIME: May, June
LIFE ZONE: Plains, Foothills

Date _____
Where found _____
_____

Silver Mat Penstemon
Penstemon linarioides ssp. *coloradoensis*
Low-growing with silvery leaves and stems; leaves linear, ½ to ¾ inch long; flowers ½ inch long on slender but plentiful spikes 6–12 inches tall, soft lavender. Found in the sunny dry soils of piñon/juniper woodlands in our southwestern plateaus, and well adapted to rock gardens and xeric borders with good drainage. The cultivar 'Silverton' is widely available.
BLOOM TIME: June
LIFE ZONE: High Desert, Foothills, Montane

ate _____
here found _____
_____

Water Speedwell
Veronica americana
Small deep-blue flowers, ⅛ inch across, 4 rounded petals, 2 stamens; flowers in clusters in axils of leaves; leaves opposite, stems erect or trailing, 8–20 inches. Common in shallow water, muddy places along streams, on the plains and lower foothills.
BLOOM TIME: July, August
LIFE ZONE: Plains, Foothills

Date _____
Where found _____
_____

Figwort Family (Scrophulariaceae)

Blue Flax

Linum lewisii

Flowers pale blue to sky blue, open in the morning, with 5 fragile petals that fall easily by afternoon; ball-shaped seed capsules; numerous narrow leaves ½ to 1 inch long, on upright stems. Widespread. Named for Captain Meriwether Lewis of the Lewis and Clark Expedition. Nearly indistinguishable from its European counterpart, *Linum perenne,* which is found in gardens and "wildflower" seed mixes.

BLOOM TIME: May, June, July, August

LIFE ZONE: Plains, Foothills

Date _____

Where found _____

_____

Arctic Gentian

Gentiana algida

Low plants 2–7 inches tall, deep cup-shaped flowers in clusters, up-facing, 1½ to 1¾ inches long, greenish-white and streaked with purple. Found in moist, high meadows. One of the latest alpine plants to bloom.

BLOOM TIME: August

LIFE ZONE: Subalpine, Alpine

Date _____

Where found _____

_____

Moss Gentian

Gentiana prostrata

Blue, star-shaped, 4 or 5-lobed tubular flowers, ⅓ inch wide, lobes flat when open; single flower on slender stem, ½ to 4 inches tall. So light sensitive, it is said that flowers close if shaded, even momentarily. (My experience has been mixed.) Found on grassy alpine meadows.

BLOOM TIME: June, July, August

LIFE ZONE: Alpine

Date _____

Where found _____

_____

Parry Gentian

Gentiana parryi

Flowers bright blue, goblet-shaped, 1½ to 2 inches long; each stem with 1 to few flowers partially hidden in large leafy bracts; leaves oval and opposite; stems in clumps 6–15 inches tall. Found in moist meadows and along stream banks and bogs. Probably found more often than other gentians because of its large size and attractive color.

BLOOM TIME: August

LIFE ZONE: Montane, Subalpine

Date _____

Where found _____

_____

Pleated Gentian

Gentiana affinis

Flowers several to many at tip of stems or in upper leaf axils; pale to medium blue, ¾ to 1¼ inches long, cylindrical, opening slightly only in bright sunlight; leafy stems in clumps 4–12 inches high; leaves opposite, without stalks. Found on moist soil, fields, and slopes.

BLOOM TIME: August, September

LIFE ZONE: Foothills, Montane

Date _____

Where found _____

_____

Rocky Mountain Fringed Gentian

Gentianopsis thermalis

Deep bluish-purple upfacing flowers, 1 to 1½ inches, with 4 spreading lobes, fringed around the edges; stems with a single flower; petal twisted in the bud; leaves opposite; plants 6–15 inches tall. Found in wet meadows and along stream margins.

BLOOM TIME: August

LIFE ZONE: Montane, Subalpine

Date _____

Where found _____

_____

Rose Gentian

Gentianella amarelle ssp. *acuta*

Small bluish-lavender to rose-pink tubular flowers, with 4–5 pointed lobes, few to numerous up-facing flowers clustered on leafy stem; plants 4–15 inches tall. Found in moist ground; very common in aspen groves.

BLOOM TIME: July, August
LIFE ZONE: Montane, Subalpine

Date _____

Where found _____

Star Gentian

Swertia perennis

Flowers blue, star-shaped, with 5 spreading lobes (sometimes 4), in narrow cluster at top of stem; stems 6–12 inches tall rising from rosette of smooth, narrow leaves. Found along stream banks and in moist meadows.

BLOOM TIME: August
LIFE ZONE: Montane, Subalpine

Date _____

Where found _____

Tulip Gentian

Eustoma grandiflorum

Showy large deep-purple tulip-shaped flowers, 5 petals, 1 to 1½ inches long; stems with opposite bluish-green leaves; plants 8–24 inches tall. Found in wet meadows on eastern plains. Formerly a common species, now threatened because of increasing land use and development, especially mining of sand and gravel in broad river valleys along the Front Range. Please help protect it in the wild. Horticultural varieties sold as florist plants lack the hardiness and grace of the species.

BLOOM TIME: July, August, September
LIFE ZONE: Plains

Date _____

Where found _____

Blue Flag
Iris missouriensis

Flowers pale blue, purplish, or nearly white, similar to cultivated iris; on leafless stalks, 8–12 inches tall, which emerge from slender blue-green leaves; brown woody seed pods are persistent. Plants grow in dense clumps, abundant in wet meadows, streams, and hillside seeps.

BLOOM TIME: May, June
LIFE ZONE: Foothills, Montane

Date _____

Where found _____

_____

Blue-Eyed Grass
Sisyrinchium montanum

Flowers starry with 6 violet to pale-blue petals; sepals and petals nearly equal in size and shape, less than ½ inch broad, at the tips of stems, open only in bright sunlight; stems somewhat flattened and winged, 10–20 inches in height; leaves very narrow and grass-like. Found on moist meadows and slopes.

BLOOM TIME: June, July, August
LIFE ZONE: Foothills, Montane

Date _____

Where found _____

_____

American or Blue Vetch
Vicia americana

Showy purple pea-like flowers, 3 or more in a raceme; flat pods; slender scrambling vine under 3 feet, only attaining the height of plants it climbs on; pinnately compound leaves with tendrils at tips. Common and found on brushy hillsides.

BLOOM TIME: May, June, July, August
LIFE ZONE: Plains, Foothills

Date _____

Where found _____

_____

Low Lupine
Lupinus pusillus

Similar to silvery lupine, but much shorter, 3–8 inches tall; flowers pea-like, pale blue–lavender to nearly white; foliage and stems with stiff hairs; seed pods with only 2 seeds. An annual plant found in sandy soil from the Kansas plains throughout the Rocky Mountains and the West, sometimes forming large patches.

BLOOM TIME: July, August
LIFE ZONE: High Desert, Plains

Date _____

Where found _____

_____

Scurf Pea
Psoralea tenuiflora

Small blue-purple pea-like flowers in loose racemes or clusters, 1 to 3 flowers at a node; leaflets in threes with glandular dots; much-branched erect stems 8 inches to 2 feet tall. Likes sandy soil. Sometimes called breadroot.

BLOOM TIME: July, August
LIFE ZONE: Plains, Foothills

Date _____

Where found _____

_____

Silvery Lupine
Lupinus argenteus

Flowers light bluish-lavender to purple, sometimes bicolored, pea-like, ½ inch long, in spike-like clusters; stems slender, 12–30 inches tall; leaves palmately compound with 5–9 leaflets. Common, providing large splashes of rich blue throughout the mountains in open woods, fields, and along roadsides.

BLOOM TIME: July, August
LIFE ZONE: Plains, Foothills, Montane, Subalpine

Date _____

Where found _____

_____

Skullcap
Scutellaria brittonii
Flowers rich blue-purple in pairs in upper leaf axils, ½ to ¾ inch long, distinctly 2-lipped, upper lip of sepals bearing a conspicuous crest; stems branching at the base, 4–10 inches tall; leaves opposite, oval. Common name derived from sepals united to form a "cap." Prefers dry soil, dying back in summer heat. Spreads widely via stolons if conditions suit it, especially in sandy soil.
BLOOM TIME: May, June, July
LIFE ZONE: Plains, Foothills, Montane

Date _____

Where found _____

_____

Wild Mint
Mentha arvensis
Small tubular 2-lipped flowers, pale blue to light pink, clustered in leaf axils; leaves oval, pointed at the tip, with sharp teeth; stems square, leaves opposite—both characteristics of the mint family. The aromatic foliage when steeped makes a pleasant beverage. Found along stream banks, bogs, and wet meadows.
BLOOM TIME: July, August, September
LIFE ZONE: Plains, Foothills

Date _____

Where found _____

_____

Purple-Flowered Groundcherry
Quincula lobata
Violet to purple saucer-shaped 5-petaled flowers, ½ to 1 inch wide, with woolly star in center; stems branched and sprawling, leaves fleshy and scurfy (covered with scale-like particles). Common plant, often in large patches in sandy soil, fields, and along roadsides.
BLOOM TIME: April, May, June, July, August
LIFE ZONE: Plains

Date _____

Where found _____

_____

Jacob's Ladder

Polemonium pulcherimum ssp. *delicatum*

Sky-blue, funnel-shaped flowers, ½ inch broad, in loose clusters; stems weak and spreading, 8–12 inches tall; compound leaves mostly at base of stem, with narrow leaflets in 10–12 pairs, suggesting a ladder. Common in moist subalpine forests, often at timberline. A delicate, attractive species, but with a strong skunk-like odor.

BLOOM TIME: July, August

LIFE ZONE: Subalpine

Date _____

Where found _____

_____

Sky Pilot

Polemonium viscosum

Purple or dark blue funnel-shaped flowers, ¾ inch long, with bright orange anthers; flowers in tight clusters at top of stem; plants 4–12 inches tall; leaves basal, compound with very small oval leaflets clustered along the leaf-stalk. Some species of polemonium are often called "skunk plants" because of the disagreeable odor of the foliage.

BLOOM TIME: June, July

LIFE ZONE: Subalpine, Alpine

Date _____

Where found _____

_____

Sticky Gilia

Gilia pinnatifida

Numerous small light-blue flowers with conspicuous stamens; much-branched odorous plant, 4–20 inches tall; finely divided sticky leaves. Common on rocky slopes.

BLOOM TIME: June, July, August

LIFE ZONE: Foothills, Montane

Date _____

Where found _____

_____

Spiderwort
Tradescantia occidentalis
Dark blue flowers in clusters, 3-petaled, with 2 or 3 leafy bracts at base of flower stalks; long, tapering leaves with sheathing bases; stems 6 inches to 2 feet tall; fleshy plant with slimy sap. Often found along the base of the foothills. Related to the cultivated wandering jew. Durable and lovely addition to a border or meadow garden.
BLOOM TIME: June, July
LIFE ZONE: Plains, Foothills

Date _____

Where found _____

Blue Aspen Daisy
Erigeron speciosus
Flower heads blue to lilac, about 1 inch broad, with numerous very narrow rays and yellow disks; stems leafy, 1-2 feet tall, each bearing 1–10 heads; leaves 3-nerved, lance-shaped to oval, smooth margins. Found in moist meadows and aspen groves. The most common daisy of the montane and foothills, often called showy daisy. Wonderful naturalized in a wild garden, or as a border plant. Deadheading can extend bloom season.
BLOOM TIME: May, June, July, August
LIFE ZONE: Foothills, Montane

Date _____

Where found _____

Blue Lettuce
Lactuca tatarica ssp. *pulchella*
Light blue flower heads made up of strap-shaped ray flowers; smooth perennial with milky sap; stems 1–4 feet high topped by flower heads; leaves narrow and long, often cut or lobed but not spiny. Found in wet meadows and along roadsides.
BLOOM TIME: May, June, July, August
LIFE ZONE: Plains, Foothills

Date _____

Where found _____

Chicory

Chicorium intybus

Flower heads sky blue, 1 to 1½ inches across, composed of strap-shaped ray flowers; stems much-branched, nearly leafless, 1½ to 3 feet tall; bitter, milky juice. Its long tap root is roasted, ground, and used as coffee or an adulterant; young stems and leaves can be used as salad greens. A **non-native species** introduced from Europe, now a common roadside weed.

BLOOM TIME: June, July, August, September

LIFE ZONE: Plains

Date _____

Where found _____

_____

Pinnate-Leaved Daisy

Erigeron pinnatisectus

Plant may resemble a small fern, growing between boulders and on rocky expanses of tundra. Flowers daisy-like with purple rays and yellow disks; heads solitary, 1 inch broad; plants 4–5 inches tall; leaves small and finely divided.

BLOOM TIME: June, July, August

LIFE ZONE: Subalpine, Alpine

Date _____

Where found _____

_____

Sky Blue Aster

Symphyotrichum lanceolatum var. *hesperium*

Numerous small flower heads, pale blue (sometimes nearly white) with yellow centers on 1½ to 3 foot tall much-branched plant; leaves narrow and willow-like. Fairly common along ditch banks, streams, and ponds.

BLOOM TIME: July, August, September

LIFE ZONE: Plains, Foothills

Date _____

Where found _____

_____

Smooth Aster

Symphyotrichum laeve var. *geyeri*
Heads numerous, ½ to 1 inch broad, in flattish clusters with younger heads at center, ray flowers bright blue; stems 1–3 feet tall, branching; leaves smooth, lance-shaped to oval, the upper leaves clasping the stem. Prefers moist soil.
BLOOM TIME: August, September, October
LIFE ZONE: Foothills, Montane

Date _____

Where found _____

_____

Sunflower Family (Asteraceae)

Blue Vervain

Verbena hastata
Flowers dark blue or purple in numerous tall, slender, dense spikes 5–8 inches long, clustered at top of stem; plants tall, up to 40 inches. Common in marshy areas and along irrigation ditches on the plains and in valleys of lower foothills. Attractive perennial in damp gardens or at water's edge where it will reseed happily.
BLOOM TIME: July, August, September
LIFE ZONE: Plains, Foothills

Date _____

Where found _____

_____

Bracted Vervain

Verbena bracteata
Spikes, 4–6 inches long (not showy), of tiny light-blue to purple 5-lobed flowers intermingled with stiff, hairy bracts; stems much-branched, spreading, usually lying flat on the ground, 4–20 inches long; leaves opposite, deeply cut. A weedy plant of roadsides, fields, and waste ground at low elevations over much of North America.
BLOOM TIME: June, July, August
LIFE ZONE: Plains

Date _____

Where found _____

_____

Verbena Family (Verbenaceae)

Birdfoot Violet
Viola pedatifida
Palmately lobed leaves not typical of a violet, but classic violet flowers in early spring. Found on rocky soils along the foothills and mesas, and onto the high prairies. The rich purple-blue flowers can seem nearly hidden in the dry tan grasses of early spring.
BLOOM TIME: April, May, June, July, August
LIFE ZONE: Plains, Foothills

Date _____
Where found _____

Mountain Blue Violet
Viola adunca
Flowers blue-violet, ¼ to ½ inch across, 5 petals, with spur or sac at the back of lower petal; stems short; leaves round to oval. Found at edges of streams, on moist slopes, and meadows.
BLOOM TIME: April, May, June, July, August
LIFE ZONE: Montane, Subalpine

Date _____
Where found _____

Sweet Violet
Viola odorata
Heart-shaped leaves; deep blue or white flowers; most often encountered in lawns or where human habitation has occurred in recent decades, or in adjacent moist wildlands. **Non-native species**—this imported cousin to our native violet spreads by runners or seed. This is a tough survivor and can be aggressive in a garden setting. Native species are generally more restrained.
BLOOM TIME: April, May, June, July, August, September
LIFE ZONE: Plains, Foothills

Date _____
Where found _____

Purple Pincushion or Purple Fringe

Phacelia sericea

Showy flowers are dark purple, in spike-like clusters; protruding yellow stamens make a striking contrast; plants 4–12 inches tall; leaves are silky gray and finely divided; plant has an unpleasant odor. Common along roadsides and in disturbed soils, usually above 10,000 feet.

BLOOM TIME: July, August

LIFE ZONE: Subalpine, Alpine

Date _____

Where found _____

_____

What Do These Scientific Names Mean?

Correct plant names are the life-long pursuit of dedicated plant taxonomists. In many cases, opinions can differ on which Latin name should be applied to a given plant. New research can indicate that a plant actually deserves a different name. Sometimes very closely related plants are lumped together under one genus or species; sometimes they are split apart with distinct names. This process keeps a lot of people busy!

It also keeps ordinary people like you and me guessing! Over the course of time, a single plant may have had a dozen or more names that are considered synonyms. To further complicate matters, some authorities excel in one group of plants and their work is widely accepted, while other plant names seem to be endlessly disputed by many experts. Using the most recent assessment is very important to some people, and of little concern to others.

To simplify this edition, we've used the U.S. Department of Agriculture as our primary authority, and list plants according to the names that they accept as "correct." Their website offers a wealth of information, including the synonyms that others have used for each plant over the years. If you see a plant listed by a name that you are not familiar with, a bit of investigation may help to clarify its identity.

On a more practical note, most Latin names do carry some meaning—some simple and some quite complex. They typically reflect either the name of a person who worked with or discovered the plant; a location; or a particular characteristic of the plant. These meanings thankfully do not change, and learning some of the more common meanings can help you remember a plant's identity and features.

What Do These Scientific Names Mean?

acer-	sharp	-cephalus	head
acuminata	long-pointed	cereum	waxy
adeno-	gland	cernuum	nodding
aduncus	hooked	chamae-	on the ground
aggregata	clustered	chima-	winter
agrestis	growing wild	chrysanthus	golden-flowered
alatus	winged	cinereus	ash-colored
albidus, alba	white	cinque-	five
alpinus	alpine	coccineus	scarlet
alta	tall	cordi-	heart-shaped
amplexicaulis	stem-clasping	cornuta	horned
angusti-	narrow	corona	crown
anserina	goose	crassi-	fleshy
anthus	flower	croceus	saffron-yellow
aprica	exposed to the sun	cunei-	wedge-shaped
aquifolium	needle-leaved	cuspidata	tipped with a sharp and stiff point
arenaria	sand-loving		
argentea	silvery		
arguta	sharp (toothed)	dasy-	rough, thick
arvense	field	decumbens	lying down
asper-	rough	dendro-	tree-like
atro-	dark	-denta	tooth
atrosanguineus	dark blood-red	didymo-	twin-like
aurantiacus	orange-colored	discolor	of different colors
aureum	golden	divari-	diverse
		divergens	wide-spreading
bi-	two	dumosus	bushy
bilobus	two-lobed		
blanda	white	edulis	edible
boreale	northern	elatior	tall and slender
brachy-	short	eremo-	solitary, lonely
brevi-	short	erigeron	early old
		erio-	woolly
caerulea	sky blue	erythro-	red
caespitosus	tufted, sod-forming	exigua	small
canescens	white-hairy	exscapa	stemless
-capitatum	headed		
-carpum	fruit(ed)	fili-	thread-like
caudata	tailed	flagellaris	whip-like
-caulus	stem	flavo-	yellow

-flora	flower(ed)	*mega-*	large
floribundus	free flowering	*melano-*	black
foetidissima	very ill-smelling	*micro-*	small
-folium	leaved	*mille-*	thousands, many
formosa	handsome	*mono-*	one
fruticosa	shrubby, bushy	*mucronatus*	sharp-pointed
		multi-	many
galericulata	covered with a helmet		
glaber	smooth	*nana*	dwarf
glauca	bluish-green	*niger*	black
-glottis	tongue	*nitidus*	shining
-gonum	corner, knee	*nivale*	snow
graveolens	rank-smelling	*nuda*	naked
guttatus	spotted, drop-like		
-gynus	seed	*occidentalis*	western
		octo-	eight
hetero-	mixed, varied	*officinalis*	healing
hirsut-	rough-hairy	*-oides*	like
hirta	short-hairy	*oligo-*	few
hydro-	water	*-opsis*	head
hyper-	above	*oreo-*	mountain
hypo-	under	*oreophilus*	mountain-loving
humifusa	spread over the ground	*osmo-*	odorous
humilis	dwarf		
		pallida	pale
-ifera	bearing	*palustris*	marsh-loving
inerme	unarmed	*parri-*	leek-like
integra-	whole	*parva-*	small
-issima	very (superlative)	*patens*	spreading
		pauci-	few
lacti-	milk-like	*pectinata*	with narrow, comb-like divisions
laevigatus	smooth		
lanatus	woolly	*-philus*	loving
lanceolatus	lance-leaf	*-phylla*	leaf
lasio-	hairy	*platy-*	broad
lati-	broad	*plena-*	plentiful, many
lepto-	slender, small	*-pleura*	rib
leuco-	whitish	*poli-*	polished
luteus	yellow	*poly-*	many
		pratensis	meadow-
macro-	large	*procerus*	tall
maculata	spotted		

procumbens	lying on its face	*spectabilis*	beautiful
prunifolia	plum-leaved	*-sperma*	seed
pseudo-	false, similar to	*squarrosus*	parts spreading or recurving at ends
-pteri	winged		
pulcherrima	very beautiful	*-stella*	star-shaped
punctata	dotted	*stenopetala*	with small petals
pumila	dwarf	*stolonifera*	bearing runners
purpureus	purple	*strepto-*	twisted, curved
pusillus	dwarf	*stricta*	stiff
pygmaea	dwarf	*sub-*	just below
		sylvestris	wild, of the woods
racemosus	branched		
reni-	kidney	*tenella*	frail
repens	creeping	*tenue-*	thin, frail
reptans	creeping	*-thamnos*	bush
rostrata	beaked	*thele-*	nipple
rotundi-	round, plump	*tinctoria*	paint, used for dye
rupestris	of the rocks	*toxi-*	poisonous
rupicola	living among rocks	*trachy-*	rough
rubra	red	*tri-*	three
rugosa	wrinkled		
		uliginosus	marsh
saligna	willow-leaved	*umbellata*	umbrella-shaped
salsuginosus	growing in brackish places	*uncinatus*	hooked
		uva-ursi	bear-berry
sanguineus	bloody, blood-red		
sativa	cultivated	*varians*	variable
saxatile	found among stones	*villosa*	downy
saxi-	stone	*virens, viridis*	green
saxifraga	rock-breaker	*viscosa*	sticky
scoparius	broom-like	*vulgatum*	common
scopulorum	of the mountains		
secunda-	facing one-side	*xanthum*	yellow
senecio	old, old man		
sepium	growing in hedges		
septentrionale	northern		
sericea	silky soft-hairy		
serotina	late		
serra	saw-toothed		
speciosa	beautiful		

Glossary of Botanical Terms

Areole A modified node, visible as small depressions on the surface of cacti from which spines grow.

Alternate Plant parts that occur singly at a node. *See* opposite and whorled.

Annual plant A plant that grows, matures, sets seed, and dies within a year.

Anther The pollen-bearing part of a stamen.

Banner The large upper petal of a pea-like flower. *See* wings and keel for other parts of a pea flower.

Biennial A plant completing its growth in two years.

Blade The expanded portion of a leaf.

Bract A small modified leaf; bracts usually circle the base of a flower cluster, or a composite flower head.

Calyx The collective term for the circle of sepals in a single flower.

Capsule A dry fruit that splits open when ripe, with one or more seed-containing compartments.

Catkin A spike of tiny pollen-bearing or seed-producing flowers, commonly found on willow, aspen or birch.

Composite Flowers very small that are crowded into tightly compact heads superficially resembling a single flower, as in the sunflower family.

Compound A leaf in which the blade is subdivided into separate portions or leaflets. *See* pinnate and palmate.

Corolla Collective term for all the petals in an individual flower, which may be separate or united.

Cultivar A named form or hybrid of a species, usually selected for specific desirable traits and propagated asexually for horticultural purposes.

Deciduous Refers to a plant that loses its leaves at the end of a growing season.

Disk flower The tubular flowers in the center of composite flower heads, such as sunflowers and asters. Some heads like thistle and rabbitbrush have only disk flowers.

Entire Descriptive term for a leaf that has smooth edges without teeth, notches, or being otherwise divided.

Alternate

Anther

Banner

Blade

Capsule or Pod

Catkin

Corolla

Calyx

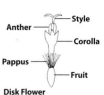

Anther — Style

Pappus — Corolla

Fruit

Disk Flower

251

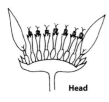

Head

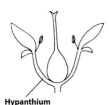

Hypanthium

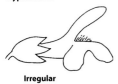

Irregular

Keel

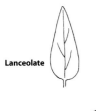

Lanceolate

Leaf Axil

Linear

Evergreen   A plant bearing green leaves throughout the year.

Frond   A fern leaf.

Fruit   Botanically, any ripened ovary whether fleshy, like apples and berries, or dry, like capsules or sunflower seeds.

Glaucous   A covering of the outer surface of leaves or fruits of a bluish-white, waxy powder, which can be rubbed off.

Glochid   Fine stiff hairs, often barbed, arising from the areoles at the base of spines in the cactus genus *Opuntia, Cylindropuntia*, and related cacti.

Head   A dense cluster of small flowers surrounded at the base by bracts; used most often to describe flowers of the sunflower family.

Hemiparasitic   Attached to, and relying on, the roots of another plant for some of its nutrients.

Herb   Plants are herbs (or herbaceous) if they have no woody stems.

Hypanthium   A cup or tube-shaped enlargement at the base of a flower bearing on its rim the stamens, petals, and sepals.

Inflorescence   Refers to the flowering parts of a plant that can be grouped in variously arranged clusters; a flower cluster.

Involucre   A circle of bracts at the base of a flower head or flower cluster.

Irregular   Said of flowers that are bilaterally symmetrical, like snapdragons.

Keel   In pea flowers, the lower boat-shaped pair of united petals that enclose the stamens and pistil. Found in all pea-like flowers of the legume family.

Lanceolate   Lance-shaped, long and narrow, broadest toward the base.

Leaf axil   The upper angle between the leaf stalk and the stem.

Lenticel   A small spot or line of loose corky cells allowing an exchange of gases between living tissue of the stem and the atmosphere.

Linear   Refers to a long, narrow leaf with nearly parallel margins.

Lobe   Divisions of a leaf, especially if rounded; or the corolla of a flower with united petals.

Mat plant A form of plant growth in which stems and leaves are very low and interwoven into a dense mass, like moss campion, or a spreading thick tangle, like alpine clover.

Much-branched A stem or branch that divides into smaller branches many times.

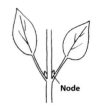

Node

Node On stems, the point at which a leaf or flower cluster is, or has been, attached. Sometimes the word "joint" is appropriate when there is a swelling at the node.

Oblanceolate Lance-shaped leaf, but broadest above the middle and tapering toward the base.

Obovate Oval leaf shape, more slender near the base.

Opposite Refers to leaf or stem arrangement where two like units are attached to opposite sides of the same node.

Palmate

Ovary The part of the pistil that contains ovules and, after fertilization, ripens into a fruit containing the seed.

Palmate Said of a leaf when leaflets, lobes, or veins all spread from the top of the leaf petiole like fingers of a hand.

Panicle An inflorescence in which individual flowers are attached to a much-branched flower stalk.

Panicle

Pappus The modified and mature calyx of florets (tiny flowers making up the flowerhead) in the sunflower family (Asteraceae), usually comprised of hairs, bristles, or scales (dandelion, salsify, sunflower).

Pedicel The flower stalk of an individual flower in a cluster.

Perennial Plants that live for several years, even though they may die back to underground living parts in winter.

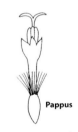

Pappus

Petal One of the colored or white segments making up the corolla of a flower.

Pinnate A compound leaf with leaflets attached on a long axis (featherlike).

Pistil The seed-producing organ of a flower, made up of ovary, ovules, stigma, and style.

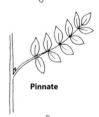

Pinnate

Pod A dry fruit that splits open along two sides, releasing seed (legume).

Pollen Tiny yellow grains produced in the anther and transferred to the stigma in pollination.

Raceme An elongated inflorescence or flower cluster in which the individual flowers are attached by their stalks to a central axis.

Raceme

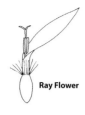

Ray Flower

Ray flowers   Refers to the strap-shaped marginal flowers around a center disk as in the sunflower family; often thought of as "petals."

Regular   Radially symmetrical. Said of a flower when the parts of the calyx are alike in size and form, and the parts of the corolla are also alike in size and form.

Rosette   A dense flat circular cluster of leaves at the base of a stem, as dandelion or mullein.

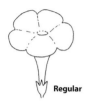

Regular

Saprophyte   Relying on decomposing organic materials as a source of food.

Sepal   The part of a flower, usually green, that encloses the flower bud; a segment of the calyx.

Simple leaf   Said of a leaf that is not compound. *See* Compound.

Shrub   A perennial woody plant smaller than a tree, with several to many stems.

Sorus (sori, pl.)   Spore-producing structures appearing as dots on the underside of fern fronds (leaves).

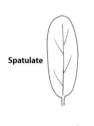

Spatulate

Spatulate   Said of a leaf broader at the tip and tapering to the base; spatula-shaped.

Species   A group containing individual plants of the same kind. The word is both singular and plural.

Sp. (spp., pl.) An abbreviation indicating that the exact species or type of plant is not named. For example *Rosa* sp. for one species, or *Rosa* spp. referring to several species.

Ssp.   Abbreviation for subspecies. *See* variety.

Spur

Spore   A microscopic reproductive body produced by non-flowering plants, such as ferns, horsetails, spikemosses.

Spur   A hollow, nectar-containing projection sometimes found as a part of a sepal or petal, as in larkspur or violet.

Stalk   The flower-supporting structure; a specialized flower stem.

Anther

Flament

Stamen

Stamen   The pollen-producing organ of a flower, composed of anther and filament.

Stigma   The pollen receiving part of the pistil.

Stolon   Underground stems that spread from the original plant, producing new above-ground plants as they go.

Stoloniferous   Able to spread via stolons to form expanding colonies.

Style   The stalk-like part of the pistil connecting the ovary and stigma.

Stipules   Small appendages at the base of a leaf or leaf stalk in many plants; may be leaf-like or thorn-like, generally in pairs.

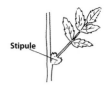

Stipule

Toothed   Refers to leaf margins that have points or serrations of various shapes, like the teeth of a saw.

Tendril   A slender twining outgrowth from the tip of a leaf or stem, or sometimes at a node.

Tendril

Two-lipped   Describes a type of flower found in the figwort and mint families; the petals are united or joined into a tube that is expanded at the open end into two lobes, usually of unequal size and rounded or notched, like penstemons or snapdragons.

Toothed

Tufted   Stems or leaves in a very tight cluster.

Umbel   A type of flat-topped or rounded inflorescence in which the flower stalks all arise from the same point, like umbrella spokes.

Two-Lipped

Variety or var.   A term denoting a minor variation of a species.

Whorled   Three or more leaves or branches arising from a single node are said to be whorled. Examples are bedstraw, field horsetail, whorl-leaf loco.

Umbel

Wings   In the pea-like flowers, the two similar petals at the sides of the flower, between the banner and keel.

Woody   Said of plants with firm stems and branches remaining alive from season to season.

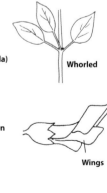

Whorled

Wings

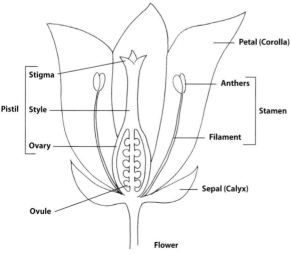

Pistil — Stigma, Style, Ovary
Petal (Corolla)
Anthers
Stamen
Filament
Sepal (Calyx)
Ovule
Flower

Elevations of Towns, Peaks, Passes, and Parks*

*Where state is not indicated, location is in Colorado.

Zones

P – Plains (4,000 to 6,000 feet, east of the Continental Divide)

H – High Desert (5,000 to 7,000 feet, west of the Continental Divide)

F – Foothills (6,000 to 8,000 feet)

M – Montane (8,000 to 10,000 feet)

S – Subalpine (10,000 to 11,500 feet, or timberline)

A – Alpine (11,500 up)

Location	Zone	Elev. ft.
Mt. Abrams	A	12,800
Mt. Achonee	A	12,656
Aguilar	F	6,700
Akron	P	4,662
Alamosa	F	7,544
Albuquerque, NM	PH	4,950
Allen's Park	M	8,513
Alma	S	10,353
Animas City	F	6,500
Mt. Antero	A	14,269
Antonito	F	7,888
Apache Pass	S	9,060
Arapahoe Peak	A	13,506
Arvada	P	5,337
Aspen	F	7,908
Aurora	P	5,400
Bailey	F	7,725
Barr Lake	P	5,104
Basalt	F	6,624
Bayfield	F	6,500
Mt. Belford	A	14,197
Bergen Park	F	7,643
Berthoud	P	5,029

Location	Zone	Elev. ft.
Berthoud Pass	S	11,314
Mt. Bierstadt	A	14,060
Bierstadt Lake	S	10,500
Blackhawk	M	8,042
Black Canyon Natl. Park (Gunnison)	HF	7,500
Blanca	F	7,746
Blanca Peak	A	14,317
Bonanza	FM	8,000
Boulder	PF	5,349
Breckenridge	M	9,578
Brighton	P	4,982
Brook Forest	F	8,000
Mt. Bross	A	14,169
Brush	P	4,231
Buena Vista	F	7,954
Buffalo Creek	F	6,631
Burlington	P	4,167
Calhan	F	6,508
Mt. Cameron	A	14,238
Cameron Pass	S	10,285
Cañon City	P	5,333
Capital Peak	A	14,137
Carbondale	HF	6,181
Casper, WY	P	5,123
Castle Peak	A	14,259
Castle Rock	F	6,202
Cedaredge	HF	6,175
Centennial	P	5,883
Center	M	7,645
Central City	M	8,419
Cerro Summit	F	7,964
Cheyenne Mountain	M	9,407

Location	Zone	Elev. ft.	Location	Zone	Elev. ft.
Cheyenne Wells	P	4,296	Eagle	F	6,602
Cheyenne, WY	F	6,062	East Canyon	P	5,343
Clayton, NM	P	5,050	Eaton	P	4,839
Cochetopa Pass	S	10,032	Echo Lake	S	10,600
Collbran	HF	5,988	Edgewater	P	5,353
Colo. Natl. Monument	H	6,000	Mt. Elbert	A	14,431
Colorado Springs	PF	6,012	Mt. Eolus	A	14,086
Mt. Columbia	A	14,073	El Diente	A	14,159
Como	M	9,787	Eldora	M	8,700
Conejos	F	7,880	Eldorado Springs	PF	5,900
Conifer	M	8,052	Elizabeth	F	6,448
Cortez	H	6,200	Empire	M	8,603
Crags (The)	S	10,500	Englewood	P	5,306
Craig	F	6,186	Estes Park	F	7,522
Crater Lake	S	10,500	Eureka	M	9,800
Crawford	HF	6,666	Mt. Evans	A	14,264
Creede	M	8,842	Evanston, WY	F	6,748
Crested Butte	M	8,855	Evergreen	F	7,500
Crestone	F	7,860	Fairplay	M	9,953
Crestone Needle	A	14,191	Fall River Pass	A	11,797
Crestone Peak	A	14,291	Farmington, NM	H	5,300
Cripple Creak	M	9,494	Farmington, UT	H	4,231
Culebra Peak	A	14,069	Fillius Park	F	7,700
Cumbres Pass	S	10,022	Florence	PF	5,187
Dalhart, TX	P	3,985	Florissant	M	8,193
Dallas Divide	M	8,970	Fort Collins	P	5,000
Daniels Park	F	6,200	Fort Garland	F	7,936
De Beque	H	4,935	Fort Logan	P	5,438
Deckers	F	6,250	Fort Lupton	P	4,906
Deertrail	P	5,183	Fort Morgan	P	4,265
Del Norte	F	7,872	Fowler	P	4,337
Delta	H	4,961	Fraser	M	8,560
Mt. Democrat	A	14,142	Fremont Pass	S	11,318
Denver	P	5,280	Frisco	M	9,097
Devils Head	M	9,348	Fruita	H	4,498
Dillon	M	8,858	Garden of the Gods	F	6,500
Dolores	F	6,936	Genesee Mountain	M	8,270
Douglas, WY	P	4,815	Georgetown	M	8,506
Durango	F	6,512	Glenwood Springs	HF	5,747

Location	Zone	Elev. ft.
Golden	P	5,675
Gore Pass	M	9,524
Granby	F	7,935
Grand Junction	H	4,587
Grand Lake	M	8,369
Grand Mesa	M	9,000 to 10,000
Grand Valley	H	5,095
Grant	M	8,567
Grays Peak	A	14,270
Greeley	P	4,655
Green Mtn. Falls	F	7,964
Green River, WY	HF	6,100
Grizzly Mountain	A	14,000
Guffy	M	8,400
Gunnison	F	7,703
Gypsum	HF	6,333
Handies Peak	A	14,049
Mt. Harvard	A	14,420
Haxtun	P	4,000
Hayden	F	6,336
Highlands Ranch	P	5,680
Holly	P	3,400
Holyoke	P	3,745
Hoosier Pass	A	11,541
Hotchkiss	H	5,351
Hot Sulphur Springs	F	7,667
Hudson	P	5,000
Hugo	P	5,046
Humboldt Peak	A	14,044
Huron Peak	A	14,005
Hygiene	P	5,086
Idaho Springs	F	7,536
Ignacio	F	6,432
Independence Pass	A	12,095
James Peak	A	13,260
Jefferson	M	9,500
Johnstown	P	4,820
Julesburg	P	3,477

Location	Zone	Elev. ft.
Kebler Pass	MS	10,000
Keenesburg	P	4,958
Kelso Mountain	A	13,200
Kemmerer, WY	F	6,927
Kenosha Pass	MS	10,001
Kiowa	F	6,347
Kit Carson	P	4,285
Kit Carson Peak	A	14,100
Kokomo	A	10,672
Kremmling	F	7,356
Lafayette	P	5,237
La Junta	P	4,066
Lake City	M	8,664
La Manga Pass	S	10,230
Lamar	P	3,616
La Plata Peak	A	14,340
Lander, WY	P	5,357
Laramie, WY	F	7,165
La Salle	P	4,676
Las Animas	P	3,901
Las Vegas, NM	PF	6,435
La Veta	F	7,013
La Veta Pass	M	9,382
Leadville	S	10,152
Little Bear Mountain	A	14,040
Limon	P	5,366
Mt. Lincoln	A	14,284
Mt. Lindsey	A	14,125
Littleton	P	5,362
Lizard Head Pass	MS	10,222
Logan, UT	H	4,535
Longmont	P	4,979
Longs Peak	A	14,256
Lookout Mountain (near Denver)	F	7,375
Loveland	P	4,982
Loveland Pass	A	11,992
Lyons	PF	5,374
Manassa	F	7,683

Location	Zone	Elev. ft.
Mancos	HF	6,993
Manitou	F	6,414
Marble	F	7,800
Maroon Peak	A	14,158
Marshall Pass	S	10,856
Mt. Massive	A	14,418
Meeker	F	6,249
Mesa Verde Natl. Park	HFM	7,500
Middle Park	M	8,500
Milner Pass	S	10,759
Minturn	FM	7,817
Missouri Mountain	A	14,067
Moab, UT	H	4,000
Molas Divide	MS	10,910
Monarch Pass	S	11,312
Monticello, UT	HF	7,050
Monte Vista	F	7,658
Montrose	H	5,795
Monument	F	6,960
Morrison	PF	5,767
Muddy Pass	M	8,772
Nederland	M	8,236
North Maroon Peak	A	14,000
North Park	M	8,000 to 9,000
Oak Creek	F	7,413
Ogden, UT	H	4,370
Olathe	H	5,346
Old Baldy	A	14,125
Ordway	P	4,312
Ouray	F	7,811
Mt. Oxford	A	14,153
Pagosa Springs	F	7,105
Palisade	H	4,731
Palmer Park	F	6,500
Palmer Lake	F	7,225
Pikes Peak	A	14,110
Poncha Pass	M	9,010
Poncha Springs	F	7,469
Price, UT	H	5,545
Mt. Princeton	A	14,197
Provo, UT	H	4,510
Pueblo	P	4,695
Pyramid Peak	A	14,000
Quandary Peak	A	14,252
Rabbit Ears Pass	M	9,680
Raton, NM	P	6,660
Raton Pass	F	7,834
Redcloud Peak	A	14,050
Red Cliff	M	8,596
Red Mountain Pass	S	11,018
Red Rocks Park	PF	6,000
Red River Pass, WY	S	10,004
Ridgway	HF	6,985
Rifle	H	5,345
Rock Springs, WY	F	6,271
Rocky Ford	P	4,178
Rocky Mtn. Natl. Park	FMSA	7,500 to 14,000
Rollinsville	M	8,367
Roswell, NM	P	3,600
Royal Gorge	P	5,500 to 6,000
Rye	F	6,725
Saguache	F	7,697
Salida	F	7,036
Salt Lake City, UT	H	4,366
Sangre de Cristo Range (see Blanca Peak)		
San Luis Peak	A	14,014
San Luis Valley	F	7,500 to 8,000
Santa Fe, NM	HF	7,000
Sapinero	F	7,240
Mt. Shavano	A	14,229
Mt. Sherman	A	14,037
Silver Cliff	FM	8,000
Silver Plume	M	9,114
Silverton	M	9,302

Location	Zone	Elev. ft.
Simla	PF	5,968
Slumgullion Pass	S	11,361
Mt. Sneffels	A	14,150
Snowmass Peak	A	14,077
South Park	M	9,000 to 10,000
E. Spanish Peak	A	12,683
W. Spanish Peak	A	13,623
Spring Creek Pass	S	10,901
Springfield	P	4,350
Squaw Pass	M	9,807
Steamboat Springs	F	6,695
Sterling	P	3,940
Stewart Peak	A	14,032
Stratton	P	4,411
Sulphur Springs	F	7,667
Sunlight Peak	A	14,060
Sunshine Peak	A	14,018
Tabeguache Peak	A	14,155
Taos, NM	F	6,950
Taos Pass, NM	M	9,282
Telluride	M	8,876
Tennessee Pass	S	10,424
Thermopolis, WY	H	4,326
Torreys Peak	A	14,267
Torrington, WY	P	4,104
Trail Ridge Road	A	12,183
Trappers Lake	MS	9,604
Trinidad	PF	5,994
Trout Creek Pass	M	9,346
Twin Lakes	M	9,367
Uncompahgre Peak	A	14,301
Vail Pass	S	10,603
Vail Village	M	8,160
Vernal, UT	H	5,325
Victor	M	9,692
Wagon Wheel Gap	M	8,449

Location	Zone	Elev. ft.
Walsenburg	F	6,182
Walden	M	8,101
Walsh	P	3,954
Ward	M	9,253
Wellington	P	5,201
Westcliffe	F	7,888
Westminster	P	5,280
Wetterhorn Peak	A	14,017
Whitehouse Mountain	A	13,498
Willow Creek Pass	M	9,683
Wilkerson Pass	M	9,525
Wilson Peak	A	14,017
Mt. Wilson	A	14,246
Windom Peak	A	14,091
Windsor	P	4,800
Wolcott	HF	6,976
Woodland Park	M	8,494
Wolf Creek Pass	S	10,850
Wray	P	3,516
Mt. Yale	A	14,194
Yampa	F	7,892
Yuma	P	4,132

References

Many of the references below were also listed in previous editions, and though their freshness may have been surpassed by more recent works, they still provide relevant information and enjoyable reading. Some are unique for their historical perspective and context.

This edition includes websites that provide up-to-date information and endless browsing opportunities. The broad fields of wildflower study, gardening, and conservation have never had such a wealth of informational resources at their disposal.

Arnberger, Leslie P. 1982. *Flowers of the Southwest Mountains.* Southwest Parks and Monuments Association, Tucson, Ariz.

Barr, Claude A. 1983. *Jewels of the Plains: Wild Flowers of the Great Plains and Hills.* University of Minnesota Press, Minneapolis, Minn.

Busco, Janice, and Nancy R. Morin. 2003. *Native Plants for High Elevation Western Gardens.* Fulcrum Publishing, Denver, Colo.

Carter, Jack L. 2006. *Trees and Shrubs of Colorado.* Mimbres Press, Silver City, New Mexico.

Craighead, John J., Frank C. Craighead, Jr., and Ray J. Davis. 1998. *A Field Guide to Rocky Mountain Wildflowers.* Peterson Field Guide Series. Houghton Mifflin Co., Boston, Mass.

Dorn, Robert D., and Jane L. Dorn. 2007. *Growing Native Plants of the Rocky Mountain Area.* Self-published via Lulu.com

Duft, Joseph F. and Robert K. Moseley. 1989. *Alpine Wildflowers of the Rocky Mountains.* Mountain Press Publishing Co., Missoula, Mont.

Elmore, Francis. 1976. *Shrubs and Trees of the Southwest Uplands.* Southwest Parks and Monuments Association, Tucson, Ariz.

Fagan, Damian. 1998. *Canyon Country Wildflowers: Including Arches and Canyonlands National Parks.* Falcon Press, Guilford, Conn.

Freeman, Craid C., and Eileen K. Schofield. 1991. *Roadside Wildflowers of the Southern Great Plains.* University Press of Kansas, Lawrence, Kan.

Harrington, Harold D. 1957. *How to Identify Plants.* Sage Press, Denver, Colo.

Harrington, Harold D. 1964. *Manual of the Plants of Colorado.* Sage Press, Denver, Colo.

Irish, Mary and Gary. 2000. *Agaves, Yuccas, and Related Plants: A Gardener's Guide.* Timber Press, Portland, Ore.

Kelly, George W. *A Guide to the Woody Plants of Colorado.* 1970. Pruett Publishing Co., Boulder, Colo.

Kershaw, Linda K., Pojar, Jim, and Andy Mackinnon. 1998. *Plants of the Rocky Mountains.* Lone Pine Publishing, Auburn, Wash.

Ladd, Doug. 2005. *Tallgrass Prairie Wildflowers 2: A Field Guide to Common Wildflowers and Plants of the Prairie Midwest.* Falcon Press, Guilford, Conn.

Lamb, Samuel H. 1975. *Woody Plants of the Southwest.* Sunstone Press.

McPherson, Alan and Sue McPherson. 1979. *Edible and Useful Wildplants of the Urban West.* Pruett Publishing Co., Boulder, Colo.

Marinos, Nic, and Helen Marinos. 1981. *Plants of the Alpine Tundra.* Rocky Mountain Nature Association, Inc., Estes Park, Colo.

Martin, William C., and Charles R. Hutchins. 1984. *Spring Wildflowers of New Mexico.* University of New Mexico Press, Albuquerque, N.M.

Martin, William C., and Charles R. Hutchins. 1986. *Summer Wildflowers of New Mexico.* University of New Mexico Press, Albuquerque, N.M.

Mielke, Judy. 1993. *Native Plants for Southwestern Landscapes.* University of Texas Press, Austin, Tex.

Mutel, Cornelia F., and John C. Emerick. 1992. *From Grassland to Glacier: The Natural History of Colorado and the Surrounding Region.* Johnson Books, Boulder, Colo.

Nelson, Ruth Ashton. 2000. *Plants of Rocky Mountain National Park.* Rocky Mountain Nature Association, Inc., Estes Park, Colo.

Nelson, Ruth Ashton. 1992. *Handbook of Rocky Mountain Plants.* 4th edition, revised by Roger L. Williams. Roberts Rinehart Publishers, Niwot, Colo.

Nold, Robert. 1999. *Penstemons.* Timber Press, Portland, Ore.

Owensby, Clenton E. 1980. *Kansas Prairie Wildflowers.* Iowa State University Press, Ames, Iowa.

Phillips, Judith. 1995. *Plants for Natural Gardens: Southwestern Native & Adaptive Trees, Shrubs, Wildflowers & Grasses.* Museum of New Mexico Press, Albuquerque, N.M.

Phillips, Judith. 1995. *Natural by Design: Beauty and Balance in Southwest Gardens.* Museum of New Mexico Press, Albuquerque, N.M.

Spackman, S.; Jennings, B.; Coles, J.; Dawson, C.; Minton, M.; Kratz, A.; and C. Spurrier. 1997. *Colorado Rare Plant Field Guide.* Prepared for the Bureau of Land Management, the U.S. Forest Service, and the U.S. Fish and Wildlife Service by the Colorado Natural Heritage Program.

Taylor, Ronald J. 1992. *Sagebrush Country: A Wildflower Sanctuary.* Mountain Press Publishing Co., Missoula, Mont.

Wasowski, Sally. 2002. *Gardening with Prairie Plants: How to Create Beautiful Native Landscapes.* University of Minnesota Press, Minneapolis, Minn.

Weber, William A. 1976. *Rocky Mountain Flora.* Colorado Associated University Press, Boulder, Colo.

Weber, William A., and Ronald C. Wittmann. 2001. *Colorado Flora: Eastern Slope.* University Press of Colorado, Boulder, Colo.

Weber, William A., and Ronald C. Wittmann. 2001. *Colorado Flora: Western Slope.* University Press of Colorado, Boulder, Colo.

West, Steve. 2000. *Northern Chihuahuan Desert Wildflowers.* Falcon Press, Guilford, Conn.

Williams, Sara. 1997. *Creating the Prairie Xeriscape: Low-maintenance, Water-efficient Gardening.* Lone Pine Publishing, Auburn, Wash.

Wingate, Janet L. *Rocky Mountain Flower Finder.* 1990. Wilderness Press, Berkeley, Calif.

Young, R.G. and Joann Young. *Colorado West—Land of Geology and Wildflowers.* Wheelwright Lithographing Co., Salt Lake City, Utah.

Zwinger, Ann H. 2002. *Beyond the Aspen Grove.* Johnson Books, Boulder, Colo.

Zwinger, Ann H. and Beatrice E. Willard. 1996. *Land Above the Trees: A Guide to American Alpine Tundra.* Johnson Books, Boulder, Colo.

Websites

Colorado Native Plant Society
www.conps.org/conps.html

Colorado Natural Heritage Program
www.cnhp.colostate.edu

CSU Herbarium Wildflower Photo Album
www.herbarium.biology.colostate.edu/photo.htm

Denver Botanic Gardens
www.botanicgardens.org/high-altitude-gardener

Denver Plants: Colorado Rocky Mountain Wildflowers
www.denverplants.com/wflwr/index.htm

USDA Forest Service and International Society of Arboriculture
www.forestyimages.org

Southwest Colorado Wildflowers, Ferns, and Trees
www.swcoloradowildflowers.com/

USDA Plants Database
plants.usda.gov/

Plant Reference Chart

HOW ORGANIZED:

Plants are listed alphabetically by common family name, then by genus, then species.

A = primary color
B = secondary color

*Where no cultivation rating is given, plant is generally not cultivated or recommended. Chart includes only native plants.

Family, *Latin Name*	Common Name
Agave Family, *Yucca baccata* (Agavaceae)	Banana Yucca
Agave Family, *Yucca glauca* (Agavaceae)	Soapweed Yucca
Agave Family, *Yucca harrimaniae* (Agavaceae)	Harriman's Yucca, Dollhouse Yucca
Barberry Family, *Berberis fendleri* (Berberidaceae)	Fendler's Barberry
Barberry Family, *Berberis repens* (Berberidaceae)	Oregon Grape
Barberry Family, *Mahonia fremontii* (Berberidaceae)	Fremont's Mahonia
Bellflower Family, *Campanula parryi* (Campanulaceae)	Parry Harebell
Bellflower Family, *Campanula rotundifolia* (Campanulaceae)	Harebell, Bluebell
Bellflower Family, *Lobelia cardinalis* ssp. *graminea* (Campanulaceae)	Cardinal Flower
Bellflower Family, *Lobelia syphilitica* var. *ludoviciana* (Campanulaceae)	Great Blue Lobelia
Birch Family, *Alnus incana* ssp. *tenuifolia* (Betulaceae)	Rocky Mountain Alder
Birch Family, *Betula glandulosa* (Betulaceae)	Bog Birch
Birch Family, *Betula occidentalis* (Betulaceae)	Western River Birch
Borage Family, *Cryptantha virgata* (Boraginaceae)	Miner's Candle
Borage Family, *Eritrichium nanum* var. *elongatum* (Boraginaceae)	Alpine Forget-Me-Not
Borage Family, *Hackelia floribunda* (Boraginaceae)	False Forget-Me-Not
Borage Family, *Lithospermum incisum* (Boraginaceae)	Narrow-Leaf Puccoon
Borage Family, *Lithospermum multiflorum* (Boraginaceae)	Many-Flowered Puccoon
Borage Family, *Mertensia ciliata* (Boraginaceae)	Tall Chiming Bells
Borage Family, *Mertensia lanceolata* (Boraginaceae)	Lanceleaf Chiming Bells
Borage Family, *Mertensia viridis* (Boraginaceae)	Alpine Chiming Bells
Buckthorn Family, *Ceanothus fendleri* (Rhamnaceae)	Fendler Ceanothus
Buckthorn Family, *Ceanothus velutinus* (Rhamnaceae)	Mountain Balm

West Slope	East Slope	Uncommon	Sunny, Open	Cool, Shady	Riparian	Moist Meadows	Aquatic, Wetlands	Green-Brown	White, Cream	Yellow	Orange	Red, Maroon	Reddish-Purple	Pink	Blue, Bluish-Purple	Easy	Challenging
X	X		X						A							X	
X	X		X						A							X	
X			X						A							X	
X	X		X							A							
X	X		X	X						A						X	
X			X							A						X	
X	X		X	X											A	X	
X	X		X						B						A	X	
	X	X	X	X		X						A					X
	X		X			X									A	X	
X	X				X		A									X	
X	X		X			X	A										X
X	X		X	X	X		A									X	
X	X		X						A								X
X	X		X											A			X
X	X		X											A			X
X	X		X							A						X	
X	X		X							A						X	
X	X		X			X	X								A		X
X	X		X											B	A	X	
X	X		X			X									A		X
X	X		X						A							X	
X	X	X	X						A								X

Family, *Latin Name*	Common Name
Buckwheat Family, *Eriogonum alatum* (Polygonaceae)	Winged Buckwheat
Buckwheat Family, *Eriogonum annuum* (Polygonaceae)	Annual Buckwheat
Buckwheat Family, *Eriogonum arcuatum* var. *arcuatum* (Polygonaceae)	James' Yellow Buckwheat
Buckwheat Family, *Eriogonum arcuatum* var. *xanthum* (Polygonaceae)	Alpine Golden Buckwheat
Buckwheat Family, *Eriogonum effusum* (Polygonaceae)	Prairie Baby's Breath, Spreading Buckwheat
Buckwheat Family, *Eriogonum inflatum* (Polygonaceae)	Desert Trumpet
Buckwheat Family, *Eriogonum jamesii* var. *jamesii* (Polygonaceae)	James' Wild Buckwheat
Buckwheat Family, *Eriogonum umbellatum* (Polygonaceae)	Sulphur Flower
Buckwheat Family, *Oxyria digyna* (Polygonaceae)	Alpine Sorrel
Buckwheat Family, *Polygonum amphibium* (Polygonaceae)	Water Buckwheat
Buckwheat Family, *Polygonum bistortoides* (Polygonaceae)	Bistort
Buckwheat Family, *Polygonum pensylvanicum* (Polygonaceae)	Smartweed
Buckwheat Family, *Rumex salicifolius* (Polygonaceae)	Willow-Leaved Dock
Buckwheat Family, *Rumex venosus* (Polygonaceae)	Showy Dock, Wild Begonia
Buttercup Family, *Aconitum columbianum* (Ranunculaceae)	American Monkshood
Buttercup Family, *Actaea rubra* (Ranunculaceae)	Baneberry
Buttercup Family, *Anemone canadensis* (Ranunculaceae)	Northern Anemone
Buttercup Family, *Anemone multifida* var. *multifida* (Ranunculaceae)	Red Anemone
Buttercup Family, *Anemone narcissiflora* (Ranunculaceae)	Alpine Anemone
Buttercup Family, *Aquilegia chrysantha* (Ranunculaceae)	Golden Columbine
Buttercup Family, *Aquilegia coerulea* (Ranunculaceae)	Colorado Columbine
Buttercup Family, *Aquilegia elegantula* (Ranunculaceae)	Western Red Columbine
Buttercup Family, *Aquilegia saximontana* (Ranunculaceae)	Dwarf Columbine

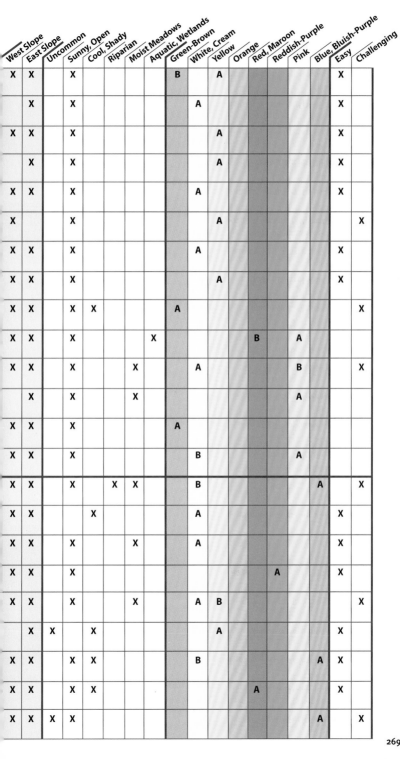

West Slope	East Slope	Uncommon	Sunny, Open	Cool, Shady	Riparian	Moist Meadows	Aquatic, Wetlands	Green-Brown	White, Cream	Yellow	Orange	Red, Maroon	Reddish-Purple	Pink	Blue, Bluish-Purple	Easy	Challenging
X	X		X					B		A						X	
	X		X						A							X	
X	X		X							A						X	
	X		X							A						X	
X	X		X						A							X	
X			X							A							X
X	X		X						A							X	
X	X		X							A						X	
X	X		X	X				A									X
X	X		X			X						B		A			
X	X		X			X			A					B			X
	X		X			X								A			
X	X		X					A									
X	X		X						B					A			
X	X		X		X	X			B						A		X
X	X			X					A							X	
X	X		X			X			A							X	
X	X		X										A			X	
X	X		X			X			A	B							X
	X	X		X						A						X	
X	X		X	X					B						A	X	
X	X		X	X								A				X	
X	X	X	X												A		X

269

Family, *Latin Name*	Common Name
Buttercup Family, *Caltha leptosepala* (Ranunculaceae)	White Marsh Marigold
Buttercup Family, *Clematis columbiana* (Ranunculaceae)	Rock Clematis
Buttercup Family, *Clematis hirsutissima* (Ranunculaceae)	Leather Flower, Sugarbowls
Buttercup Family, *Clematis ligusticifolia* (Ranunculaceae)	Virgins Bower
Buttercup Family, *Delphinium barbeyi* (Ranunculaceae)	Subalpine Larkspur
Buttercup Family, *Delphinium carolinianum* ssp. *virescens* (Ranunculaceae)	Plains Larkspur
Buttercup Family, *Delphinium glaucum* (Ranunculaceae)	Tall Larkspur
Buttercup Family, *Delphinium nuttallianum* (Ranunculaceae)	Two-Lobe Larkspur
Buttercup Family, *Pulsatilla patens* (Ranunculaceae)	Pasque Flower
Buttercup Family, *Ranunculus adoneus* (Ranunculaceae)	Snow Buttercup
Buttercup Family, *Ranunculus glaberrimus* var. *ellipticus* (Ranunculaceae)	Sagebrush Buttercup
Buttercup Family, *Ranunculus trichophyllus* (Ranunculaceae)	Water Crowfoot
Buttercup Family, *Thalictrum fendleri* (Ranunculaceae)	Meadow-Rue
Buttercup Family, *Trollius laxus* (Ranunculaceae)	Globeflower
Cactus Family, *Coryphantha missouriensis* var. *missouriensis* (Cactaceae)	Nipple Cactus, Beehive Cactus
Cactus Family, *Coryphantha vivipara* var. *vivipara* (Cactaceae)	Beehive Cactus
Cactus Family, *Cylindropuntia imbricata* (Cactaceae)	Candelabra Cactus, Cholla
Cactus Family, *Echinocereus fendleri* (Cactaceae)	Fendler's Hedgehog
Cactus Family, *Echinocereus reichenbachii* var. *perbellus* (Cactaceae)	Lace Cactus
Cactus Family, *Echinocereus triglochidiatus* (Cactaceae)	Claret Cup
Cactus Family, *Echinocereus viridiflorus* (Cactaceae)	Green Hedgehog Cactus
Cactus Family, *Opuntia fragilis* (Cactaceae)	Dwarf Prickly Pear
Cactus Family, *Opuntia heakockii* (Cactaceae)	Hair-Spine Prickly Pear

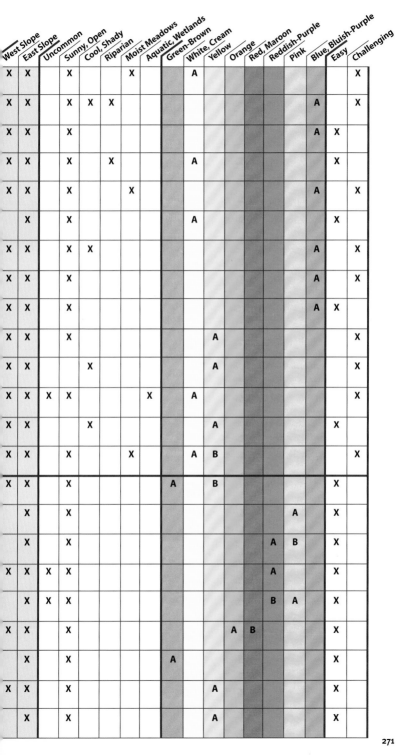

West Slope	East Slope	Uncommon	Sunny, Open	Cool, Shady	Riparian	Moist Meadows	Aquatic, Wetlands	Green-Brown	White, Cream	Yellow	Orange	Red, Maroon	Reddish-Purple	Pink	Blue, Bluish-Purple	Easy	Challenging
X	X		X			X			A								X
X	X		X	X	X									A			X
X	X		X											A		X	
X	X		X		X				A							X	
X	X		X			X								A			X
	X		X						A							X	
X	X		X	X										A			X
X	X		X											A			X
X	X		X											A		X	
X	X		X							A							X
X	X			X						A							X
X	X	X	X				X		A								X
X	X			X						A						X	
X	X		X		X				A	B							X
X	X		X					A	B							X	
	X		X											A		X	
	X		X										A	B		X	
X	X	X	X										A			X	
	X	X	X										B	A		X	
X	X		X								A	B				X	
	X		X					A								X	
X	X		X							A						X	
	X		X							A						X	

Family, *Latin Name*	Common Name
Cactus Family, *Opuntia macrorhiza* (Cactaceae)	Prickly Pear
Cactus Family, *Opuntia phaeacantha* (Cactaceae)	New Mexican Prickly Pear
Cactus Family, *Opuntia polyacantha* (Cactaceae)	Hunger Cactus, Plains Prickly Pear
Cactus Family, *Opuntia polyacantha* var. *erinacea* (Cactaceae)	Hedgehog Prickly Pear
Cactus Family, *Pediocactus simpsonii* (Cactaceae)	Mountain Ball Cactus
Cactus Family, *Sclerocactus parviflorus* (Cactaceae)	Fishhook Cactus, Devil Claw Cactus
Caper Family, *Cleome lutea* (Capparidaceae)	Yellow Bee Plant
Caper Family, *Cleome serrulata* (Capparidaceae)	Rocky Mountain Bee Plant
Caper Family, *Polanisia dodecandra* (Capparidaceae)	Clammy-Weed
Cattail Family, *Typha latifolia* (Typhaceae)	Cattail
Currant or **Gooseberry Family**, *Ribes aureum* (Grossulariaceae)	Golden Currant
Currant or **Gooseberry Family**, *Ribes cereum* (Grossulariaceae)	Wax Currant
Currant or **Gooseberry Family**, *Ribes coloradense* (Grossulariaceae)	Subalpine Black Currant
Currant or **Gooseberry Family**, *Ribes inerme* (Grossulariaceae)	Wild Gooseberry
Currant or **Gooseberry Family**, *Ribes montigenum* (Grossulariaceae)	Red Prickly Currant
Cypress Family, *Juniperus communis* (Cupressaceae)	Common Juniper
Cypress Family, *Juniperus monosperma* (Cupressaceae)	One-Seeded Juniper
Cypress Family, *Juniperus osteosperma* (Cupressaceae)	Utah Juniper
Cypress Family, *Juniperus scopulorum* (Cupressaceae)	Rocky Mountain Juniper
Dogbane Family, *Apocynum androsaemifolium* (Apocynaceae)	Dogbane
Dogbane Family, *Apocynum cannabinum* (Apocynaceae)	Dogbane, Indian Hemp
Dogwood Family, *Cornus canadense* (Cornaceae)	Bunchberry
Dogwood Family, *Cornus sericea* ssp. *sericea* (Cornaceae)	Red-Osier Dogwood

West Slope	East Slope	Uncommon	Sunny, Open	Cool, Shady	Riparian	Moist Meadows	Aquatic, Wetlands	Green-Brown	White, Cream	Yellow	Orange	Red, Maroon	Reddish-Purple	Pink	Blue, Bluish-Purple	Easy	Challenging
	X		X							A						X	
X	X		X							A	B			B		X	
X	X		X						B	A	B		B	B		X	
X			X											A		X	
X	X		X											A		X	
X		X	X											A			X
X			X							A						X	
X	X		X										B	A		X	
X	X		X						B					A		X	
X	X		X			X	X	A									
X	X		X							A						X	
X	X		X											A		X	
X	X		X	X										A		X	
X	X			X						A						X	
X	X		X						B					A		X	
X	X		X					A								X	
	X		X					A								X	
X			X					A								X	
X	X		X					A								X	
X	X		X											A			
X	X		X						A							X	
X	X	X		X					A								X
X	X		X		X				A							X	

Family, *Latin Name*	Common Name
Duckweed Family, *Lemna minor* (Lemnaceae)	Duckweed
Dwarf Mistletoe Family, *Arceuthobium* spp. (Viscaceae)	Mistletoe
Elm Family, *Celtis reticulata* (Ulmaceae)	Hackberry
Evening Primrose Family, *Calylophys lavandulifolius* (Onagraceae)	Sundrops
Evening Primrose Family, *Calylophus serrulatus* (Onagraceae)	Dainty Sundrops
Evening Primrose Family, *Chamerion angustifolium* (Onagraceae)	Fireweed
Evening Primrose Family, *Epilobium* ssp. (Onagraceae)	Willow-Herb
Evening Primrose Family, *Gaura coccinea* (Onagraceae)	Scarlet Gaura
Evening Primrose Family, *Oenothera albicaulis* (Onagraceae)	Plains Evening Primrose
Evening Primrose Family, *Oenothera brachycarpa* (Onagraceae)	Yellow Stemless Evening Primrose
Evening Primrose Family, *Oenothera caespitosa* (Onagraceae)	White Stemless Evening Primrose
Evening Primrose Family, *Oenothera canescens* (Onagraceae)	Spotted Evening Primrose
Evening Primrose Family, *Oenothera coronopifolia* (Onagraceae)	Cut-Leaf Evening Primrose
Evening Primrose Family, *Oenothera flava* (Onagraceae)	Golden Evening Primrose
Evening Primrose Family, *Oenothera villosa* (Onagraceae)	Common Evening Primrose
False Hellebore Family, *Veratrum tenuipetalum* (Melanthiaceae)	Cornhusk Lily, False Hellebore
Figwort Family, *Besseya alpina* (Scrophulariaceae)	Alpine Kittentails
Figwort Family, *Besseya plantaginea* (Scrophulariaceae)	Kittentails
Figwort Family, *Castilleja chromosa* (Scrophulariaceae)	Desert Paintbrush
Figwort Family, *Castilleja integra* (Scrophulariaceae)	Orange Paintbrush
Figwort Family, *Castilleja linariaefolia* (Scrophulariaceae)	Indian Paintbrush
Figwort Family, *Castilleja miniata* (Scrophulariaceae)	Scarlet Paintbrush
Figwort Family, *Castilleja occidentalis* (Scrophulariaceae)	Western Yellow Paintbrush

West Slope	East Slope	Uncommon	Sunny, Open	Cool, Shady	Riparian	Moist Meadows	Aquatic, Wetlands	Green-Brown	White, Cream	Yellow	Orange	Red, Maroon	Reddish-Purple	Pink	Blue, Bluish-Purple	Easy	Challenging
X	X		X			X	X	A									
X	X		X					A									
X	X		X		X			A									
	X		X							A					X		
X	X		X							A					X		
X	X		X	X									A				
X	X		X			X								A			
X	X		X											A		X	
X	X		X						A					B		X	
	X		X							A						X	
X	X		X							A						X	
	X		X											A		X	
X	X		X						A							X	
X	X		X							A						X	
X	X		X		X					A						X	
X	X		X			X		B	A								X
X	X		X												A		X
X	X			X					A					B			X
X			X								B	A					X
X	X		X								B	A					X
X	X		X									A					X
X	X		X									A					X
X	X		X					B	B	A							X

275

Family, *Latin Name*	Common Name
Figwort Family, *Castilleja rhexifolia* (Scrophulariaceae)	Rosy Paintbrush
Figwort Family, *Chionophila jamesii* (Scrophulariaceae)	Snowlover
Figwort Family, *Collinsia parviflora* (Scrophulariaceae)	Blue-Eyed Mary
Figwort Family, *Mimulus glabratus* (Scrophulariaceae)	Plains Monkeyflower
Figwort Family, *Mimulus guttatus* (Scrophulariaceae)	Yellow Monkeyflower
Figwort Family, *Orthocarpus luteus* (Scrophulariaceae)	Owl Clover
Figwort Family, *Pedicularis bracteosa* (Scrophulariaceae)	Bracted Lousewort
Figwort Family, *Pedicularis groenlandica* (Scrophulariaceae)	Elephant Heads, Little Red Elephants
Figwort Family, *Pedicularis parryi* (Scrophulariaceae)	Parry Lousewort
Figwort Family, *Pedicularis racemosa* (Scrophulariaceae)	Ram's-Horn, Sickletop Lousewort
Figwort Family, *Pedicularis sudetica* (Scrophulariaceae)	Alpine Lousewort
Figwort Family, *Penstemon albidus* (Scrophulariaceae)	White Penstemon
Figwort Family, *Penstemon angustifolius* (Scrophulariaceae)	Narrow-Leaf Penstemon
Figwort Family, *Penstemon barbatus* (Scrophulariaceae)	Scarlet Penstemon
Figwort Family, *Penstemon caespitosus* (Scrophulariaceae)	Mat Penstemon
Figwort Family, *Penstemon eatonii* (Scrophulariaceae)	Firecracker Penstemon
Figwort Family, *Penstemon glaber* var. *alpinus* (Scrophulariaceae)	Alpine Penstemon
Figwort Family, *Penstemon grandiflorus* (Scrophulariaceae)	Shell-Leaf Penstemon
Figwort Family, *Penstemon hallii* (Scrophulariaceae)	Hall's Penstomen
Figwort Family, *Penstemon linarioides* ssp. *coloradoensis* (Scrophulariaceae)	Silver-Mat Penstemon
Figwort Family, *Penstemon rostriflorus* (Scrophulariaceae)	Bridges' Penstemon
Figwort Family, *Penstemon secundiflorus* (Scrophulariaceae)	Side-Bells Penstemon
Figwort Family, *Penstemon strictus* (Scrophulariaceae)	Rocky Mountain Penstemon

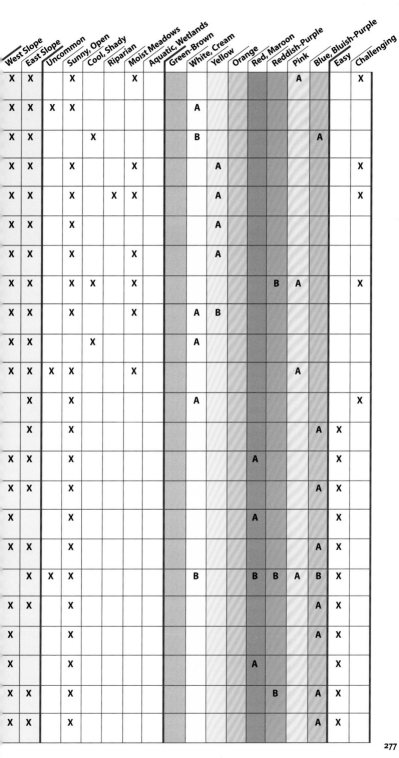

West Slope	East Slope	Uncommon	Sunny, Open	Cool, Shady	Riparian	Moist Meadows	Aquatic, Wetlands	Green-Brown	White, Cream	Yellow	Orange	Red, Maroon	Reddish-Purple	Pink	Blue, Bluish-Purple	Easy	Challenging
X	X		X			X								A			X
X	X	X	X						A								
X	X			X					B						A		
X	X		X			X				A							X
X	X		X		X	X				A							X
X	X		X							A							
X	X		X			X				A							
X	X		X	X		X						B	A				X
X	X		X			X		A	B								
X	X			X				A									
X	X	X	X			X								A			
	X		X					A									X
	X		X												A	X	
X	X		X									A				X	
X	X		X												A	X	
X			X									A				X	
X	X		X												A	X	
	X	X	X					B				B	B	A	B	X	
X	X		X												A	X	
X			X												A	X	
X			X									A				X	
X	X		X										B		A	X	
X	X		X												A	X	

Family, *Latin Name*	**Common Name**
Figwort Family, *Penstemon virens* (Scrophulariaceae)	Blue Mist Penstemon
Figwort Family, *Penstemon virgatus* ssp. *asa-grayi* (Scrophulariaceae)	One-Side Penstemon
Figwort Family, *Penstemon whippleanus* (Scrophulariaceae)	Dusky Beard-Tongue, Whipple's Penstemon
Figwort Family, *Scrophularia lanceolata* (Scrophulariaceae)	Bunny In The Grass, Western Figwort
Figwort Family, *Veronica americana* (Scrophulariaceae)	Water Speedwell
Flax Family, *Linum lewisii* (Linaceae)	Blue Flax
Four O'Clock Family, *Abronia fragrans* (Nyctaginaceae)	Sand Verbena, Prairie Snowball
Four O'Clock Family, *Mirabilis multiflora* (Nyctaginaceae)	Desert Four-O'clock
Four O'Clock Family, *Mirabilis rotundifolia* (Nyctaginaceae)	Round-leaf Four-O'clock
Frankenia Family, *Frankenia jamesii* (Frankeniaceae)	Frankenia
Fumitory Family, *Corydalis aurea* (Fumariaceae)	Golden Smoke
Gentian Family, *Eustoma grandiflorum* (Gentianaceae)	Tulip Gentian
Gentian Family, *Frasera speciosa* (Gentianaceae)	Green Gentian
Gentian Family, *Gentiana affinis* (Gentianaceae)	Pleated Gentian
Gentian Family, *Gentiana algida* (Gentianaceae)	Arctic Gentian
Gentian Family, *Gentiana parryi* (Gentianaceae)	Parry Gentian
Gentian Family, *Gentiana prostrata* (Gentianaceae)	Moss Gentian
Gentian Family, *Gentianella amarelle* ssp. *acuta* (Gentianaceae)	Rose Gentian
Gentian Family, *Gentianopsis thermalis* (Gentianaceae)	Rocky Mountain Fringed Gentian
Gentian Family, *Swertia perennis* (Gentianaceae)	Star Gentian
Geranium Family, *Geranium caespitosum* (Geraniaceae)	Pineywoods Geranium
Geranium Family, *Geranium caespitosum* var. *fremontii* (Geraniaceae)	Fremont's Geranium
Geranium Family, *Geranium richardsonii* (Geraniaceae)	White Geranium

West Slope	East Slope	Uncommon	Sunny, Open	Cool, Shady	Riparian	Moist Meadows	Aquatic, Wetlands	Green-Brown	White, Cream	Yellow	Orange	Red, Maroon	Reddish-Purple	Pink	Blue, Bluish-Purple	Easy	Challenging
X	X		X	X											A	X	
	X		X												A	X	
X	X		X	X					B						A		X
X	X		X					A				B					
X	X		X		X										A		
X	X		X												A	X	
X	X		X						A							X	
X	X		X											A		X	
X	X	X	X											A			
X	X	X	X						A								X
X	X		X							A						X	
	X	X	X		X										A		X
X	X		X		X			A	B								X
X	X		X		X										A		X
X	X		X		X										A		X
X	X		X		X										A		X
X	X		X												A		X
X	X			X										A	B		X
X	X		X		X										A		X
X	X		X		X										A		X
X	X		X											A		X	
X	X		X										A			X	
X	X			X					A							X	

Family, *Latin Name*	Common Name
Goosefoot Family, *Atriplex canescens* (Chenopodaceae)	Four-Wing Saltbush
Goosefoot Family, *Atriplex corrugata* (Chenopodaceae)	Mat Saltbush
Goosefoot Family, *Krascheninnikovia lanata* (Chenopodiaceae)	Winter Fat
Gourd Family, *Cucurbita foetidissima* (Cucurbitaceae)	Wild Gourd, Buffalo Gourd
Gourd Family, *Echinocystis lobata* (Cucurbitaceae)	Mock Cucumber
Grape Family, *Parthenocissus vitacea* (Vitaceae)	Virginia Creeper
Grape Family, *Vitis riparia* (Vitaceae)	Riverbank Grape
Grass Family, *Achnatherum hymenoides* (Poaceae)	Indian Ricegrass
Grass Family, *Andropogon gerardii* (Poaceae)	Big Bluestem
Grass Family, *Aristida purpurea* (Poaceae)	Purple Three-Awn
Grass Family, *Blepharoneuron tricholepis* (Poaceae / Graminaceae)	Pine Dropseed
Grass Family, *Bothriochloa laguroides* ssp. *torreyana* (Poaceae)	Silver Beardgrass
Grass Family, *Bouteloua curtipendula* (Poaceae)	Sideoats Grama
Grass Family, *Bouteloua dactyloides* (Poaceae)	Buffalo Grass
Grass Family, *Bouteloua gracilis* (Poaceae)	Blue Grama
Grass Family, *Elymus canadensis* (Poaceae)	Canada Wild Rye
Grass Family, *Heterostipa comata* (Poaceae)	Needle And Thread Grass
Grass Family, *Heterostipa neomexicana* (Poaceae)	New Mexican Feather Grass
Grass Family, *Hordeum jubatum* (Poaceae)	Foxtail Barley
Grass Family, *Muhlenbergia torreyi* (Poaceae)	Ring Muhly
Grass Family, *Nassella viridula* (Poaceae)	Green Needle Grass
Grass Family, *Panicum virgatum* (Poaceae)	Switch Grass
Grass Family, *Pascopyrum smithii* (Poaceae)	Western Wheatgrass

West Slope	East Slope	Uncommon	Sunny, Open	Cool, Shady	Riparian	Moist Meadows	Aquatic, Wetlands	Green-Brown	White, Cream	Yellow	Orange	Red, Maroon	Reddish-Purple	Pink	Blue, Bluish-Purple	Easy	Challenging
X	X	X								A						X	
X	X	X						A									X
X	X	X							A							X	
X	X	X								A						X	
	X	X	X							A						X	
X	X	X	X	X				A								X	
	X	X	X	X				A								X	
X	X	X						A								X	
X	X	X			X			B				A				X	
X	X	X						A				B				X	
X	X	X							A								X
	X	X							A							X	
X	X	X						A								X	
	X	X						A								X	
X	X	X						A								X	
X	X	X	X	X				A								X	
X	X	X						A								X	
X	X	X						A								X	
X	X	X			X			A								X	
	X	X						B						A			X
X	X	X						A								X	
X	X	X						A								X	
X	X	X						A									

Family, Latin Name	Common Name
Grass Family, *Pleuraphis jamesii* (Poaceae)	Galeta Grass
Grass Family, *Schizachyrium scoparium* (Poaceae)	Little Bluestem
Grass Family, *Sorghastrum nutans* (Poaceae)	Indian Grass
Grass Family, *Sporobolus airoides* (Poaceae)	Alkali Sacaton
Heath Family, *Arctostaphylos patula* (Ericaceae)	Manzanita
Heath Family, *Arctostaphylos uva-ursi* (Ericaceae)	Kinnikinnick
Heath Family, *Kalmia polifolia* (Ericaceae)	Mountain Laurel
Heath Family, *Moneses uniflora* (Ericaceae)	Woodnymph, Single Delight
Heath Family, *Orthilia secunda* (Ericaceae)	One-Sided Wintergreen, Pyrola
Heath Family, *Pterospora andromeda* (Ericaceae)	Woodnymph, Single Delight
Heath Family, *Pyrola asarifolia* (Ericaceae)	Bog Wintergreen
Heath Family, *Pyrola chlorantha* (Ericaceae)	Green Pyrola
Heath Family, *Pyrola minor* (Ericaceae)	Least Wintergreen
Heath Family, *Vaccinium myrtillus* (Ericaceae)	Mountain Blueberry
Honeysuckle Family, *Linnaea borealis* (Caprifoliaceae)	Twinflower
Honeysuckle Family, *Lonicera involucrata* (Caprifoliaceae)	Bush Honeysuckle
Honeysuckle Family, *Sambucus racemosa* (Caprifoliaceae)	Red-Berried Elder
Honeysuckle Family, *Symphoricarpos oreophilus* (Caprifoliaceae)	Mountain Snowberry
Hopps Family, *Humulus lupulus* var. *lupuloides* (Cannabaceae)	Native Hops
Hydrangea Family, *Fendlera rupicola* (Hydrangeaceae)	Cliff Fendlerbush
Hydrangea Family, *Jamesia americana* (Hydrangeaceae)	Waxflower
Hydrangea Family, *Philadelphus microphyllus* (Hydrangeaceae)	Little-Leaf Mock Orange
Iris Family, *Iris missouriensis* (Iridaceae)	Blue Flag

West Slope	East Slope	Uncommon	Sunny, Open	Cool, Shady	Riparian	Moist Meadows	Aquatic, Wetlands	Green-Brown	White, Cream	Yellow	Orange	Red, Maroon	Reddish-Purple	Pink	Blue, Bluish-Purple	Easy	Challenging
X	X		X					A								X	
X	X		X		X			A								X	
	X		X		X			B	A							X	
X	X		X					A								X	
X		X	X						B					A			X
X	X		X						B					A			X
X	X	X	X			X								A			X
X	X			X						A							X
X	X			X				A	B								X
X	X			X				B				A					X
X	X			X										A			X
X	X			X		X		A	B								X
X	X			X		X			A					B			X
X	X		X	X										A			X
X	X			X										A			X
X	X		X	X	X					A						X	
X	X		X	X	X				A							X	
X	X			X										A		X	
X	X		X		X			A								X	
X			X						A							X	
X	X			X					A							X	
X	X		X						A							X	
X	X		X			X									A	X	

Family, *Latin Name*	Common Name
Iris Family, *Sisyrinchium montanum* (Iridaceae)	Blue-Eyed Grass
Jointfir Family, *Ephedra viridis* (Ephedraceae)	Mormon Tea, Jointfir
Legume Family, *Amorpha canescens* (Fabaceae)	Leadplant
Legume Family, *Amorpha fruticosa* var. *angustifolia* (Fabaceae)	False Indigo
Legume Family, *Amorpha nana* (Fabaceae)	Dwarf Leadplant
Legume Family, *Astragalus crassicarpus* (Fabaceae)	Ground Plum
Legume Family, *Astragalus drummondii* (Fabaceae)	Drummond Milkvetch
Legume Family, *Astragalus flexuosus* (Fabaceae)	Limber Vetch
Legume Family, *Astragalus Shortianus* (Fabaceae)	Leather-Pod Loco
Legume Family, *Dalea candida* (Fabaceae)	White Prairie Clover
Legume Family, *Dalea purpurea* (Fabaceae)	Prairie Clover
Legume Family, *Desmanthus illinoensis* (Fabaceae)	Bundle Flower
Legume Family, *Glycyrrhiza lepidota* (Fabaceae)	Wild Licorice
Legume Family, *Lathyrus eucosmos* (Fabaceae)	Purple Peavine
Legume Family, *Lathyrus leucanthus* (Fabaceae)	White Peavine
Legume Family, *Lathyrus polymorphus* (Fabaceae)	Wild Sweet Pea
Legume Family, *Lupinus argenteus* (Fabaceae)	Silvery Lupine
Legume Family, *Lupinus pusillus* (Fabaceae)	Low Lupine
Legume Family, *Oxytropis lambertii* (Fabaceae)	Lambert's Loco
Legume Family, *Oxytropis sericea* (Fabaceae)	Rocky Mountain Loco
Legume Family, *Oxytropis splendens* (Fabaceae)	Whorl-Leaf Loco
Legume Family, *Psoralea tenuiflora* (Fabaceae)	Scurf Pea
Legume Family, *Robinia neomexicana* (Fabaceae)	New Mexico Locust

West Slope	East Slope	Uncommon	Sunny, Open	Cool, Shady	Riparian	Moist Meadows	Aquatic, Wetlands	Green-Brown	White, Cream	Yellow	Orange	Red, Maroon	Reddish-Purple	Pink	Blue, Bluish-Purple	Easy	Challenging
X	X		X		X				B						A	X	
X			X							A						X	
	X		X												A	X	
	X		X	X	X							A				X	
	X		X									A		B		X	
	X		X					A									X
X	X		X					A									X
X	X		X											A			X
X	X		X									A					X
X	X		X					A								X	
	X		X										B	A		X	
	X		X					A								X	
X	X		X		X			A									
X	X		X						B						A	X	
X	X		X					A									X
	X		X						B					A			X
X	X		X												A		X
X	X		X						B						A		X
X	X		X									A	B				X
X	X		X					A									X
X	X		X									A					X
X	X		X												A		
X	X		X											A		X	

Family, *Latin Name*	Common Name
Legume Family, *Sophora nuttaliana* (Fabaceae)	White Loco
Legume Family, *Thermopsis montana* (Fabaceae)	Mountain Golden Banner
Legume Family, *Thermopsis rhombifolia* (Fabaceae)	Prairie Golden Banner
Legume Family, *Trifolium dasyphyllum* (Fabaceae)	Alpine Clover
Legume Family, *Trifolium nanum* (Fabaceae)	Dwarf Clover
Legume Family, *Trifolium parryi* (Fabaceae)	Rose Clover, Parry's Clover
Legume Family, *Vicia americana* (Fabaceae)	American Vetch, Blue Vetch
Lily Family, *Calochortus gunnisonii* (Liliaceae)	Mariposa Lily, Sego Lily
Lily Family, *Calochortus nuttallii* (Liliaceae)	Sego Lily, Nuttall's Mariposa
Lily Family, *Erythronium grandiflorum* (Liliaceae)	Avalanche Lily
Lily Family, *Leucocrinum montanum* (Liliaceae)	Sand Lily
Lily Family, *Lilium philadelphicum* (Liliaceae)	Wood Lily
Lily Family, *Lloydia serotina* (Liliaceae)	Alpine Lily, Alplily
Lily Family, *Maianthemum stellatum* (Liliaceae)	False Solomon's Seal
Lily Family, *Streptopus amplexifolius* (Liliaceae)	Twisted Stalk
Lily Family, *Zigadenus venenosus* (Liliaceae)	Death Camas, Wand Lily
Lily Family, *Zygadenus elegans* (Liliaceae)	Death Camas, Wand Lily
Loasa Family, *Mentzelia albicaulis* (Loasaceae)	Small-Flowered Stickleaf, Evening Star
Loasa Family, *Mentzelia decapetala* (Loasaceae)	Evening Star
Loasa Family, *Mentzelia multiflora* (Loasaceae)	Yellow Evening Star
Loasa Family, *Mentzelia nuda* (Loasaceae)	White Evening Star
Madder Family, *Galium boreale* (Rubiaceae)	Bedstraw
Mallow Family, *Callirhoe involucrata* (Malvaceae)	Winecups

West Slope	East Slope	Uncommon	Sunny, Open	Cool, Shady	Riparian	Moist Meadows	Aquatic, Wetlands	Green-Brown	White, Cream	Yellow	Orange	Red, Maroon	Reddish-Purple	Pink	Blue, Bluish-Purple	Easy	Challenging
X	X		X						A							X	
X	X		X		X				A							X	
X	X		X							A						X	
X	X		X											A			X
X	X		X											A			X
X	X		X											A			X
X	X		X												A	X	
X	X		X						A								X
X			X						A					B			X
X	X		X	X						A							X
X	X		X						A								X
X	X	X	X			X					A						X
X	X		X						A								X
X	X			X					A							X	
X	X			X	X				A								X
X	X		X						A								X
X	X		X						A								X
X	X		X							A						X	
	X		X						A							X	
X	X		X							A						X	
	X		X						A							X	
X	X		X						A							X	
	X		X									A				X	

287

Family, *Latin Name*	Common Name
Mallow Family, *Sidalcea candida* (Malvaceae)	Modest Mallow, White Checker Mallow
Mallow Family, *Sidalcea neomexicana* (Malvaceae)	Wild Hollyhock
Mallow Family, *Sphaeralcea coccinea* (Malvaceae)	Cowboy's Delight
Maple Family, *Acer glabrum* (Aceraceae)	Rocky Mountain Maple
Maple Family, *Acer grandidentatum* (Aceraceae)	Big-Tooth Maple
Maple Family, *Acer negundo* (Aceraceae)	Boxelder
Milkweed Family, *Asclepias cryptocerus* (Asclepiadaceae)	Antelope Horns
Milkweed Family, *Asclepias incarnata* (Asclepiadaceae)	Swamp Milkweed
Milkweed Family, *Asclepias pumila* (Asclepiadaceae)	Dwarf Milkweed
Milkweed Family, *Asclepias speciosa* (Asclepiadaceae)	Showy Milkweed
Milkweed Family, *Asclepias subverticillata* (Asclepiadaceae)	Whorled Milkweed
Milkweed Family, *Asclepias tuberosa* (Asclepiadaceae)	Butterfly Weed
Milkweed Family, *Asclepias viridiflora* (Asclepiadaceae)	Green Comet Milkweed
Mint Family, *Mentha arvensis* (Lamiaceae)	Wild Mint
Mint Family, *Monarda fistulosa* var. *menthaefolia* (Lamiaceae)	Horsemint
Mint Family, *Poliomintha incana* (Lamiaceae)	Frosted Mint
Mint Family, *Prunella vulgaris* (Lamiaceae)	Self-Heal
Mint Family, *Scutellaria brittonii* (Lamiaceae)	Skullcap
Morning Glory Family, *Evolvulus nuttalianus* (Convolvulaceae)	Shaggy Dwarf Morning Glory
Morning Glory Family, *Ipomoea leptophylla* (Convolvulaceae)	Bush Morning Glory
Mustard Family, *Barbarea orthoceras* (Brassicaceae)	Winter Cress
Mustard Family, *Cardamine cordifolia* (Brassicaceae)	Bitter Cress
Mustard Family, *Draba aurea* (Brassicaceae)	Golden Draba

West Slope	East Slope	Uncommon	Sunny, Open	Cool, Shady	Riparian	Moist Meadows	Aquatic, Wetlands	Green-Brown	White, Cream	Yellow	Orange	Red, Maroon	Reddish-Purple	Pink	Blue, Bluish-Purple	Easy	Challenging
X	X		X			X			A							X	
X	X		X		X									A		X	
X	X		X								A					X	
X	X			X				A								X	
X		X	X	X	X			A								X	
X	X		X	X	X							A				X	
X			X						B			A					X
	X		X		X									A		X	
	X		X						A							X	
X	X		X		X									A		X	
X	X		X						A							X	
	X		X							B	A					X	
	X		X					A								X	
X	X		X			X								B	A	X	
X	X		X											A		X	
X		X	X						B						A		X
X	X		X	X		X							A				
	X		X												A	X	
	X		X											A			
	X		X											A			X
X			X			X				A							
X	X		X						A								X
X	X		X	X						A						X	

Family, *Latin Name*	Common Name
Mustard Family, *Draba streptocarpa* (Brassicaceae)	Twisted-Pod Draba
Mustard Family, *Erysimum asperum* (Brassicaceae)	Western Wallflower
Mustard Family, *Erysimum capitatum* (Brassicaceae)	Wallflower
Mustard Family, *Lepidium montanum* (Brassicaceae)	Pepperweed
Mustard Family, *Lesquerella ludoviciana* (Brassicaceae)	Plains Bladderpod
Mustard Family, *Lesquerella montana* (Brassicaceae)	Bladderpod
Mustard Family, *Noccaea montanum* (Brassicaceae)	Mountain Candytuft
Mustard Family, *Physaria bellii* (Brassicaceae)	Bell's Bladderpod
Mustard Family, *Physaria vitulifera* (Brassicaceae)	Fiddle-Leaf Twin Pod
Mustard Family, *Stanleya albescens* (Brassicaceae)	White Bottlebrush
Mustard Family, *Stanleya pinnata* (Brassicaceae)	Prince's Plume
Nightshade Family, *Datura wrightii* (Solanaceae)	Angel's Trumpet
Nightshade Family, *Quincula lobata* (Solanaceae)	Purple-Flowered Groundcherry
Oak Family, *Quercus gambelii* (Fagaceae)	Scrub Oak
Oak Family, *Quercus turbinella* (Fagaceae)	Shrub Live Oak
Oak Family, *Quercus x pauciloba* (Fagaceae)	Wavyleaf Oak
Oleaster Family, *Shepherdia argentea* (Elaeagnaceae)	Silver Buffaloberry
Oleaster Family, *Shepherdia canadensis* (Elaeagnaceae)	Canada Buffaloberry
Onion Family, *Allium cernuum* (Alliaceae)	Nodding Onion
Onion Family, *Allium geyeri* (Alliaceae)	Geyer Onion
Onion Family, *Allium textile* (Alliaceae)	Sand Onion
Orchid Family, *Calypso bulbosa* (Orchidaceae)	Fairy Slipper
Orchid Family, *Corallorhiza maculata* (Orchidaceae)	Coral-Root Orchid

West Slope	East Slope	Uncommon	Sunny, Open	Cool, Shady	Riparian	Moist Meadows	Aquatic, Wetlands	Green-Brown	White, Cream	Yellow	Orange	Red, Maroon	Reddish-Purple	Pink	Blue, Bluish-Purple	Easy	Challenging
X	X		X							A							X
X	X		X							B	A					X	
X	X		X							A	B	B				X	
X	X		X						A								
X	X		X							A							X
X	X		X							A						X	
X	X		X						A							X	
	X	X	X							A						X	
	X		X							A						X	
X			X						A							X	
X	X		X							A						X	
X	X		X						A							X	
	X		X												A		
X	X		X					A								X	
X	X	X	X					A								X	
	X		X					A								X	
X	X		X		X					A						X	
X	X		X	X						A						X	
X	X		X											A		X	
X	X		X											A		X	
X	X		X						A							X	
X	X	X		X										A			X
X	X	X		X				A									X

Family, *Latin Name*	Common Name
Orchid Family, *Cypripedium parviflorum* var. *pubescens* (Orchidaceae)	Yellow Ladyslipper
Orchid Family, *Goodyera oblongifolia* (Orchidaceae)	Rattlesnake Plantain
Orchid Family, *Platanthera dilatata* ssp. *albiflora* (Orchidaceae)	White Bog Orchid
Orchid Family, *Platanthera stricta* (Orchidaceae)	Green Bog Orchid
Orchid Family, *Spiranthes diluvialis* (Orchidaceae)	Ute Lady's Tresses
Orchid Family, *Spiranthes romanzoffiana* (Orchidaceae)	Lady's Tresses
Parsley Family, *Angelica ampla* (Apiaceae)	Giant Angelica
Parsley Family, *Cicuta douglasii* (Apiaceae)	Water Hemlock
Parsley Family, *Harbouria trachypleura* (Apiaceae)	Whiskbroom Parsley
Parsley Family, *Heracleum maximum* (Apiaceae)	Cow Parsnip
Parsley Family, *Ligusticum porteri* (Apiaceae)	Wild Lovage
Parsley Family, *Lomatium orientale* (Apiaceae)	Salt-And-Pepper
Parsley Family, *Oreoxis alpina* (Apiaceae)	Alpine Parsley
Parsley Family, *Osmorhiza depauperata* (Apiaceae)	Sweet Cicely
Parsley Family, *Pseudocymopterus montanus* (Apiaceae)	Yellow Mountain Parsley
Phlox Family, *Collomia linearis* (Polemoniaceae)	Tiny Trumpet, Collomia
Phlox Family, *Gilia pinnatifida* (Polemoniaceae)	Sticky Gilia
Phlox Family, *Ipomopsis aggregata* (Polemoniaceae)	Fairy Trumpet, Scarlet Gilia
Phlox Family, *Ipomopsis aggregata* ssp. *candida* (Polemoniaceae)	White Fairy Trumpet
Phlox Family, *Leptodactylon pungens* (Polemoniaceae)	Pungent Gilia
Phlox Family, *Microsteris gracilis* (Polemoniaceae)	Microsteris
Phlox Family, *Phlox caespitosa* ssp. *pulvinata* (Polemoniaceae)	Alpine Phlox
Phlox Family, *Phlox hoodii* ssp. *canescens* (Polemoniaceae)	Early Moss Phlox

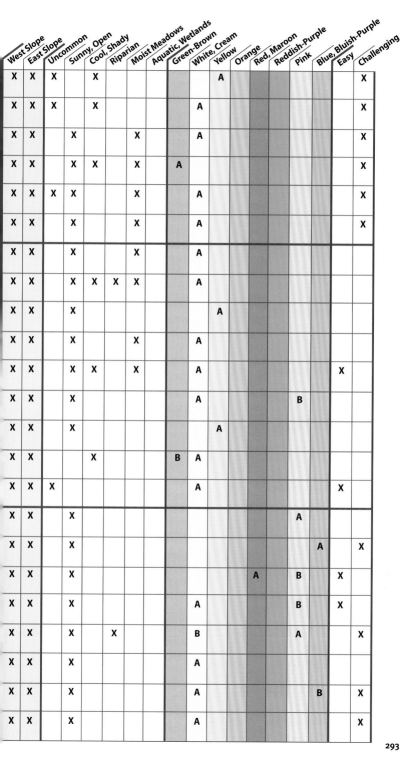

West Slope	East Slope	Uncommon	Sunny, Open	Cool, Shady	Riparian	Moist Meadows	Aquatic, Wetlands	Green-Brown	White, Cream	Yellow	Orange	Red, Maroon	Reddish-Purple	Pink	Blue, Bluish-Purple	Easy	Challenging
X	X	X		X						A							X
X	X	X		X					A								X
X	X		X			X			A								X
X	X		X	X		X		A									X
X	X	X	X			X			A								X
X	X		X			X			A								X
X	X		X			X			A								
X	X		X	X	X	X			A								
X	X		X							A							
X	X		X			X			A								
X	X		X	X		X			A							X	
X	X		X						A					B			
X	X		X							A							
X	X			X				B	A								
X	X	X							A							X	
X	X		X											A			
X	X		X												A		X
X	X		X									A	B		X		
X	X		X						A				B		X		
X	X		X		X				B					A			X
X	X		X						A								
X	X		X						A						B		X
X	X		X						A								X

Family, *Latin Name*	Common Name
Phlox Family, *Phlox multiflora* (Polemoniaceae)	Rocky Mountain Phlox
Phlox Family, *Polemonium pulcherimum* var. *delicatum* (Polemoniaceae)	Jacob's Ladder
Phlox Family, *Polemonium viscosum* (Polemoniaceae)	Sky Pilot
Pine Family, *Abies concolor* (Pinaceae)	White Fir
Pine Family, *Abies lasiocarpa* (Pinaceae)	Subalpine Fir
Pine Family, *Picea engelmannii* (Pinaceae)	Engelmann Spruce
Pine Family, *Picea pungens* (Pinaceae)	Colorado Blue Spruce
Pine Family, *Pinus aristata* (Pinaceae)	Bristlecone Pine
Pine Family, *Pinus contorta* ssp. *latifolia* (Pinaceae)	Lodgepole Pine
Pine Family, *Pinus edulis* (Pinaceae)	Pinon Pine
Pine Family, *Pinus flexilis* (Pinaceae)	Limber Pine
Pine Family, *Pinus ponderosa* (Pinaceae)	Ponderosa Pine, Western Yellow Pine
Pine Family, *Pinus strobiformis* (Pinaceae)	Southwestern White Pine
Pine Family, *Pseudotsuga menziesii* var. *glauca* (Pinaceae)	Douglas Fir
Pink Family, *Arenaria fendleri* (Caryophyllaceae)	Fendler's Sandwort
Pink Family, *Arenaria hookeri* (Caryophyllaceae)	Sandwort
Pink Family, *Cerastium arvense* (Caryophyllaceae)	Mouse-Ear Chickweed
Pink Family, *Minuartia obtusiloba* (Caryophyllaceae)	Alpine Sandwort
Pink Family, *Paronychia pulvinata* (Caryophyllaceae)	Nailwort
Pink Family, *Paronychia sessiliflora* (Caryophyllaceae)	Creeping Nailwort, Whitlow-Wort
Pink Family, *Silene acaulis* ssp. *subacaulescens* (Caryophyllaceae)	Moss Campion, Cushion Pink
Poppy Family, *Argemone polyanthemos* (Papaveraceae)	Prickly Poppy
Primrose Family, *Androsace chamaejasme* (Primulaceae)	Rock Jasmine

West Slope	East Slope	Uncommon	Sunny, Open	Cool, Shady	Riparian	Moist Meadows	Aquatic, Wetlands	Green-Brown	White, Cream	Yellow	Orange	Red, Maroon	Reddish-Purple	Pink	Blue, Bluish-Purple	Easy	Challenging
X	X		X						B					A	B		X
X	X		X	X											A		X
X	X		X												A	X	
X	X		X	X				A								X	
X	X		X					B				A					X
X	X		X					A								X	
X	X		X		X			B				A				X	
X	X		X					A								X	
X	X		X					A								X	
X	X		X					A								X	
X	X		X					A								X	
X	X		X					A								X	
X	X		X					A								X	
X	X		X	X				A								X	
X	X		X						A								X
X	X		X						A								X
X	X		X						A								X
X	X		X						A								X
X	X		X							A							X
X	X		X						A	B						X	
X	X		X											A		X	
	X		X					A								X	
X	X		X					A									X

295

Family, *Latin Name*	Common Name
Primrose Family, *Androsace septentrionalis* (Primulaceae)	Rock Primrose
Primrose Family, *Dodecatheon pulchellum* (Primulaceae)	Shooting Star
Primrose Family, *Primula angustifolia* (Primulaceae)	Fairy Primrose
Primrose Family, *Primula parryi* (Primulaceae)	Parry Primrose
Purslane Family, *Claytonia lanceolata* (Portulacaceae)	Spring Beauty
Purslane Family, *Claytonia megarhiza* (Portulacaceae)	Alpine Spring Beauty
Purslane Family, *Lewisia pygmaea* (Portulacaceae)	Pygmy Bitterroot
Purslane Family, *Lewisia rediviva* (Portulacaceae)	Bitterroot
Purslane Family, *Montia chamissoi* (Portulacaceae)	Water Spring Beauty
Purslane Family, *Talinum calycinum* (Portulacaceae)	Large Flowered Rock Pink
Purslane Family, *Talinum parviflorum* (Portulacaceae)	Prairie Fameflower
Rose Family, *Amelanchier alnifolia* (Rosaceae)	Serviceberry, Shadbush
Rose Family, *Cercocarpus montanus* (Rosaceae)	Mountain Mahogany
Rose Family, *Crataegus erythropoda* (Rosaceae)	Shiny-Leaved Hawthorn
Rose Family, *Dryas octopetala* ssp. *hookeriana* (Rosaceae)	Mountain Dryad
Rose Family, *Fallugia paradoxa* (Rosaceae)	Apache Plume
Rose Family, *Fragaria virginiana* var. *glauca* (Rosaceae)	Wild Strawberry
Rose Family, *Geum macrophyllum* (Rosaceae)	Bur Avens
Rose Family, *Geum rossii* (Rosaceae)	Alpine Avens
Rose Family, *Geum triflorum* (Rosaceae)	Prairie Smoke
Rose Family, *Holodiscus dumosus* (Rosaceae)	Rock Spirea
Rose Family, *Peraphyllum ramosissimum* (Rosaceae)	Squaw Apple
Rose Family, *Physocarpus monogynus* (Rosaceae)	Ninebark

West Slope	East Slope	Uncommon	Sunny, Open	Cool, Shady	Riparian	Moist Meadows	Aquatic, Wetlands	Green-Brown	White, Cream	Yellow	Orange	Red, Maroon	Reddish-Purple	Pink	Blue, Bluish-Purple	Easy	Challenging
X	X		X						A							X	
X	X		X		X									A			X
X	X		X											A			X
X	X		X		X									A			X
X	X		X	X					A					B		X	
X	X		X						A					B			X
X	X		X											A			X
X	X		X											A			X
X	X		X			X	X		A					B			
	X	X	X										B	A		X	
X	X		X											A			X
X	X		X						A							X	
X	X		X						A							X	
X	X		X	X	X				A							X	
X	X		X						A								X
X			X						A							X	
X	X		X						A							X	
X	X		X			X				A							
X	X		X							A							X
X	X		X	X										A		X	
X	X		X						A					B		X	
X			X						B					A		X	
X	X			X					A							X	

Family, *Latin Name*	**Common Name**
Rose Family, *Potentilla arguta* (Rosaceae)	Creamy Cinquefoil
Rose Family, *Potentilla diversifolia* and other species (Rosaceae)	Glaucous Cinquefoil
Rose Family, *Potentilla fissa* (Rosaceae)	Leafy Cinquefoil
Rose Family, *Potentilla fruticosa* ssp. *floribunda* (Rosaceae)	Shrubby Cinquefoil
Rose Family, *Potentilla hippeana* (Rosaceae)	Silver Cinquefoil
Rose Family, *Prunus americana* (Rosaceae)	Wild Plum
Rose Family, *Prunus pensylvanica* (Rosaceae)	Pin Cherry
Rose Family, *Prunus pumila* ssp. *besseyi* (Rosaceae)	Sand Cherry
Rose Family, *Prunus virginiana* var. *melanocarpa* (Rosaceae)	Western Chokecherry
Rose Family, *Purshia stansburiana* (Rosaceae)	Cliff Rose
Rose Family, *Purshia tridentata* (Rosaceae)	Antelope Brush
Rose Family, *Rosa woodsii* (Rosaceae)	Wild Rose
Rose Family, *Rubus deliciosus* (Rosaceae)	Boulder Raspberry
Rose Family, *Rubus idaeus* (Rosaceae)	Wild Raspberry
Rose Family, *Rubus parviflorus* (Rosaceae)	Thimbleberry
Rose Family, *Sibbaldia procumbens* (Rosaceae)	Sibbaldia
Rose Family, *Sorbus scopulina* (Rosaceae)	Mountain Ash
Rush Family, *Juncus* spp. (Juncaceae)	Rushes
Sandalwood Family, *Comandra umbellata* (Santalaceae)	Bastard Toadflax
Saxifrage Family, *Heuchera hallii* (Saxifragaceae)	Small-Leaved Alumroot
Saxifrage Family, *Heuchera parvifolia* (Saxifragaceae)	Small-Leaved Alumroot
Saxifrage Family, *Mitella pentandra* (Saxifragaceae)	Mitrewort, Bishop's Cap
Saxifrage Family, *Parnassia parviflora* (Saxifragaceae)	Grass Of Parnassus

West Slope	East Slope	Uncommon	Sunny, Open	Cool, Shady	Riparian	Moist Meadows	Aquatic, Wetlands	Green-Brown	White, Cream	Yellow	Orange	Red, Maroon	Reddish-Purple	Pink	Blue, Bluish-Purple	Easy	Challenging
X	X	X							A							X	
X	X	X	X		X					A						X	
X	X	X								A						X	
X	X	X			X					A						X	
X	X	X								A						X	
	X	X							A							X	
	X	X	X	X					A							X	
	X	X							A							X	
X	X	X	X						A							X	
X		X						B	A							X	
X	X	X						B	A							X	
X	X	X		X										A		X	
X	X		X	X					A							X	
X	X	X	X						A							X	
X	X		X						A							X	
X	X	X								A							X
X	X		X						A							X	
X	X	X			X			A									
	X	X							A								
	X		X						A							X	
X	X		X					B	A								X
X	X		X		X			A									X
X	X	X			X				A								X

Family, *Latin Name*	Common Name
Saxifrage Family, *Saxifraga bronchialis* (Saxifragaceae)	Dotted Saxifrage
Saxifrage Family, *Saxifraga cernua* (Saxifragaceae)	Nodding Saxifrage
Saxifrage Family, *Saxifraga chrysantha* (Saxifragaceae)	Fairy Saxifrage, Golden Saxifrage
Saxifrage Family, *Saxifraga flagellaris* (Saxifragaceae)	Whiplash Saxifrage
Saxifrage Family, *Saxifraga rhomboidea* (Saxifragaceae)	Snowball Saxifrage
Saxifrage Family, *Telesonix jamesii* (Saxifragaceae)	Telesonix
Sedge Family, *Carex heliophila* (Cyperaceae)	Early Sedge
Sedge Family, *Carex* spp. (Cyperaceae)	Sedges
Sedge Family, *Scirpus* spp. (Cyperaceae)	Bulrush
Soapberry Family, *Sapindus saponaria* var. *drummondii* (Sapindaceae)	Western Soapberry
Spiderwort Family, *Tradescantia occidentalis* (Commelinaceae)	Spiderwort
Spurge Family, *Croton texensis* (Euphorbiaceae)	Croton
Spurge Family, *Euphorbia marginata* (Euphorbiaceae)	Snow On The Mountain
Staff-tree Family, *Paxistima myrsinites* (Celastraceae)	Mountain Lover
Stonecrop Family, *Rhodiola integrifolia* (Crassulaceae)	King's Crown
Stonecrop Family, *Rhodiola rhodantha* (Crassulaceae)	Rose Crown, Queen's Crown
Stonecrop Family, *Sedum lanceolatum* (Crassulaceae)	Yellow Stonecrop
Sumac Family, *Rhus glabra* (Anacardiaceae)	Smooth Sumac
Sumac Family, *Rhus trilobata* (Anacardiaceae)	Three-Leaf Sumac
Sumac Family, *Toxicodendron radicans* (Anacardiaceae)	Poison Ivy
Sunflower Family, *Achillea millefolium* (Asteraceae)	Yarrow
Sunflower Family, *Agoseris aurantiaca* (Asteraceae)	Burnt-Orange Dandelion
Sunflower Family, *Agoseris glauca* (Asteraceae)	Tall False Dandelion

West Slope	East Slope	Uncommon	Sunny, Open	Cool, Shady	Riparian	Moist Meadows	Aquatic, Wetlands	Green-Brown	White, Cream	Yellow	Orange	Red, Maroon	Reddish-Purple	Pink	Blue, Bluish-Purple	Easy	Challenging
X	X			X					A								X
X	X		X						A	B							X
X	X		X							A							X
X	X		X							A							X
X	X		X						A							X	
	X	X	X	X									A	B			X
X	X		X	X						A							
X	X		X			X		A									
X	X		X			X		A									
	X	X	X		X			B	A							X	
X	X		X												A	X	
	X		X						A								
	X		X					B	A							X	
X	X			X				B				A				X	
X	X		X				X					A					X
X	X		X				X							A			X
X	X		X							A						X	
X	X		X						A							X	
X	X		X							A						X	
X	X		X	X					A								
X	X		X						A							X	
X	X		X								A						X
X	X		X							A							X

301

Family, *Latin Name*	**Common Name**
Sunflower Family, *Ambrosia acanthicarpa* (Asteraceae)	Flat Spine Bur Ragweed
Sunflower Family, *Ambrosia tomentosa* (Asteraceae)	Skeleton Bur Ragweed
Sunflower Family, *Anaphalis margaritacea* (Asteraceae)	Pearly Everlasting
Sunflower Family, *Antennaria parvifolia* (Asteraceae)	Sun-Loving Pussytoes
Sunflower Family, *Antennaria rosea* (Asteraceae)	Pussytoes
Sunflower Family, *Arnica cordifolia* (Asteraceae)	Heart-Leaved Arnica
Sunflower Family, *Arnica fulgens* (Asteraceae)	Meadow Arnica
Sunflower Family, *Artemisia filifolia* (Asteraceae)	Sand Sage
Sunflower Family, *Artemisia frigida* (Asteraceae)	Fringed Sage
Sunflower Family, *Artemisia ludoviciana* (Asteraceae)	Prairie Sage
Sunflower Family, *Artemisia tridentata* (Asteraceae)	Sagebrush
Sunflower Family, *Bahia dissecta* (Asteraceae)	Wild Chrysanthemum
Sunflower Family, *Balsamorhiza sagittata* (Asteraceae)	Balsam Root
Sunflower Family, *Berlandiera lyrata* (Asteraceae)	Chocolate Flower
Sunflower Family, *Bidens cernua* (Asteraceae)	Beggar's Tick, Bur Marigold
Sunflower Family, *Brickellia grandiflora* (Asteraceae)	Tasselflower
Sunflower Family, *Chaetopappa ericoides* (Asteraceae)	Heather Daisy
Sunflower Family, *Chrysothamnus viscidiflorus* (Asteraceae)	Dwarf Rabbitbrush
Sunflower Family, *Cirsium canescens* (Asteraceae)	Creamy Thistle
Sunflower Family, *Cirsium scariosum* (Asteraceae)	Elk Thistle
Sunflower Family, *Cirsium scopulorum* (Asteraceae)	Woolly Thistle, Frosty Ball
Sunflower Family, *Coreopsis tinctoria* (Asteraceae)	Plains Coreopsis
Sunflower Family, *Dyssodia papposa* (Asteraceae)	Fetid Marigold

West Slope	East Slope	Uncommon	Sunny, Open	Cool, Shady	Riparian	Moist Meadows	Aquatic, Wetlands	Green-Brown	White, Cream	Yellow	Orange	Red, Maroon	Reddish-Purple	Pink	Blue, Bluish-Purple	Easy	Challenging
X	X	X								A							
	X	X								A							
X	X	X							A							X	
X	X	X							A					B		X	
X	X	X							B					A		X	
X	X	X	X							A							X
X	X	X								A							X
	X	X								A						X	
X	X	X						B		A						X	
X	X	X								A						X	
X	X	X								A						X	
X	X	X								A						X	
X	X	X								A							X
	X	X								A						X	
	X	X			X					A						X	
X	X	X							A							X	
X	X	X							A					B		X	
X	X	X								A						X	
X	X	X							A								X
X	X	X				X			A								X
X	X	X							A								X
	X	X								A		B				X	
X	X	X								A						X	

303

Family, *Latin Name*	Common Name
Sunflower Family, *Encelia nutans* (Asteraceae)	Sleepyhead
Sunflower Family, *Engelmannia peristenia* (Asteraceae)	Engelmann Daisy
Sunflower Family, *Ericameria nauseosus* ssp. *nauseosus* var. *nauseosus* (Asteraceae)	Rabbitbrush
Sunflower Family, *Erigeron belidiastrum* (Asteraceae)	Western Fleabane
Sunflower Family, *Erigeron divergens* (Asteraceae)	Spreading Daisy
Sunflower Family, *Erigeron flagellaris* (Asteraceae)	Whiplash Daisy
Sunflower Family, *Erigeron melanocephalus* (Asteraceae)	Blackheaded Daisy
Sunflower Family, *Erigeron peregrinus* (Asteraceae)	Subalpine Daisy
Sunflower Family, *Erigeron pinnatisectus* (Asteraceae)	Pinnate-Leaved Daisy
Sunflower Family, *Erigeron simplex* (Asteraceae)	One-Flowered Daisy
Sunflower Family, *Erigeron speciosus* (Asteraceae)	Blue Aspen Daisy
Sunflower Family, *Gaillardia aristata* (Asteraceae)	Gaillardia, Blanket Flower
Sunflower Family, *Gaillardia pinnatifida* (Asteraceae)	Cut-Leaf Gaillardia
Sunflower Family, *Grindelia squarrosa* (Asteraceae)	Gumweed
Sunflower Family, *Grindelia subalpina* (Asteraceae)	Mountain Gumweed
Sunflower Family, *Gutierrezia sarothrae* (Asteraceae)	Snakeweed
Sunflower Family, *Helianthella quinquenervis* (Asteraceae)	Aspen Sunflower
Sunflower Family, *Helianthus annuus* (Asteraceae)	Kansas Sunflower, Common Sunflower
Sunflower Family, *Helianthus maximilian's* (Asteraceae)	Maximillion's Sunflower
Sunflower Family, *Helianthus nuttallii* (Asteraceae)	Tall Marsh Sunflower
Sunflower Family, *Helianthus pauciflorus* ssp. *pauciflorus* (Asteraceae)	Stiff Sunflower
Sunflower Family, *Helianthus petiolaris* (Asteraceae)	Prairie Sunflower
Sunflower Family, *Helianthus pumilus* (Asteraceae)	Dwarf Sunflower

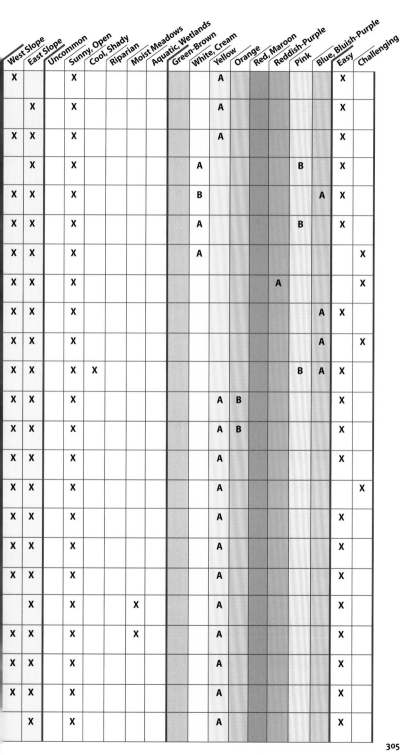

West Slope	East Slope	Uncommon	Sunny, Open	Cool, Shady	Riparian	Moist Meadows	Aquatic, Wetlands	Green-Brown	White, Cream	Yellow	Orange	Red, Maroon	Reddish-Purple	Pink	Blue, Bluish-Purple	Easy	Challenging
X			X							A						X	
	X		X							A						X	
X	X		X							A						X	
	X		X						A					B		X	
X	X		X						B						A	X	
X	X		X						A					B		X	
X	X		X						A								X
X	X		X										A				X
X	X		X												A	X	
X	X		X												A		X
X	X		X	X										B	A	X	
X	X		X						A	B						X	
X	X		X						A	B						X	
X	X		X						A							X	
X	X		X						A								X
X	X		X						A							X	
X	X		X						A							X	
X	X		X						A							X	
	X		X			X			A							X	
X	X		X			X			A							X	
X	X		X						A							X	
X	X		X						A							X	
	X		X						A							X	

Family, *Latin Name*	Common Name
Sunflower Family, *Heliomeris multiflora* (Asteraceae)	Sunspots, Goldeneye
Sunflower Family, *Heterotheca fulcrata* (Asteraceae)	Golden Aster
Sunflower Family, *Heterotheca villosa* (Asteraceae)	Golden Aster
Sunflower Family, *Hymenopappus filifolius* (Asteraceae)	Cream Tips
Sunflower Family, *Hymenoxys grandiflora* (Asteraceae)	Old Man Of The Mountain, Rydbergia
Sunflower Family, *Hymenoxys hoopesii* (Asteraceae)	Orange Sneezeweed
Sunflower Family, *Hymenoxys richardsonii* (Asteraceae)	Colorado Rubber Plant
Sunflower Family, *Lactuca tatarica* ssp. *pulchella* (Asteraceae)	Blue Lettuce
Sunflower Family, *Liatris punctata* (Asteraceae)	Dotted Gay Feather, Blazing Star
Sunflower Family, *Lygodesmia juncea* (Asteraceae)	Skeleton Plant
Sunflower Family, *Machaeranthera bigelovii* (Asteraceae)	Tansy Aster
Sunflower Family, *Melampodium leucanthum* (Asteraceae)	White Paper Flower, Black-Footed Daisy
Sunflower Family, *Nothocalais cuspidata* (Asteraceae)	Wavy-Leaf False Dandelion
Sunflower Family, *Packera fendleri* (Asteraceae)	Fendler's Senecio
Sunflower Family, *Palafoxia sphacelata* (Asteraceae)	Palafoxia
Sunflower Family, *Psilostrophe bakeri* (Asteraceae)	Paperflower
Sunflower Family, *Ratibida columnifera* (Asteraceae)	Prairie Coneflower
Sunflower Family, *Ratibida tagetes* (Asteraceae)	Short-Rayed Coneflower
Sunflower Family, *Rudbeckia hirta* (Asteraceae)	Black-Eyed Susan
Sunflower Family, *Rudbeckia laciniata* var. *ampla* (Asteraceae)	Tall Coneflower
Sunflower Family, *Rudbeckia montana* (Asteraceae)	Naked Coneflower
Sunflower Family, *Senecio atratus* (Asteraceae)	Black-Tipped Senecio
Sunflower Family, *Senecio bigelovii* (Asteraceae)	Rayless Senecio

West Slope	East Slope	Uncommon	Sunny, Open	Cool, Shady	Riparian	Moist Meadows	Aquatic, Wetlands	Green-Brown	White, Cream	Yellow	Orange	Red, Maroon	Reddish-Purple	Pink	Blue, Bluish-Purple	Easy	Challenging
X	X	X								A						X	
X	X	X								A						X	
X	X	X								A						X	
X	X	X							A							X	
X	X	X								A							X
X	X	X								A	B					X	
X	X	X								A							X
X	X	X			X									A			
X	X	X										A				X	
X	X	X											A				X
X	X	X										A				X	
	X	X							A							X	
X	X									A							X
X	X	X								A							X
	X	X											A				X
X		X								A						X	
X	X	X								A		B				X	
	X	X										A					X
X	X	X			X					A						X	
X	X	X		X						A						X	
X		X			X			A									X
X	X	X								A							X
X	X	X	X		X					A							X

Family, *Latin Name*	Common Name
Sunflower Family, *Senecio eremophilus* (Asteraceae)	Western Golden Ragwort
Sunflower Family, *Senecio fremontii* var. *blitoides* (Asteraceae)	Rock Ragwort
Sunflower Family, *Senecio integerrimus* (Asteraceae)	Early Spring Senecio
Sunflower Family, *Senecio spartioides* (Asteraceae)	Broom Senecio
Sunflower Family, *Senecio triangularis* (Asteraceae)	Triangle-Leaved Ragwort
Sunflower Family, *Solidago gigantea* (Asteraceae)	Tall Goldenrod
Sunflower Family, *Solidago missouriensis* (Asteraceae)	Smooth Goldenrod
Sunflower Family, *Solidago simplex* var. *nana* (Asteraceae)	Dwarf Goldenrod
Sunflower Family, *Symphyotrichum ericoides* (Asteraceae)	Many-Flowered Aster
Sunflower Family, *Symphyotrichum laeve* var. *geyeri* (Asteraceae)	Smooth Aster
Sunflower Family, *Symphyotrichum lanceolatum* var. *hesperium* (Asteraceae)	Sky Blue Aster
Sunflower Family, *Symphyotrichum porteri* (Asteraceae)	Porters Aster
Sunflower Family, *Tetraneuris acaulis* (Asteraceae)	Actinea, Perky Sue
Sunflower Family, *Tetraneuris acaulis* var. *caespitosa* (Asteraceae)	Woolly Actinella
Sunflower Family, *Thelesperma filifolium* (Asteraceae)	Greenthread
Sunflower Family, *Townsendia grandiflora* (Asteraceae)	Large-Flowered Townsendia, Showy Townsendia
Sunflower Family, *Townsendia hookeri* (Asteraceae)	Easter Daisy
Sunflower Family, *Verbesina encelioides* (Asteraceae)	Goldweed
Sunflower Family, *Wyethia amplexicaulis* (Asteraceae)	Smooth Mule's Ears
Sunflower Family, *Wyethia Arizonica* (Asteraceae)	Mule's Ears
Sunflower Family, *Zinnia grandiflora* (Asteraceae)	Wild Zinnia
Trillium Family, *Trillium ovatum* (Trilliaceae)	Trillium
Valerian Family, *Valeriana edulis* (Valerianaceae)	Tall Valerian

West Slope	East Slope	Uncommon	Sunny, Open	Cool, Shady	Riparian	Moist Meadows	Aquatic, Wetlands	Green-Brown	White, Cream	Yellow	Orange	Red, Maroon	Reddish-Purple	Pink	Blue, Bluish-Purple	Easy	Challenging
X	X		X							A						X	
X	X		X							A							X
X	X		X							A							X
X	X		X							A						X	
X	X			X		X				A							X
X	X		X			X				A						X	
X	X		X							A						X	
X	X		X							A						X	
X	X		X						A							X	
X	X		X												A	X	
X	X		X			X		B							A	X	
X	X		X					A								X	
X	X		X							A						X	
X	X		X							A						X	
	X		X							A						X	
	X		X						A								X
X	X		X						A					B			X
X	X		X							A						X	
X	X									A							X
X			X							A							X
	X		X							A						X	
X	X	X		X				A									X
X	X		X			X		A									X

309

Family, *Latin Name*	Common Name
Verbena Family, *Glandularia bipinnatifida* (Verbenaceae)	Prairie Verbena
Verbena Family, *Phyla cuneifolia* (Verbenaceae)	Phyla, Fog-Fruit, Frog Fruit
Verbena Family, *Verbena bracteata* (Verbenaceae)	Bracted Vervain
Verbena Family, *Verbena hastata* (Verbenaceae)	Blue Vervain
Violet Family, *Viola adunca* (Violaceae)	Mountain Blue Violet
Violet Family, *Viola canadensis* (Violaceae)	Canada Violet
Violet Family, *Viola nuttallii* (Violaceae)	Yellow Violet
Violet Family, *Viola pedatifida* (Violaceae)	Birdfoot Violet
Water Lily Family, *Nuphar luteum* (Nymphaeaceae)	Yellow Pond Lily
Water Plantain Family, *Sagittaria latifolia* (Alismataceae)	Arrowhead
Waterleaf Family, *Hydrophyllum fendleri* (Hydrophyllaceae)	Waterleaf
Waterleaf Family, *Phacelia hastata* (Hydrophyllaceae)	Silver Scorpionweed
Waterleaf Family, *Phacelia heterophylla* (Hydrophyllaceae)	Scorpion Weed
Waterleaf Family, *Phacelia sericea* (Hydrophyllaceae)	Purple Pincushion, Purple Fringe
Willow Family, *Populus angustifolia* (Salicaceae)	Narrow-Leaf Cottonwood
Willow Family, *Populus deltoids* (Salicaceae)	Plains Cottonwood
Willow Family, *Populus tremuloides* (Salicaceae)	Quaking Aspen
Willow Family, *Salix amygdaloides* (Salicaceae)	Peachleaf Willow
Willow Family, *Salix arctica* (Salicaceae)	Arctic Willow
Willow Family, *Salix exigua* (Salicaceae)	Sandbar Willow
Willow Family, *Salix planifolia* (Salicaceae)	Diamond Leaf Willow
Willow Family, *Salix reticulata* ssp. *nivalis* (Salicaceae)	Snow Willow
Willow Family, *Salix scouleriana* (Salicaceae)	Scouler Willow

West Slope	East Slope	Uncommon	Sunny, Open	Cool, Shady	Riparian	Moist Meadows	Aquatic, Wetlands	Green-Brown	White, Cream	Yellow	Orange	Red, Maroon	Reddish-Purple	Pink	Blue, Bluish-Purple	Easy	Challenging
X	X		X									A	B	B		X	
	X		X		X									A		X	
	X		X		X										A		
	X		X		X										A	X	
X	X		X	X	X										A	X	
X	X			X					A							X	
	X		X							A						X	
X	X	X	X												A		X
X	X	X	X				X			A							X
X	X		X			X	X		A							X	
X	X			X					A								X
	X		X	X					A							X	
X	X		X						A								
X	X		X												A		X
X	X		X		X			A								X	
	X		X		X			A								X	
X	X		X	X		X		A								X	
X	X		X		X	X		A								X	
X	X		X			X		A									X
X	X		X		X	X		A									
X	X		X		X	X		A								X	
X	X		X			X		A									X
X	X		X		X	X		A									X

Family, *Latin Name*	Common Name
Willow Family, *Salix* ssp. (Salicaceae)	Tundra Willows
Willow Family, *Salix* spp. (Salicaceae)	Alpine Thicket Willows
Woodsia Family, *Woodsia oregano* ssp. *cathcartiana* (Woodsiaceae)	Oregon Cliff Fern

West Slope	East Slope	Uncommon	Sunny, Open	Cool, Shady	Riparian	Moist Meadows	Aquatic, Wetlands	Green-Brown	White, Cream	Yellow	Orange	Red, Maroon	Reddish-Purple	Pink	Blue, Bluish-Purple	Easy	Challenging
X	X	X				X		A									
X	X	X				X		A									
X	X			X													X

Photo Credits

All photos in this book are by Loraine Yeatts and Dan Johnson except those listed below.

Apocynum androsaemifolium, Mary Ellen (Mel) Harte, bugwood.org
Arceuthobium spp., William Jacobi, Colorado State University, bugwood.org
Balsamorhiza sagittata, Steve Dewey, Utah State University, bugwood.org
Barbarea orthoceras, Joseph M. DiTomaso, University of California-Davis, bugwood.org
Berberis vulgaris, Leslie J. Mehrhoff, University of Connecticut, bugwood.org
Bidens cernua, Richard Old, SID Services, Inc., bugwood.org
Calylophus serrulatus, Sandy Smith, Lady Bird Johnson Wildflower Center
Capsella bursa-pastoris, Phil Westra, Colorado State University, bugwood.org
Castilleja linariaefolia, Dave Powell, USDA Forest Service, bugwood.org
Chaetopappa ericoides, © Gary A. Monroe, USDA-NRCS Plants Database, bugwood.org
Chorispora tenella, Steve Dewey, Utah State University, bugwood.org
Cicuta douglasii, Mary Ellen (Mel) Harte, bugwood.org
Clematis orientalis, Jan Loechell Turner
Collomia linearis, Richard Old, SID Services, Inc., bugwood.org
Coreopsis tinctoria, Charles T. Bryson, USDA Agricultural Research Service, bugwood, org
Cynoglossum officinale, Mary Ellen (Mel) Harte, bugwood.org
Cypripedium parviflorum, Arnold T. Drooz, USDA Forest Service, bugwood.org
Delphinium glaucum, William and Wilma Follette, USDA-NRCS Plants Database,
    bugwood.org
Echinocystis lobata, Barbara Tokarska-Guzik, University of Silesia, bugwood.org
Eleagnus angustifolia, Norbert Frank, University of West Hungary, bugwood.org
Encelia nutans, Panayoti Kelaidis, Denver Botanic Gardens
Erigeron bellidiastrum, Harry T. Cliffe, Lady Bird Johnson Wildflower Center
Eriogonum jamesii, Dave Powell, USDA Forest Service, bugwood.org
Euphorbia myrsinites, Steve Dewey, Utah State University, bugwood.org
Evolvulus nuttallianus, Campbell and Lynn Loughmiller, Lady Bird Johnson
    Wildflower Center
Frankenia jamesii, Dave Powell, USDA Forest Service, bugwood.org
Gaillardia pinnatifida, David Cappaert, Michigan State University, bugwood.org
Galium boreale, Dave Powell, USDA Forest Service, bugwood.org
Geranium caespitosum, Dave Powell, USDA Forest Service, bugwood.org
Geum macrophyllum, Mary Ellen (Mel) Harte, bugwood.org
Gilia pinnatifida, Mary Ellen (Mel) Harte, bugwood.org
Grindelia subalpina, Dave Powell, USDA Forest Service, bugwood.org
Hackelia floribunda, Mary Ellen (Mel) Harte, bugwood.org
Hesperostipa neomexican, Campbell and Lynn Loughmiller, Lady Bird Johnson
    Wildflower Center
Hesperus matronalis, Tom Heutte, USDA Forest Service, bugwood.org
Heuchera parvifolia, Dave Powell, USDA Forest Service, bugwood.org
Hymenopappus filifolius, Dave Powell, USDA Forest Service, bugwood.org
Hypericum perforatum, L.L. Berry, bugwood.org
Lactuca tatarica, Mary Ellen (Mel) Harte, bugwood.org
Lathyrus leucanthus, Dave Powell, USDA Forest Service, bugwood.org
Lepidium montanum, Steve Dewey, Utah State University, bugwood.org
Leptodactylon pungens, Margaret Williams, USDA-NRCS Plants Database, bugwood.org

Leucanthemum vulgare, Keith Weller, USDA Agricultural Research Service, bugwood.org

Lithospermum multiflorum, Dave Powell, USDA Forest Service, bugwood.org

Mentha arvensis, Richard Old, SID Services, Inc., bugwood.org

Montia chamissoi, Sheri Hagwood, USDA-NRCS Plants Database, bugwood.org

Nasturtium officinale, Mary Ellen (Mel) Harte, bugwood.org

Oenothera flava, Dave Powell, USDA Forest Service, bugwood.org

Osmorhiza depauperata, Dave Powell, USDA Forest Service, bugwood.org

Pedicularis parryi, Mary Ellen (Mel) Harte, bugwood.org

Penstemon linarioides var *coloradoensis,* Silverton® bluemat penstemon, David Winger for Plant Select®

Phacelia heterophylla, Dave Powell, USDA Forest Service, bugwood.org

Phemeranthus parviflorus, Robert L. Stone, Lady Bird Johnson Wildflower Center

Poliomintha incana, © Al Schneider, www.swcoloradowildflowers.com

Polygonum pensylvanicum, Dan Tenaglia, missouriplants.com

Potentilla cinquefoil, Mary Ellen (Mel) Harte, bugwood.org

Pyrola asarifolia, Dave Powell, USDA Forest Service, bugwood.org

Pyrola chlorantha, Dave Powell, USDA Forest Service, bugwood.org

Ranunculus aquatilis, William and Wilma Follette © USDA-NRCS Database/USDA NRCS 1992

Ratibida peduncularis, Harry T. Cliffe, Lady Bird Johnson Wildflower Center

Rudbeckia occidentalis, Mrs. W.D. Bransford, Lady Bird Johnson Wildflower Center

Rumex acetosella, Forest and Kim Starr, US Geological Survey, bugwood.org

Rumex salicifolius, Richard Old, XID Services, Inc., bugwood.org

Sagittaria latifolia, Graves Lovell, Alabama Department of Conservation and Natural Resources, bugwood.org

Salix scouleriana, Dave Powell, USDA Forest Service, bugwood.org

Saxifraga rhomboidea, Dave Powell, USDA Forest Service, bugwood.org

Scirpus spp., Graves Lovell, Alabama Department of Conservation and Natural Resources, bugwood.org

Scrophularia lanceolata, Dave Powell, USDA Forest Service, bugwood.org

Selaginella densa, Dave Powell, USDA Forest Service, bugwood.org

Senecio bigelovii, Joy Viola, Northeastern University, bugwood.org

Senecio eremophilus, Dave Powell, USDA Forest Service, bugwood.org

Sidalcea candida, Dave Powell, USDA Forest Service, bugwood.org

Solidago gigantean, Robert Vidéki, Doronicum kft, bugwood.org

Spiranthes cernua, Mrs. W.D. Bransford, Lady Bird Johnson Wildflower Center

Stanleya albescens, Mrs. W.D. Bransford, Lady Bird Johnson Wildflower Center

Symphyotrichum lanceolatum ssp. *Hesperium,* Campbell and Lynn Loughmiller, Lady Bird Johnson Wildflower Center

Thermopsis montana, Mary Ellen (Mel) Harte, bugwood.org

Thermopsis rhombifolia, William M. Ciesla, Forest Health Management International, bugwood.org

Thlaspi arvense, Steve Dewey, Utah State University, bugwood.org

Verbena hastate, Steve Dewey, Utah State University, bugwood.org

Verbesina encelioides, Dave Powell, USDA Forest Service, bugwood.org

Veronica americana, Mary Ellen (Mel) Harte, bugwood.org

Viola pedatifida, James Henderson, Gulf South Research Corp, bugwood.org

Woodsia obtusa, John Triana, Regional Water Authority, bugwood.org

Wyethia arizonica, Mary Ellen (Mel) Harte, bugwood.org

Index of Latin Names

Index of Common Names

VICKIE DANIELSON

Dan Johnson has filled his life with gardening, hiking, travel, and photography, always exploring new interests in plants, natural habitats, and garden styles. He has worked in the "green industry" for thirty years, the last fourteen spent as Curator of Native Plants at Denver Botanic Gardens. His broad interests have taken him throughout the western U.S., and to such far-flung places as the Karakoram and Himalaya mountains of Pakistan, the Drakensberg and Karoo of South Africa, rugged Andalucia in Spain, and the wind-blown steppe and Andes mountains in Patagonia, observing wildflowers and their unique habitats. Still, Colorado and the West are home. Durable native plants are the mainstay in many of his gardens, combining the best of our native plants with compatible species from around the globe. Three decades of gardening and observation in the West have provided the insights that only experience can give, though he will be the first to admit that there is far more yet to learn.

Loraine Yeatts combines botanical expertise with a life-long interest in nature and macro photography. Years of volunteer work in the Kathryn Kalmbach Herbarium at Denver Botanic Gardens and floristic surveys of Rocky Mountain National Park and other Colorado wildlands has nurtured a love affair with the Colorado flora and a deep concern for disappearing habitat. With Janet Wingate she coauthored *Alpine Flower Finder*.